ROUNDUP
at the
DOUBLE
DIAMOND

Also by Bill Surface

THE HOLLOW
THE POISONED IVY
INSIDE INTERNAL REVENUE

ROUNDUP

at the

DOUBLE DIAMOND

The American Cowboy Today

BY BILL SURFACE

Illustrated by Lorence F. Bjorklund

HOUGHTON MIFFLIN COMPANY BOSTON

1974

FIRST PRINTING   V

Library of Congress Cataloging in Publication Data

Surface, William.
    Roundup at the Double Diamond.

    1. Cowboys.   2. Ranch life.   I. Title.
F596.S94   917.8'03'3   74-3360
ISBN 0-395-18499-1

PRINTED IN THE UNITED STATES OF AMERICA

for
Elizabeth Cullen Surface

Preface / Finding the American Cowboy Today

THE AMERICAN COWBOY remains the most enduring and universal folk hero of all time. The country's first migrant laborer, the working cowboy has been shrouded with mystique and envy simply for what he does, not what he owns or receives. He epitomizes the swashbuckling man, a ruggedly romantic breed whose life-style and working uniforms are emulated around the world. Yet the same lack of visibility that often clouded the image of the working cowboy during his most colorful era, the late nineteenth century, also fosters the impression that he is, by now, nearly extinct or obsolete. With the working cowboy seldom living even a comfortable drive from a city, let alone the short gallop by horse that is a feature of western movies, it has always been simpler to model him after the more sanitized men found in the accessible cattle towns. For the same reason today, the cattlemen photographed beside airplanes parked on ranches located near highways, or corporate feedlots used to fatten at one time 75,000 steers brought in from ranches, suggest that there is little need for a cowboy in the United States. When outsiders portray the contemporary cowboy, they invariably settle for the members of professional rodeos.

To find the authentic working cowboy, I initially focused my research on ranches in the brushy areas of southeast Texas where the American cowboy originated and the valleys of New Mexico that cowmen took during the infamous range wars. The variety of men contacted included employees of rodeos, cowboy reunions, and cattlemen's associations from Texas to Wyoming; an elderly United States Customs agent who often worked on horseback in the rugged edges of ranches along the Texas-Mexico border; a sheriff who keeps drifting cowboys from rustling cattle in a mountainous county of Nevada; and four cowboys, now working as inspectors, who look for rustlers sneaking onto ranches in Texas and Oklahoma. Despite the rich personality of each area of the cattle country, it was obvious that many cowboys and former cowboys favored the huge ranches of West Texas. Typically, as he recited the names of more than a dozen ranches in West Texas, a man from Laredo grew thoughtful: "I sure wouldn't mind riding with some of 'em old boys in the rough country 'round the Texas and New Mexico state line. They say they don't take nothing off nobody."

Turning westward, I rode so long through Texas that it soon became apparent why even a cowboy from East Texas has little opportunity to see his counterpart in West Texas. I rode all day through West Texas and nothing really changed. I was still in West Texas, marveling at the stamina of the men and women who traveled the country by horse. I no longer looked for anyone. The terrain — flat, dusty, and treeless — still baked under the ultraviolet sun. Deep creek beds remained dry and cracked, almost white. In the only diversion to the open land, stunted mesquite shrubs perched atop small sand hills; blades of pale grass became visible on the shady side of reddish brown sandstone or tall yucca. Abruptly, bearing southward in the high plains, bare, pyramid-shaped hills filled the horizon. With the hills growing into jagged mountains, I was in the expanse between the end of the Rocky Mountains and the beginning of the chain of stony mountains that rise into the awesome Sierra Madre in Mexico. Interchangeably known as the Big Bend, the Highlands, or West Texas, these mountains often conceal a valley as immense as an eastern state, a canyon or ranch the size of a dozen counties. Though in Big Bend, I still needed to drive at least 400 miles to reach, say, the area's six largest ranches. To find my way, I arranged to meet an old cowboy, driving a pickup truck from the foothills of the Apache Mountains, at the crossroads town of Van Horn. Later, when the slopes drew closer, I observed: "Pretty country, ain't it? " Smiling, the cowboy's eyes darted back to the horse stirring in a small gray trailer. "Yeah, but it'll fool you good if you're a town boy," he drawled. "Tough country kinda. If you gonna work cattle in 'is high country, you gotta be kinda tougher'n it is."

Here, from the canyons to county seats, it was equally apparent that cowboys are hired because of necessity, not nostalgia. Take, for example, the afternoon that I went into Marfa, a cattle supply town with an imposing stone courthouse dominating the end of Main Street. As I glanced up at the Texas longhorns and buffalo head mounted in the lobby of the El Paisano Hotel, a stucco Spanish-style building, eighty-two-year-old Elmer Husted rose from his chair. Unlocking a glass case, he offered to sell 1851- and 1872-model Colt revolvers, gold-trimmed derringers, a palm-size gambler's pistol, and a dozen other guns that had helped to settle the cattle country. "If I'm going to sell 'em, it got to be to somebody like you coming through," he said. "Ranch people here aren't interested in western antiques — they just want what it takes to get the job done now."

Across the lobby, Rube Evans, a fifth-generation cattleman now operating his wife's ranch, piled his boots atop a bare desk in the office of the Rio Grande Cattle Company. Still scratching the dust from his eyebrows, Evans thought that I looked tired from just watching him help another cowman and his two cowboys round up and treat 200 steers that were ill from weeds and worms. "You can go to the back pastures a hundred times and you'll spend a hundred days chasing something that needs something done to them." Later, in the cattlemen's coffee shop, Hayes Mitchell, Jr., a fourth-generation rancher now grazing 1500 cattle on pastures spread ninety miles apart, adjusted both his hat and toothpick. He turned solemn as he was told that his Cessna plane and several head of France's white Limousin cattle give him a reputation as a modern and innovative cowman. "About the best thing a plane's good for is acting like a big-shot rancher," he said, pausing to bite into a plug of tobacco. "And maybe to check your water way off somewhere's. But there's no two ways about it — this is a cowboys-and-horse business. The only way you can make it is with hard work, good cattle, and good hands."

Within a week, as I moved on, there was a need to avoid cattlemen and cattlewomen. Earlier, farther east, both owners of large ranches with reputations for "pulling the rug out from under people" and the polished men who control or operate ranches for the absentee heirs viewed any questions about them, or the cowboys, with all the concern of a teller surprised by auditors. Conversely, ranchers enjoying reputations as "good hard workers" were highly cooperative. As they drove, ate, or drank, they recalled adventures with rattlesnakes or cockleburs, droughts, or drunken cowhands. Understandably, the conversations always gravitated toward a portrait of the owners' or their ancestors' life on the ranch. In any area of Texas, it was not easy for cowmen and cowwomen who have inherited or leased 200,000 acres to sustain an interest in the motivation of a hired cowboy who may not even own the 1968 Ford that he drives. Plainly, few cowmen give any measure of the stature to the cowboy — a man as essential to them as grass — that is accorded him outside the cattle regions. As I walked across the courtyard of the El Paisano Hotel, a plump man looked up from a metal chair to volunteer an opinion that is prevalent in the cattle region. "You still going to talk to old cowboys 'stead of a rancher," he said. "Tell the truth, I don't know why anybody'd want to be a cowboy nohow."

Of the ranch foremen whom I contacted, two were particularly uninhibited and unpretentious men. One was Odell. Meeting me in town, while picking up some pinkeye medicine, he immediately voiced his dislike for even the title of foreman: "You're just another cowboy who has to see that your sorry old hands get their work done, too." Leaning against his truck, he explained his owner's life-long apprehension for journalists. "If I was to even let some Hereford magazine on the ranch," he said, "that'd get him thinking he's gonna get blamed for beef costing so much or somebody writing about what he thinks he's got hid out behind the outhouse but he ain't. Then you go writing up all the cussin' and fartin' on his ranch to boot. He knows I don't give a damn if he eats my ass out. But he's liable run my wife and kids off."

But, making no secret of his pride in the cowboy, Odell barely paused: "You don't need to print the owner's name or ranch for the time being. So why don't you put your stuff in the truck and come out for the night. 'morrow we'll be gettin' up load old culls — ones 'at ain't no count no more — and least you can see for yourself how cow-boying never was like it is on TV."

The next evening, after following Odell from dawn to dusk, I realized that he and his men best typified the spirit of the working cowboy. Though I promised to alter some names and descriptions, I felt that an unrestricted view of these men, obtained without the owner's permission, would be a truer portrait of how the American cowboy works and lives today than one drawn from many ranches where friendly cowmen or managers provided their guidance and guest room. "You able to write it up like 'at," Odell said, "you're sure welcome to watch all you want. Be glad to have somebody to talk to."

During subsequent trips back to the ranch and surrounding area, I observed the preparation for a roundup and enough of the different jobs at the beginning and end of it that exemplify the mechanics and dialogue of cowboys gathering cattle. Always staying as close to the activity as possible, I simply watched and listened to the men. Sometimes, if Odell thought I might get lost in a canyon, I then waited on a ridge or rode with the cook, wrangler, or an injured cowboy until meeting the men again. When unable to witness a pertinent scene, I later discussed it with the men until convinced that I had the facts to describe it. Any general point of view in the narrative represents what the cowboys expressed. Thoughts attributed to someone convey the views that he later emphasized during an interview. Where it seemed appropriate, I corroborated historical facts and interspersed the experiences and opinions of other cowboys, cowmen, and individuals in the cattle region. The name of the ranch has been changed to the "Double Diamond." Similarly, the name and description of everyone on the ranch — as well as anyone identified by only a first name or nickname — has been changed. With the exception of the

"Double Diamond," each full name, as well as the ranch or organization associated with it, is an actual name.

My thanks are owed to the cowboys, cattlemen, and cattlewomen; to Daphne A. Ehrlich of Houghton Mifflin Company, who had faith in the story of the working cowboy when the book was only an idea; to Richard Schultz for typing the handwritten drafts; and to Louise Fisher for typing the finished manuscript.

Contents

ROUNDUP
at the
DOUBLE
DIAMOND

1. Doctoring / Summer
of the Screwworm

In the world of the Double Diamond Ranch, land is not counted by the acre, but by a section of 640 acres and, even then, usually by the hundreds of sections. Rising from brushy valleys to towering red cliffs, from twisting canyons to piny mountains, the Double Diamond extends 37 miles at its longest point, 12.7 miles at its breadth. To enable the men to find the cattle, the ranch is divided into nine countries named for either the shape of mountains, rim rocks and canyons, or forgotten episodes with Indians, homesteaders, or trespassers. But, after working at the ranch for twelve years, the last seven as foreman, Odell knows that all he and his cowboys can do in one day is search part of a country.

ODELL DOES NOT LIKE what he sees. Pulling the left rein, he whirls Biscuit, his dun horse, so quickly that the black mane and tail toss in opposite directions. He keeps the horse in a gallop until reaching a scorched mesa, where the seemingly endless miles of bumpy valleys and plateaus of the Mule Bunch Country unfold before him. Now, as he studies the specks floating in the vast blue sky, his suspicion proves to be correct. Three thick clusters of turkey vultures, so far away that their huge wingspans seem little larger than those of sparrows, are descending into the searing heat of midmorning instead of rising, as usual, with the cooler air currents. "Well, it's too late to do no doctoring when the old buzzards waitin' for their dinner to get good and cooked," he said. "Ain't one yet ever wanted to take on a grown mouse 'at could still kick some."

His twenty-nine years as a cowboy tell him that, at the least, he is beset with the same trouble afflicting other cattle ranches in the Big Bend of Texas throughout the summer. But in this deceptive land, where distances are much greater than they initially appear, he must wait before he can see if his problem is any worse. The vultures are just too far away, he reasons, to ride back toward them now. With the Double Diamond's six other cowboys flanking him, he must continue to sweep across the valley and trap cattle to either treat or cull. Looking around, he knows that it will be another hour before everyone begins to converge near the cliff where Big Springs crosses both this pasture used for mother cows and the corner of another grazed by yearling steers.

He canters on until, rimming a circular depression in the terrain, he draws the attention of seven Hereford cows emerging from a clump of desert willow. Heads rising alertly, the cows retreat toward their calves that they entrusted with another mother cow. Splendidly proportioned, their dark red bodies contrasting handsomely with their uniformly white faces, feet, and bellies, each of the cows and calves appears in excellent health. Still, almost intuitively, Odell's eyes follow the last cow to maneuver into the group. He shakes both reins to send Biscuit sprinting forward just enough to scatter the cows and calves. Bawling replies to each distressed cry, every cow but the one Odell watches hurriedly claims a calf. Glancing around, he first sees that there is no bush or gulch to conceal any calf that this cow bore. Then, easing closer, he notices that she has the slightly ringed horns of an eleven- or twelve-year-old cow and a small udder that has not nursed a calf this year. "You missed your shot, you old bitch," he says, "so you might as well go to town 'fore the rush."

Pressing his spurs into Biscuit's ribs, he charges directly at the cow to force her to run farther away from him. Desperate, she whirls around to rejoin the group of cows that now are trotting away. But Odell quickly shifts his horse to block her. Lunging, the cow drives her left horn up at Biscuit's stomach. A spur digging deeper, Odell spins the horse with such precision that the cow stabs into the empty space and stumbles. Fighting to regain her balance, the cow looks up to find the horse snorting and snapping, Odell yelling and slapping his coiled lariat. The cow turns to escape. As Odell continues to chase her across the pasture, her eyes are glassy, her body defecating, from the terror of being singled out for removal from the bunch.

Seeing the cow, one of the cowboys gallops toward her on a coppery chestnut horse. The plaid shirt and black hat indicate that the rider is Woody. A young, loose-jointed, and exuberant man who always works with an open smile, Woody circles around the cow and drives her about 200 yards. He stops when he sees that, as planned, she is fleeing toward the trap formed by four strands of barbed wire extending from the red, rippled wall of the canyon.

Odell lets his reins sag until Woody can gallop back toward him. "Got a pretty good piece a load yet?" he hollers.

Woody's arm sweeps toward the canyon. " 'bout eighteen already penned up against 'em rocks over 'ere," he answers in a slow, relaxed tone. "Mostly bad-eyed. Cancer. Not countin' some calves 'at's cut up kinda. Anoth-er'n too — if you give me help gettin' 'at old broke-prick bull way over in 'at brush. Hell, you could half tell how his old eyes looked 'at somethin' was wrong."

Angling toward a thicket of prickly mesquite and cat's-claw, Odell shakes his head dispassionately as he stops several yards from a bulging, brick-colored bull that seems larger than a buffalo. "Swelled up like a musk-melon is *right*," he says, his soft voice laced with sarcasm. "Yeah, 'at's the price he's got to pay for goin' after all the tail like he did. They just pay more attention to 'at feeler on their old thing then 'ey do to their brain. Ever see how their whole body just jumps off the ground when 'ey start to jab it in a cow?"

Woody nods. " 'Course ever'body misses once in a while."

"Yeah, but not like 'at old son-bitch did," Odell snaps. "When 'ey miss and hit 'round a bone — 'at's all she wrote. You slam over two thousand pounds even against their old thing and it just breaks the muscle. Heals back all crooked and got a grist 'round it."

His smile widening, Woody removes his hat and rakes away the perspiration coating both short, black sideburns. "Yeah, he'll know it won't work right no more."

"Just old dead weight now, eating up good grass," Odell says, moving toward the bull. "We'll run him over 'ere with rest the culls."

The bull, lowering his horns into attacking position, appears agitated by the men. Staring and snorting belligerently, he begins to scratch a forefoot into the ground, as if marking off the boundary of a territory that he is guarding from intruders. "Well, lookie here," Odell says in a mocking, high-pitched voice.

Such a threat seems only to inspire a man with the terrain and job so clearly imprinted on both his clothing and short but deceptively stout forty-seven-year-old body. Ramrod straight while sitting on his saddle, Odell climbs down onto legs that are bowed from a life of hugging a horse's rib cage. With his springy gait, he seems to rise from pointed boots that, except for the narrow strip under the spurs, rocks have changed from dark brown into a scuffed eggshell gray. His angular, ruggedly handsome face that appears totally bronzed by the sun suddenly turns white midway on the forehead when he swats his hat at a horsefly. The crinkly, wide-brim hat — all vestiges of its original color and shape long obliterated — is jauntily perched askew. Unstrapping a rope, his powerful, seemingly leatherized hands reveal no weakness from one right finger that has been shortened by a coiling lariat and another that grew back crooked after it was broken during a roundup. Drawing back the rope, he walks toward the bull exuding such confidence that his buckskin chaps, etched by mesquite, prickly pear, and yucca, flap with each step that he takes.

Repeating his eagerness to attack, the bull takes two short steps. To Odell, the gesture seems feeble in comparison to the way that many proud bulls, muscles expanding, charge directly toward any man or animal that they really intend to gore. "You ain't gonna whip nobody," he says confidently.

His gaze intensifying, the bull seems engrossed by the way he is challenged. Suddenly, he hears Woody slipping up behind him. But he does not turn around in time. Woody punches an old, barkless oak pole into the bull's belly, near his swollen organ. Stung by the pain, the bull pivots and lumbers across the valley. With Odell galloping toward the bull, waving his lariat, Woody manages to slip close enough from the other side to jab the pole into his belly once again and turn him toward the cattle being culled. " 'at took the bull outta him good," Woody says, waving an arm.

"I want to see what Chili and 'em boys other side 'em rocks got to go with the momma cows," Odell replies. Reaching the sloping area, he quickly finds that he has enough cattle to either fill a truck or move to another pasture.

A stubby, well-fed Mexican-American cowboy, with a round face enlivened by mischievous eyes, Chili is driving several steers along a barbed wire fence separating the pastures. Quickly he turns to scare away the heavier steers. "Sissies," he says, pointing to the thinner steers.

"You boys done found 'is many queer steers already?" Odell asks in the Tex-Mex dialect of pidgin Spanish and English. Moving toward the cattle, he sees that much of the hair has been rubbed off at least seven steers' flanks or tails. Only the number of these steers, not their condition, surprises him. Though every bull calf in the pasture was castrated while only three months old, Odell knows that a few, even as steers, never lose their desire for sex. With no heifers in their pasture, bands of four or five steers work together to use a weaker steer, usually one with the size and scent closest to that of a heifer, as their private female. In taking turns simulating the sexual act, Odell notices, several steers have mounted one gaunt steer so often that he has had little time to graze. Though a side is inflamed from scraping hooves, he finds it useless to resist a steer climbing upon him; another steer has already blocked his path. Odell nods approvingly. "Yeah, if we don't send 'em someplace else," he said, "they just gonna get rode to death."

Chili shakes his rope. "Yeo-o-o-o," he yells, in a shrill tone that frightens the steers into running toward the trap.

Three of the aggressive steers also start in the same direction only to have Odell, spurting forward, jerk a boot from his stirrup in time to kick at their heads. One, feeling a boot strike an eye, wheels around with such velocity that he drives the two other steers back into the pasture.

Free to see what the vultures are circling, Odell turns back toward the floor of the valley. Squinting as he rides along a slight ridge, he waves his hat until gaining the attention of J.J., another cowboy silhouetted against a reddish brown butte shaped much like an oil storage tank. Showing the instincts that make him Odell's "right-hand man," J.J. quickly angles toward the second group of vultures.

By the time he winds around a hill, Odell finds that the vultures' keen vision has drawn another dozen or so of them to the group initially hovering above a dead cow. One vulture, dropping down to study the condition of the animal, soars back into the formation's lower level. This graceful motion, seeming as effortless as a glider, belies the loathsomeness of the dark brown scavengers when Odell approaches more than a dozen of them completely covering the bloated carcass. Their naked red necks and heads, accented by nostrils large enough for someone to see through, bob gluttonously as their pronounced beaks tear deeper into the softer, decomposing eyes, rectum, and genitalia. Seeing Odell, each vulture flexes its wings. But, typifying their appetites, all of them peck hurriedly for another chunk of the cow's carcass before letting their huge, flapping wings lift them into the air. Knowing that he is too late to determine what killed the cow, Odell does not bother to climb down from his horse.

He has a question that is answerable when he jogs toward J.J. A short, muscular, and serious-looking man in his early thirties, with a large cud of tobacco in the right jaw making him appear jowlier than he actually is, J.J. is standing in front of a nervous young cow. "Little old calf's just 'bout dead," J.J. says, pointing a wrinkled straw hat behind him. "I never seen a navel all caked up blood way his is."

Easing behind the cow, Odell sees that she is shielding a small, bony calf, at least two months younger than most of the others in the pasture, that is lying on its right side. A young cow, no doubt nursing only her first or second calf, she spins around to keep her body between Odell and the calf. Bawling softly, she nuzzles the calf's chin and retreats three steps.

An odor quickly warns Odell what has struck the calf. Handing his reins to J.J., he pulls at the calf's bloodied navel. The raw wound confirms his suspicion. As cowboys throughout hotter, more accessible areas of South Texas have already found during this summer of 1972, masses of screwworms — striped bluish green flies each nearly three times the size of houseflies — have swarmed up from Central America and Mexico for virtually the first time in thirteen years. Though the screwworm's disease, per se, is not contagious, the female fly blows so many microscopic eggs into natural openings or the slightest scratch that, if untreated, hatch into screw-shaped larvae that not only devour enough flesh and blood to kill a cow or calf within two weeks but also multiply into such overwhelming numbers of flies that they can cause an epidemic on a ranch.

Odell brushes a sleeve across his nostrils as he straightens up. "Damn if I wasn't hoping 'em old screwworms wouldn't get 'is far in the mountains," he says, speaking slowly. "You don't ever see the old worms a-tall. But way 'ey done eat up 'is little old late calf is what they'll do. I 'member when I was a kid, 'ey must've been

two hundred thousand head right in Texas got killed by
'em just in 'at one bad year — nineteen and thirty-eight.
Watch so 'is old bitch don't hook me when my back's
turned."

"Yeo, yeo," J.J. hollers, distracting the cow.

Pumping the lever on his Winchester-style .30-.30 rifle
as he walks, Odell slowly circles the calf until the angle
suits him. Then, in a continuous motion, he draws the
rifle to his right shoulder, aims, and squeezes the trigger.
The .30-.30 bullet, larger than is necessary to kill the calf,
tears into its brain, causing several muscles to jerk. Mis-
taking the brief spasm as renewed strength, the cow happily licks the calf's chin.

Odell fits the rifle back into a long holster attached to
his saddle; then, returning to the lifeless calf, he smears a
purple ointment into the navel to kill the larvae before
they can crawl out.

Her eyes studying the men, her nose sniffing, the cow finally seems to sense that her calf is dead. She bawls
mournfully for about half a minute and then, apparently
thinking of her own survival, scampers about twenty
yards.

Riding away from the calf, J.J. turns a thumb up toward
the vultures without looking at them. "They after 'nother
calf over yonder where you rode past?"

"Old cow. But it's too late to tell if it's screwworms 'at
got her," Odell says, exhaling lightly. "But bad off as 'is
calf was means one thing for sure — 'ey done got least a
ten-, maybe twelve-day head start on 'is pasture."

Reaching the trap, holding the cattle that the men have
culled, Odell's attentive blue eyes study the nearest calf
even as he ties Biscuit to a fence post. "Somethin' matter
with 'em little calves or their mommas?" he asks, raising
his voice above the chorus of bawls. Though speaking to
no one in particular, Odell instinctively looks for an an-

swer from Virgil, the most seasoned of the cowboys at the Double Diamond.

Virgil nods. A tall, cheerful and unhurried man, with a red, pinched face and white hair turned tawny by dust, Virgil carries his sixty-five years as well as his bandanna covers the scar that the end of a Lone Star beer bottle left on his neck several years ago. He finishes squirting medicine into a calf's mouth and, arm pointing out toward the other calves, ambles toward Odell. "This'n I just wormed and bunch like 'em just plain pinworms," he says, pushing back a grimy beige hat until the brim touches his collar. "But navels, hips all sored up on 'bout six other calves 'ey brung in kinda look like screwworms 'at used to be around."

Keeping to his leisured pace, Odell drops onto his stomach. He skims away two spindly waterbugs from the widest place in the trickling stream and slurps the water. Straightening up, he throws out a palm toward the type of sudden but welcome southeasterly breeze that, if meeting certain atmospheric conditions, is what brings occasional rain to the region. "Damn if it ain't liable to get some moisture," he says, "and green up ever'thing."

Chili, not waiting until he finishes relieving himself, slaps his free hand into the wind. "Naw, it just bring back some the dirt it blow 'way yesterday."

Shaking the wrinkles from his rope as he walks, Odell eases toward the center of the pen. Holding the coil in his left hand, he nonchalantly pitches the loop over a calf's neck. His hands advancing along the rope, he dashes forward to grab the calf's forelegs; then, as Chili grasps its tail and hind legs, they flip him onto a patch of dried grass that looks almost dormant. Scowling, he swings his left fist menacingly to scare away the calf's mother. With other men pressing on each end of the calf, Odell falls to his knees to look into an egg-size sore in the calf's navel. Shaking his head, he dabs a small stone into a can of purple ointment, then pushes it far into the wound in order to kill the burrowing screwworm larvae. Odell scratches under an arm until two men wrestle another calf to the ground. "You see how 'em worms eat on his leg here?" he says, looking up at the younger men. "Least little old scratch or hole and 'ey go right to work. When you all start riding, look 'round the eyes, ass, anyplace 'at's warm. It all smells like 'is, too."

Spraying tobacco juice into the rising dust, Virgil doesn't even glance at the calf he holds under his knees. "I was a boy, a good horse could smell worms. Had a horse 'at'd light right for a cow 'at had screwworms without you sayin' nothin'."

Billy Bob, a squat twenty-three-year-old man with a square, well-tanned face, moves his eyes puckishly. Though the newest cowhand at the Double Diamond, he remains ready to offer good-natured sarcasm. " 'at's the horse you took off whole bunch Apaches, ain't it," he says, spacing out his words for emphasis. " 'em old days?"

"Shoot, had 'at horse when I was workin' over by Sanderson," replies Virgil, pausing to chase a calf away from the men. "Old blowflies what 'ey called 'em I was a boy. You just spit 'bacco juice in 'em and hope 'ey'd go som'er's else."

Odell's voice continues to sharpen. "These old flies ain't gonna go nowhere else 'less we get out to doctoring first thing tomorrow." Pausing, pressing his lips together, he turns toward the cows and steers milling nervously against the rocks. "Wanta run 'em by?"

As the remaining forty-three head of cattle are driven past him, even two or three at a time, Odell needs only to glance at them to decide whether they need a powdered medication for pinkeye, or whether they suffer from cancer or other problems that cost them their usefulness to the ranch. Finished, he squeezes a cigarette paper around his crooked finger and shakes Bull Durham tobacco into it. Then, his feet set apart, hands thrust inside his hip pockets, Odell gazes thoughtfully at the men as he decides how to assign them to ride through areas of the pastures where they have not made more than a cursory inspection in nearly two months. "J.J., first thing in the morning," he says, "you and Billy Bob and Chili — you all want to start workin' 'at big old left corner in 'at Hundred Bar country. Know all 'at prickly pear starts gettin' thicker and all. Least little scratch on a cow 'ere and 'at's screwfly heaven."

Rising to his feet, J.J. pulls up the tight, faded denim pants to the small paunch on his stomach. "There ain't none of 'at greasum over my place, you know."

Odell takes a can of ointment from his vest pocket as he twists around. "Billy Bob, you want be sure and bring out three, four cans from the tack room 'morrow?" Pausing, he looks down at Pancho, an easy-mannered, swarthy man with a long, gentle face, punching a matchstick through the air vents he has cut into his hat. "And, Pancho, you and Virgil and Woody — you all want to work out through Indian Springs? Virgil, I'll leave the extra medicine I got in your pickup — you get it when you all bring 'ese culls out to the trailers. You all keep riding till you're satisfied you've doctored ever'thing 'at you can."

Chili's eyes fasten on the large pronged rowels curving down from the end of J.J.'s Argentine gaucho spurs. "Hey," he says slowly, "how far you have to chase that nigger to get 'em rattlers, huh?"

Odell begins to smile when Billy Bob tosses his lasso around Chili's left boot.

Billy Bob pulls the rope enough to lift Chili's foot off the ground. "Think we better check Chili for screwworms, right?" he says, trying to look grim.

Odell shakes his head. "You gonna be out ridin' with Chili sometimes," he says. "And you liable to get left off some canyon you don't know your way out."

"Gringo cowboy no work," Chili replies, as tobacco juice seeps from his lips. "Welfare."

Typical of cowboys, such bantering never seems to stop; the buoyancy never seems to fade. Always congenial, often boyishly happy, these six cowboys live with the daily affirmation that they are real men. Seldom finding a job too difficult, dirty, or dangerous, each of these men visibly enjoys his work — plainly satisfying himself that what he does for a living leaves him beholden to no one.

Not even the great variance in these men's ages and physiques, as well as the fact that they receive the highest wages of their lives, has diminished their free spirit. With the exception of those who manage a large outfit, or own a few dozen cows themselves, there is little legitimate opportunity of wealth for the 126,000 men working as cowboys, fence riders, fence fixers, and at other jobs on the 51,000 cattle ranches stretching from the thick brushy flatland of South Texas to the piny mountains of northern Montana. On this day, as unprecedented prices will be paid for the 214,000 beef cattle slaughtered in the United States, the average cowboy cannot honestly claim that his wages have increased proportionately. He knows not to expect much more than $175 to $375 a month and a house — or $160 to $260 a month and board — for working at least six (and usually seven) days a week on the moderate to large ranches. He seldom receives little more than a shack and $140 a month, or eight to ten dollars a day during the strenuous seasonal jobs at the small ranches that many a cowman-cowboy operates largely with the labor of a son who vows to leave once he can buy an automobile. Yet J.J.'s dependability brings him $400 a month and the use of a pickup truck and a white frame house hidden in a hilly division of the ranch that his wife and three small children find enjoyable. Chili and Virgil each receive $340 a month, a truck, and a small shingled house that, like so many on the large ranches, is located in such a remote pasture that about the only men able to adjust to this are those who are single, widowed, or whose children are too young or too old for school. Not only are these houses far more comfortable than the batch shacks and line camps where both men have lived in past years, but Chili's wife is confident that, with some effort, she can drive out to the paved road each morning when their four children start to school. Even as young, single men, Woody and Billy Bob each receive $300 a month and a comfortable bed in the modified adobe bunkhouse equipped with running water, refrigerator, bottled gas stove, and fan.

Still, much like his own attitude before taking the responsibility of supervising the Double Diamond, Odell feels certain that at least five of these men would, if displeased by anyone or any place, move on to another ranch. Putting full faith in their masculinity, these men give little thought to saving enough money to support themselves and their families for any length of time between jobs. Head high, all have left jobs at other ranches, seldom bothering to notify the owner, with little more than a few days' wages, a saddle, and their pride. "No, buddy," is the way Billy Bob rationalized his annoyance at a cowman's orders; "I ain't takin' 'at damn old cussin' off nobody."

"You come away with anything when you quit off?" J.J. asks.

"My saddle and my ass," he replies, looking proud.

At least twenty-five years of scrambling for a living around Mexican ranchos, Odell suspects, would no doubt temper even Pancho's restive impulses. He is unlikely to walk away from the small green trailer and $300 a month (part of which he sends to his wife and children in Mexico) that he is paid to check the cattle, water, and salt on a high, stony corner of the ranch that, for all practical purposes, he can inspect only on a horse or by walking. But somewhat like a cowboy he once knew, Odell feels, Pancho would probably find a way to justify any such decision. "I never took nothin' off any old cowman in my life," the cowboy would jest, "but a few of his old calves."

Far from being eccentric, these men are probably close to what can be categorized as average working cowboys. Elsewhere, many men adopt one of two life-styles so diverse that each precludes the other from typifying the cowboy. One type needs no disagreements to "cowboy around." He remains in an orbit much like that of Dave Price, a small, happy, twenty-nine-year-old cowboy, choosing to ride saddled broncos in professional rodeos this fall instead of rounding up cattle. Propped against a gate not far from Vernon, Texas, repairing his saddle, Price enumerates some of the jobs that have enabled him to crisscross the cattle country:

"I quit this little ranch in Oklahoma. Hitchhiked to New Mexico and got on riding and fixing fences for couple months. Quit and rode a bull in a rodeo. Got on at the Double O in Oklahoma. Caught a ride up to Elko, Nevada — boy, 'at's real cattle country. Fourteen hours a day and sixty-five miles of open range. Got hold of Stanley Ellison and hired on with the Pitchfork Ranch. Quit and went with a rodeo. Got on with Wineglass. Took off with three other boys. Cut through Kansas. Worked for the CO in Arizona. Me and another boy went back to

Nevada. Two days before Christmas I was roping a steer and fell and broke my ankle. Then, second April, same horse blew up in slick weather and I fell and broke my ankle again. Fourth of July, I left Ellison again. Pulled into Mountain City, Nevada. Rodeoed little more. Labor Day, I went back to the Pitchfork gathering cattle. Got on for roundup at the Lazy S. It got down to twenty-two below zero on the trail and I wanted to go to Texas. Then me and Gene Herschel, we poured gas to that old fifty-seven Chevvy till we got to the Waggoner [Ranch] — Texas. It was suppertime and Wes O'Neal, the wagon boss, only had one set of extra horses. He put me on so he'd have thirty men working the roundup. Kinda settled down couple years — three meals a day and place to sleep and two twenty-nine a month 'fore they took things out. Twenty-five dollars extra a month when you're breaking horses. Then I quit and took off for a rodeo. Didn't do too good and I called Wes and asked if I could get my horses back. Got a five percent raise."

Price pauses briefly to dip into a can of snuff. "Some rough years," he continues. "But got my rodeo card now. Pick up fifty dollars every now and then — sometimes a hundred. Texas one night, Colorado the next. South Dakota another. Winter's coming. So I'm going to Kansas to braid saddles and take care this man's horses and keep 'em fat and practice on his real good ones. You know how it is with a cowboy. You just have to see what it's like over the next hill."

The other type of cowboy, if he likes a ranch or region, seldom travels beyond the two or three counties that make up the ranch. Nowhere is this pattern more apparent than among the seven adjoining ranches in the high, rolling plains of the West Texas Panhandle that retain much of the size and appearance they had when they were claimed soon after the Comanche and Kiowa Indians were driven from them and onto a reservation in 1875. With somewhat the same pretensions of a man volunteering that his father also attended Yale, dozens of cowboys on these ranches are proud to mention that they have spent most of their adult life "with the Pitchfork," "Four Sixes," or "Spur," or, like their fathers, always have been an "SMS," "Matador," "Waggoner," or "JA" ranch man.

Some cowboys are legendary in the region, such as Scandalous John Selman and George Humphries. A talkative man, who owed his nickname to vivid accounts of "scandalous" horses he rode, Selman could never be certain of how many years he worked in the Panhandle. His date of birth having escaped him, he always observed his birthday on the day in July that the annual Texas Cowboy Reunion began in Stamford, Texas. But, he knew, he came to the SMS Ranches when the owners purchased the Espuela Ranch where he was reared and, before he died last year, went on to work for fifty years as foreman of the SMS Flat Top Ranch. Humphries remains an imposing figure. A short, friendly man with his stomach pushing against a khaki shirt, a red bandanna flopping in the breeze, Humphries left the 6666 Ranch ("Four Sixes") not long ago after working there for fifty-two consecutive years. He might have stayed longer if he was just another cowboy. But, as head cowboy and foreman of the entire ranch for the last thirty-eight of those years — and also settling all the fights as the sheriff of King County for twenty years — Humphries found that it came time to retire in favor of a younger man.

Such cowboys, though, need not advance to foreman to spend their entire adult life at one ranch. At the Callaghan Ranch, extending across much of brushy Webb County, Texas, it is common for fence riders to stay for decades. "Cowboys who spent twenty years here have found it hard to get a lot of seniority," said Joe Finley, Jr., co-owner of the family-operated ranch. "We've got top men who've been here forty years, one over fifty years."

Whether they spend five weeks or five decades on a ranch, most such men share a common trait. Nobody did — or really can — train them to be competent cowboys. Born and growing into the job, with little practical opportunity for other employment unless they leave the region, experienced cowboys usually view themselves as preordained to tend cattle and ride horses. Much like the men working for the Double Diamond, these thoughts are similarly voiced by cowboys of all age levels as they gather to round up cattle from the 225,000 acres of H. L. Kokernot, Jr.'s 06 Ranch in Brewster and Jeff Davis counties of Texas. Asked why he has been a lifelong cowboy, sprightly seventy-one-year-old Otis Coggins reacts with an expression that alternates between amusement and amazement. Burying both thumbs inside his hand-tooled, two-toned belt, he answers while spraying enough tobacco juice to settle much of the dust around him, "I started cowboying when I was twelve year old, 'cause in 'is country you had to cowboy or else."

Given a choice of other jobs, Buzz Nichols, the forty-four-year-old foreman and head cowboy at the 06 Ranch, would still prefer being a cowhand in spite of the demands and hazards. A lean, energetic, and engaging man, insisting that he hasn't "enough ass to hold up my pants," Nichols turns philosophical as he folds his pocketknife with three right fingers that have lost their tips. He attaches little importance to the accident. Unlike many cowboys, Nichols emphasizes that he still can use the remainder of the fingers for any job that he chooses. How did he lose the tips? With one end of a rope tied to his saddle horn, he recalls, he had just tossed the noose over a steer and was preparing to jump from the horse to hopefully bind him within twelve to fifteen seconds. As the steer sprinted away from him, Nichols kept the uncoiling rope high to prevent it from falling under his horse's front legs. Suddenly, feeling as if ice was pressed to his fingers, he knew that a coil had clipped them. "Don't bother to heel him," Nichols told his partner. "I ain't got no fingers to tie him with." He glances at the remainder of the fingers as he reminisces. "The doc couldn't sew the end of the fingers back on. Time we found 'em, the ants and flies were all over 'em. But they don't even hurt except in real cold weather."

What would hurt him, Nichols quickly volunteers, is not working as a cowboy. "Listen, my dad homesteaded over yonder in the Glass Mountains in nineteen-o-three," he continues, nodding toward a series of hazy peaks, "and you just had cows and Johnson grass and when I was born my dad gave the doctor a big old fat calf for delivering me. Cowboying was the only thing I saw and all I ever liked to do. I'll never forget the day when I was seventeen and went to work for sixty dollars a month and my board chasing old cows and breaking horses and getting drug and throwed. Then I cowboyed up in Arizona and over in New Mexico and maybe a half-dozen places altogether back in this country around Alpine and Marfa and Fort Stockton. Listen, I don't have to cowboy because it's all I *can* do. My brother, for instance, went off and is the business manager of a college. I do it because I found out how I really like it. See, I got a good wife [Ruth] who taught school and played on the Flying Queens, that real good girls' basketball team, and four real nice kids — three boys and a girl. And I remembered my dad working hard cowboying till he was sixty-nine years old to get ahead. So I went to work awhile with bulldozers and doing concrete work. I was sick all the time. Weekends, I'd even cowboy someplace to keep from going crazy 'fore I came back. If you're a cowboy, you're about half coyote. You can't stand no schedule and no place but the big country and everything about it. What so important about doing something you hate? I don't want to go somewhere and sell insurance policies or something you don't believe in and the other fellow doesn't really want to buy. Biting your fingernails off all the time. But I sure like to ride a good horse and gather cattle. When you get a bunch of cattle out of the mountains and all throwed together — you can look out and see you've accomplished something."

As Nichols walks toward the barn, his eyes scan his three sons — all wearing cowboy hats, boots, and pants — milling around the pen for orphan and rejected calves. "You know, all my boys love it," he says, snapping his head. "Lord, I hope they're gonna be cowboys when they're bigger."

Still, cowboys at the 06 Ranch entertain little romanticism about their employment. Typifying the self-appraisals, Jack Phariss, a wiry thirty-eight-year-old cowboy who trains and rides cutting horses between roundups, playfully tosses his rope against a younger man's boots as he ponders a question about the image of cowboys. "Hell, a cowboy is just an old son-of-a-bitch doin' what he wants to do," he said, "when the rest of the world's tellin' you what they think you oughta do."

All that bothers Odell about this breed of men is that now, during the summer and not just the spring and fall roundups, he needs several more of them to search for ill cattle. Weighing the threat of a screwworm epidemic, he is relieved that five of the six regular cowboys have worked long enough for the Double Diamond to no longer lose themselves in the labyrinth of mountains and canyons. But Odell also is realistic about the limitations of searching a ranch with barbed wire fence stretching for

more than 280 miles; it is physically impossible for these
men to just locate the vast majority of the 15,500 cows,
calves, and steers that, for the most part, have reverted to
their wild instincts in ranging the land to find tufts of nu-
tritious grama grass or, when the spring rain is agonizingly late or light, any hardier but edible forage. No matter how many cattle the men see or treat during the next
few weeks, Odell knows an important question remains:
How many other cattle will be bitten by screwworms between the time the men search a pasture and they assemble at Echo Canyon for the fall roundup — the culmination of a year on a ranch — to gather, sort, and ship them.

Moreover, the mere possibility of screwworms compli-
cates Odell's greater concern about the entire roundup.
Even with another twenty men, the schedules of many
roundups have been disrupted by the whimsies of cowboys or cattle. Time after time, he has had to stop a cowhand from trying to fight many of the crew after drinking
his entire bottle in one evening. He has seen the same
man help drive 115 of the awesome bulls to winter pastures but then break a leg while chasing a heifer calf, or
1,500 cows driven ten miles across the ranch only to bolt
within sight of their pasture. Cows have become crazed
with grief after their calves were taken from them. Now,
besides these uncertainties, he anticipates that the need
to examine or treat cattle for screwworms will slow him
still further. If so, he wonders, will the men be able to
drive all the steers and calves down to the valleys in time
for them to refill themselves with water before they are
sold?

Maybe, Odell rationalizes, he should start the roundup
earlier than now planned. In many such situations,
Odell's position with Warren, the mild, settled seventy-
four-year-old owner of the Double Diamond Ranch,
allows him considerable authority. Though wanting to

be phoned about every two weeks, Warren leaves Odell responsible for the cattle, horses, and men on the ranch; Specks, an accountant working from an office in a bank building, is in charge of the ranch's payroll, receipts, and taxes. Dividing much of his time between homes in San Antonio and Chicago, Warren returns to his huge, elm-shrouded Spanish Colonial house on an accessible corner of the Double Diamond in the spring, the fall, and at Christmas. Generally he limits his role in the operation of the ranch to meeting large cattle buyers and approving the bloodlines of new bulls, salaries for cowboys, and dates of the roundups. Still, Odell is well aware that Warren's preference for holding the fall roundup from October 1 until early November stems as much from the Double Diamond's tradition as the practical fact, now that contracts are being prepared, that it coincides with the dates requested by the companies buying the cattle. If he starts the roundup early, Odell feels he can first gather and separate the cattle that will remain on the ranch; then he can drive into loading pens the calves and steers that will be sold on the contracted date. With characteristic decisiveness, Odell will not wait for Warren to return from San Antonio, where, as a widower, he has renewed interest in a former girl friend, to ask permission to advance the start of the roundup. Reasoning that he is responsible for "anything 'at goes wrong," Odell chooses to make plans to begin early.

To put his plan in motion, he will have the other men drive the cattle that have just been culled to the flat country on the opposite side of Cave Hill. From there, they can be hauled on two long trailers to the loading pens beside an asphalt road fourteen miles away and then wedged into a large tractor-trailer that will carry them to the stockyards in San Angelo, Texas. Turning toward three men idling against a slab of rock, Odell speaks as though he, not Warren, owns the ranch. "If we gonna whip 'ese old worms," he says in a confident voice, "I'm gonna get some more hands to help doctorin' and maybe get the roundup goin' little earlier."

Spinning, Virgil flings a stone into the face of a cow — hitting an eye — trying to slip away from the group of cattle that have been culled.

"Old Hot Shot's supposed to have truck for 'ese old culls out by the road by five o'clock," Odell continues, walking away to water Biscuit. "So you all ride 'morrow and I'll be out to help you later on. Yeah, soon as I get some more medicine and try to beat some of these other outfits to the men with any sense."

J.J. shakes his head. "I don't know where you gonna find 'nough hands 'at's any count way things are now."

Neither does Odell. Riding toward the trucks, he ponders some of the reasons behind the increasing competition to hire experienced cowhands for a roundup. Most of all, he knows, not many dependable cowboys with families can live anymore on just what they earn from occasional employment and the spring and fall roundups. Instead of waiting until they found full-time jobs as cowboys — and sometimes when they had them — nearly a dozen young men raised around cattle have been led by improved wages and roads to find quasi-cowboy jobs away from ranches. That tough, tall boy who is supposed to have nearly finished high school, Odell remembers, has left to work as a brand inspector looking for stolen cattle at county auction barns. Another who already was a first-rate cowboy now breaks and trains saddle horses near El Paso for what he calls "town people playing Sunday posse." He has heard that a dependable cowboy sought a job as one of the U.S. Department of Agriculture's sixty "river riders." This work, Odell concedes, is not too different from that on some ranches. Camping out in pairs, each man uses his own horse to ride about twenty-seven miles every day in search of Mexican cattle and horses that stray or are smuggled into the zone along the Texas side of the Rio Grande theoretically kept free of feverish cattle ticks. When someone doesn't want his cattle lassoed and checked, a river rider's job conjures up visions of bygone challenges. "Yes, sir, you get your gun out quick," Odell says, sounding impressed. "You the only law there and you hold the line."

To the envy of many men, still another popular cowboy is employed by the federal government to live for a month at a time in these mountains on just the supplies packed atop a mule in order to trap coyotes and bobcats. Much to the displeasure of Odell, it seems that about every four or five years one of those young boys who lived near a town, but showed promise of becoming a skilled cowboy, leaves to try his luck with a professional rodeo. Worse yet, some young men won't work at all.

Few of these men can be replaced by technology. The more Odell wends his way down the rocky land, the more it is evident why the working cowboy who can find and flush out cattle refuses to fade as might ordinarily be expected due to the machinations of time. Typifying the land's isolation, as he stares at what seem like several motherless calves, but prove to be pronghorn antelopes loping between two ridges, a shallow cave opens in the craggy rocks above him. Seemingly untouched by white settlers, or even contemporary hunters, the cave bears a vivid imprint of Indians who occupied it, as do hundreds of similar caves in the area, from the period of 300 to 1400 A.D. On one wall, a small picture of a deer pierced by an arrow has been painted with charcoal and animal fat. Along the bottom of the opposite wall, the red coloring in either cinnabar or iron oxide has been used to draw a woman carrying a bowl. Once told of the paintings, no doubt an archeological wealth to some, Odell flexed his right palm dismissingly. "Oh, they's all kinds of old caves 'at Indians painted and scraped things in. Little old pictures of things 'at ain't no bigger'n your hand and some big as a cow, and some 'at don't make no sense a-tall and gets some schoolteacher all worked up."

For Odell, the grandeur of the land only disguises its harshness. Even though he and his men always ride through the pastures between roundups, the disassembled, sun-bleached bones of cows from another year, now settling into the dusty soil, attest that an average of one out of every thirty head of cattle still die prematurely. Suddenly, the wind breaks the eerie silence. Dipping down like a miniature tornado, it swirls a clump of sagebrush with such force against the hind legs of a small, unsuspecting calf that it spills him.

The sense of vastness and timelessness of the cattle country remains with Odell after he reaches the trucks that were parked below Cave Hill earlier in the morning. He unsaddles Biscuit, shanking him to the shady side of a trailer, and puts three cans of the screwworm ointment into Virgil's pickup truck. Then, settling into his own pickup, he pushes the .30-.30 rifle up behind his seat, into the twin rack already holding a .22 semiautomatic rifle. Hands squeezing the steering wheel, he remains oblivious to the small ruts and ridges that bounce him over the faint path leading to a blacktop road. As he does in much of the area, where the store that sells gas and beer is seldom closer than forty miles, Odell feels comfortable driving eighty miles per hour down the middle of the road. The other visible signs of habitation are scarce: An older man waving from a tan pickup truck. A game warden. Telephone wires. An occasional cow standing behind the barbed wire paralleling the road. And, only because he knows to look between two hills, Odell can see the spinning blades of a distant windmill pumping water from a deep, subterranean stream. As he knows, the windmill is all that enabled someone to settle that and countless other plots of land so arid that they had long been considered useless — requiring today's cowboy to work in rugged areas where the pioneer cowboy never ventured.

Screened from the road, hidden behind the jagged mountains that stretch in any direction to the horizon, are other ranches so immense that some untrained men have never found their way out of them. It is the type of cattle country where myth and reality blend harmoniously: Mile after mile of land that, for the most part, the original breed of cattle barons, recall older cowboys, usually "put together by just taking" or "took off somebody else by doing 'em dirty," and, without the justice so popularly accorded them in movies and fiction, they have kept. Those who used their positions as lawyers in land grant offices often arranged to buy, cheaply, the title to certificates for some of the 200,000,000 acres of land unexplainably granted to railroad companies. Other barons purchased at negligible prices or, in the absence of dissenting evidence, claimed to have purchased blocks of scrip for land given to veterans as bonuses for service in the Mexican-American or Civil War. Cowmen with larger appetites favored arrangements with the Spanish, Mexican, or Texas governments that prevailed as legal grants to baronial empires. Deeds for a single ranch included parts of the Texas grasslands larger than all of Connecticut or a valley of New Mexico, fertilized by the Cimarron River, that was three times larger than all of Delaware.

Many other ambitious cowmen, though, seldom saw fit to act so civilly. Carrying reputations for meanness that is not always denied by descendants, these cattle kings hired adventurous men to simply drive away Mexicans or Anglo-Saxons already inhabiting a desirable plot and, when time came to obtain deeds, claimed squatters' rights for themselves. Their style was seldom impaired by the U.S. Homestead Act of 1862 that legally limited each claim for land to a maximum of 160 acres (later increased to a section of 640 acres) for a citizen over twenty-one years old who lived on it at least three years. To control the entire region, many cowmen employed "land company cowboys" to claim adjoining parcels of the range that, to prevent any belated bargaining, the cowboy usually signed away before being told the location. Or, by occupying strategic sections near the mouth of the stream, other cowmen prevented anyone from raising cattle within at least fifty miles of them. Even when many a homesteader settled land near water in this region, he often found himself fortunate to have a cowman allow him to sign away his claim for a token price. Exemplifying the tactics, accounts persist of how employees of the "Santa Fe Ring" of Confederate lawyers simply shot as trespassers men who inadvertently settled in an area of New Mexico, much of which is known today as Catron County, extending sixty-six miles from north to south, seventy-two miles from east to west.

To best grasp the immensity of these cowmen's appetites, older cowboys maintain, simply look at the remaining tracts of the ranches that are now controlled by the founders' great-grandchildren and middle-aged grandchildren or, to a lesser extent, either the men who married their daughters and granddaughters, the lawyers who arranged their mortgages and wills, or entrepreneurs or syndicates. For every large ranch that continues to buy or lease adjacent land, a dozen others have been carved by mismanagement, drought, recurring mortgages, estate taxes, division of estates, and either spending patterns or the fading interest of heirs. Still, retaining all the aura of fiefdoms, many of the ranches — extending in size up to the 570,000 acres of the Waggoner Ranch or 950,000 acres of the King Ranch — are each nearly as large as the entire state of Rhode Island or any of twenty-five small members of the United Nations.

A cowboy moving northward, through the mountainous grasslands of Arizona, Colorado, Nevada, New Mexico, Montana, and Wyoming, finds that today's well-situated cowmen control more of the enormous open range (also known as National Grasslands and National Forestlands) than their ancestors. To keep it, the cattleman's frontier force that controlled the precious accesses to water on these 220,000,000 acres of land has been replaced by the contention that any such grass belonged to the men who have used it — a position solidified since the ranges have come under the jurisdiction of either the U.S. Forest Service or Bureau of Land Management. By arranging to help draft the Federal Taylor Grazing Act, in which the policy for each "grazing district" of open range is set by an advisory board of "local stockmen recommended by the users of the range," certain old-line cattle families — some who also are governors or United States senators — have perpetual rights to the grassy regions near their ranches through leases that are, in essence, automatically renewable every ten years. The terms enabling these ranchers to graze 3,400,000 cattle a year on the open range — for an average monthly fee of sixty cents per cow — are preferable to the days when their forebears paid nothing to use it. Since the federal government underwrites nearly all expense of fences, roads, ponds, insecticides, and professional trappers to kill coyotes and bobcats, many cowmen find that banks often lend them more money on the open range that they lease than any taxable land that they own.

To find enough cowboys to gather cattle from these sprawling ranges, Odell's experience tells him that a foreman needs to know the skill of men on other ranches as well as he does on the one that he manages. It is this knowledge that leads him to suspect that he will find Frosty, a cocky but reliable cowhand, in the mood to leave his current employer in favor of working for the Double Diamond. Already Odell is surprised that Frosty's unstructured personality has allowed him to work for the past year attending cattle on 26,000 acres of land that large mountains and mortgages have separated from the central part of a medium-size ranch. From what Odell has heard, Frosty has shown little eagerness to accept the advice offered by the owner's husband, a former sewing machine salesman from Houston trying to prove himself as a cowman. In turn, Frosty's plucky independence has not endeared him to the husband.

Even if Frosty were satisfied with his current employer, Odell is also reminded that the location of the ranch — like so many where cowboys must live — will require him to either leave it or find his wife a house in town before winter so that his two children may attend school. To reach him, after speeding more than an hour over the blacktop road, Odell turns across several loose steel poles, known as a cattle guard, that support a truck but are too widely spaced for livestock to walk over. During the next hour, the thin outline of a dirt road and dry river bed take him nearly thirty miles around large rock outcroppings, a crumbled corral, and an abandoned adobe-style mortar and stone house, brown with dust; then across sandy land, its natural grass so heavily grazed and trodden during earlier days that winds have ripped away patches of the topsoil and allowed the desert scrub grass to creep across the other parts.

At the edge of a basin, he sees a thin cloud of dust spiraling above the rocks ahead of him. Careful not to frighten the cattle, he angles his truck wide to the left, around low yucca and creosote, until he can approach them from the rear. He watches a thin Mexican cowboy, yelling and waving a black hat, swerve quickly in front of a steer bolting from a herd. Just as the steer stumbles, many of the 300 or so black Angus and white-faced Herefords turn toward him. Alertly, Frosty and the two Mexican cowboys ride into the herd, their long poles stabbing repeatedly into rib cages, until the steers again move along a barbed wire fence banked with dried tumbleweed.

Satisfied that the herd is under control, Odell drives on to a gate, sagging toward him, that is held in place with wire. He waits with his hands clasped over a post until Frosty canters toward the gate, bringing a line of dust with him. "Didn't know you'd be shipping today," Odell said. "Wanted to take you back with me if I could."

A slight man in his early forties, with a wide gray hat tilted forward over a handsomely chiseled face and thin sideburns, Frosty demonstrates that he has lost none of his self-confidence. "Yeah, you look like you had enough 'perience to put you on," he says, breaking into a smile. "All the frijoles you can eat and all the good Mexican tail you can handle."

Odell shakes his head playfully. "Naw, 'em screwworms 'bout all I can handle right now," he drawls. "Wanted to see if I could hire you to help doctor calves a while and stay on for the roundup."

Frosty's expression remains noncommittal. "Old worms only got to eight head other side 'em rocks," he answered. "But we found 'em plenty of time to take care of 'em." Pausing, he twists a bony arm toward the cattle. "What I got now is a bunch of crazies — 'bout half of 'em on 'at damn old locoweed."

Familiar with all the plants that can excite, depress, stunt, or kill livestock, Odell is surprised to hear that the cattle are addicted to the bitter, poisonous locoweed. Cattle born in Southwest Texas seldom eat any of the five species of locoweed, even when it often is the only edible plant to survive a severe frost or drought. Eyes instinctively glancing toward the cattle, he asks: "Where'd 'ey come from?"

"She's pasturin' 'em for a fellow who got 'em off a old boy way over other side of Eagle Pass. 'Course, you know cows from 'at part of the country ain't seen loco before 'ey come here and think it's cow cake."

Odell stares at the extra growth of hair on the flanks of a Hereford steer. "It's sure getting to 'em. I never seen hair as dead-lookin' as 'ese."

"I'm liable to grow hair on my ass too 'less I rest it," answers Frosty, climbing down from his horse and scratching himself. "Yeah, when I first noticed how skinny-looking 'ey was getting, I thought for a minute it was a bad case of worms. Then I saw a couple wobbling 'round and eat some pop-ball loco." Finding it easy to illustrate his remark, he kicks a clump of woolish weeds, their pale yellow flowers looking as innocuous as sweet pea, about five inches high and barely larger than a man's hand. He presses his boot over a hollow pod until, when crushed, it pops.

Odell flicks an eyebrow toward a slightly darker weed that has a dried lavender bloom. "Least 'ey not on 'at old purple loco. That's so much stronger 'at a horse got on it when I worked over in Clovis and went wilder'n shit. Nearly killed somebody 'fore 'ey shot him."

Frosty smiles. "Hell, 'ese warm up on 'at pop ball for starters and go to purple loco. They just like a dope addict. Won't eat nothin' else but 'is stuff till kills 'em." Frosty's right arm stretches toward a deep gully that divides the valley. "We gonna move 'em to 'at ground over 'ere where 'ere ain't so much loco."

Odell replies quickly, "You know 'at loco's just as strong even all dried up."

"Yeah, and she knows you can't get a cow cured once 'ey been on it either," Frosty says. "But you can get 'em eatin' little and lookin' better before she ships 'em. 'at is if we can get 'em across 'is old draw without breaking their neck. Their eyesight and nerves so messed up 'at 'ey was standing good three feet away from the water and tryin' to drink it."

Walking toward the draw, Odell picks up a crooked pole that has been nearly buried with dust.

Back on his horse, Frosty rides slowly past the two men guiding the cattle. "Thing is, you gotta make 'em go slow," he says, speaking in the Tex-Mex dialect. "First one falls in down 'ere and half the rest of 'em be all piled up on top 'fore he can get back up."

With the young man prodding from the rear, and Frosty from the left side, the steers move haltingly down a slope leading into the ditch. The first dozen or so steers, seeing Frosty on their right and Odell in the gully to the left, stagger across the draw and start up the bank. Suddenly a steer stumbles while trying to step down into the draw at least two yards before reaching it. Two others, trying to move around the steer, fall across his legs. Yelling and slapping his rope, Frosty dashes in front of the oncoming steers, halting them; he prods the fallen steers to their feet before any others pile atop them.

After more than 50 steers cross the draw, the others follow behind them with little coaxing. Then, with noth-

ing to frighten him, a heavier steer not addicted to locoweed veers down the part of the gully that Odell blocks.
First, three addicted steers and then another six blindly
follow the steer, building up sufficient speed to stampede
the other cattle toward Odell. Instead of stepping aside,
Odell rushes forward with the pole behind his
neck. He swings the large end of it across the steer's
nose so forcibly that the steer winces and spins. Shifting
his hands to the middle of the stick, Odell repeatedly
drives the sharp end into the steer's neck, rib cage, and
tail. Yelping, he then aims the stick at the steer's rectum.
Though hitting only its tail, he frightens the steer into a
desperate run that, in turn, carries the other steers back
toward the herd.

His left foot swinging in one direction, a rope in the
other, Frosty maneuvers his horse down into the draw
and blocks the cattle. "Push it to 'em," he yells.

With all of the men squeezing around them, the remaining steers scramble up the bank of the draw. The elderly
Mexican cowboy, blinking to clean the dust from his eye-
lids, smiles broadly. "Loco. All loco."

Frosty points toward the cattle. "Get 'em bunched up
'cross 'at flat and I catch up with you all."

"You gonna stay on for the winter?" Odell asks. "Or
you ready to work a roundup?"

Frosty spits out a dark cud of tobacco and reaches into a
package of Mail Pouch tobacco. "Way 'is woman don't
want to hire enough help," he says, pausing to wipe the
tobacco juice from his lower lip, "I figure she's liable to
let ya go anyhow after ya got all the fall work done. But
your roundup don't start till practically first October,
doesn't it?"

Odell answers decisively, "Hell, I wanta get some good
men to doctorin' soon as 'ey can. After the roundup 'ere's
enough work breakin' colts and puttin' up for winter to

keep ya on to end of January — if you want to fix some fences."

Frosty's eyes glint.

"Yessir, 'is year we're gonna pay more'n most of 'em and not get people hired out from under us," Odell says. "Ever'body gets the same on the roundup — eleven and a half a day and chuck. Other time when 'ere ain't no cook I'll get you 'nother dollar and half a day and some of the groceries and 'bacco you can take out to the bunk-house."

"I worked for lot less lotta places," Frosty answers. "I'll be 'ere around the fifteenth of next month. Soon as I get my wife, kids settled for winter — and get ever'thing took care of here and get paid off."

Frosty is as experienced at quitting jobs, Odell remembers, as he is at tending cattle. When he has heard heavily indebted cowmen yell at anyone, or he simply disliked the man's attitude, Frosty has usually shown the spirit to do what many corporate employees, over drinks, openly aspire to do: Not just quit a job, but, in doing so, also tell the boss to go to hell. "Doesn't sound like," Odell said, "you gonna leave like you used to."

"Naw, 'at woman or her husband both ain't got a mean streak like 'at old contrary son-bitch me and you used to work for," replies Frosty. "But what galls me is way he tries to show off. I'm just gonna wait till he gets to usin' all 'at *Gunsmoke* talk front 'at woman and just say I ain't smart 'nough to work 'at way. I want to see his eyes when he finds out he's gonna get chance to wean all 'em wild-ass calves back up 'at rock country hisself."

Odell sidles toward his truck. "I better be starting on back so I can try to find couple more hands 'fore it gets on toward dark."

"You want some helluva good workin' Mexicans?" Frosty says, his voice waxing enthusiastic. " 'at old fellow 'ere — his nephew'll go in 'at brush after 'em good as cow dog. Buddy of 'at old skinny boy 'ere, too, must've run outta things to steal, I guess, and came up lookin' for work. Laid 'round here and I give'm some supper. He'll get your cows in a bunch, too."

"Where 'ey at now?"

"Back 'cross the Rio Grande. But eleven and a half a day and your kinda chuck, he'll get 'ere if he has to hide out on the Border Patrol for a week. I don't care if he was to get on at big Ruiz Ranch. He'll make lots more off your roundup then he does all year anyplace he's gonna work in Mexico."

"Way 'ey cracking down on wets, they'll have to hide out till all my hands get back to Echo Canyon," Odell says, his teeth sinking into a lip. " 'at boss of mine, why he don't get in bed with the Border Patrol, I don't know. Yeah, you get hold of 'em and I'll get you couple extra days' pay and your gas."

"You can count on me gettin' 'em up your outfit," Frosty says. "I was gonna run over to Ojinaga anyway to get me a piece of tail." Lips curling into a smile, he epitomizes the reason that wealthy cowmen generally try to keep their daughters away from cowboys. Like most, Frosty never fails to use old-fashioned manners in the presence of women, but, any other time, he thrives on the fanciful but not unfounded assumption that cowboys have a magical hold on many women in the region. "Hell, Odell," he continues, "shame you can't stick 'round and take off with me. I know couple young girls — white ones — just waiting for couple cowboys to get in their pants. When's last time you had any good twenty-year-old stuff?"

"Something 'bout a cowboy 'at sure gets to 'em, don't it?" Odell says. But, already shaking his head, he strolls toward the truck. "Naw, hell, I gotta keep 'em worms from eatin' up all the cattle first. I get the roundup over with — and I'll tie on a good one with you. O.K., I'll be seeing you 'round the fifteenth, you hear?"

Bouncing over every ridge, Odell speeds through the canyon and then, reaching the asphalt road, presses the accelerator so hard that he seems to barely control the truck. Already, the truck wobbles each time that the wind dips into Odell's path. Still, trusting the steering wheel to just his left hand, he lets the truck weave as he reaches for unfiltered cigarettes, which he smokes when it is impractical to roll them, or tunes the music on a distant radio station that fades when he passes between hills. At the sound of "Jambalaya . . . Crawdad," he hurriedly turns up the volume. A boot pats rhythmically as, against the background of an amplified steel guitar, a husky nasal voice interjects, every eight to ten seconds, "Aw!" "Oh yeah!" and "Pick it out!"

At this speed, customary among cowboys and cowmen traveling long distances, Odell needs only about one and a half hours to reach the graded gravel road that twists toward the Double Diamond's Little Hills Division. First a metal windmill comes into view. Two miles later, against the backdrop of a hill, the collection of corrals, barns, workshops, trees, and his house resembles an oasis. Weaving between the clusters of weeds, obscuring the discarded livestock trailer, tin cans, and fence posts, he parks beside an unpainted loading chute. The trucks and stock trailers that fill the powdery parking area tell him that the men have returned from the Cave Hill.

Recognizing Odell's truck, two spotted dogs rush into the road and wait to have their ears scratched. Barely flicking one dog's ear, Odell walks up to the series of maroon corrals, extending at least forty yards beyond the two white barns, and bends over the water faucet. As a screen door swings against a wall, he turns toward the long adobe-style bunkhouse that is plastered on the three sides visible from the corrals. Billy Bob, walking slowly in his bare feet, brings Odell the receipt for the cattle that a trucking company has taken to San Angelo.

Tucking the receipt inside his notebook, Odell walks past the entangled flowers, weeds, lumber, and fence that separate the barns and bunkhouse from his large stone house. To be sure, the house has weathered in the eighty years since it was built on a site dictated by the windmill. But those who have seen the house for the last half century insist that not even the modifications lessen its charm and serenity. For example, the red roofing paper on the new screened porch, extending across the rear of the house, almost matches the red Mexican tile roof on the original structure. The sixteen large oak trees, all neatly whitewashed, provide a constant shade that even motivates cattle to stare at them. With just short mesquite and silvery sagebrush standing between the trees and the horizon, the view from the front yard immediately evokes the feeling that this is the only settlement on earth.

Crossing the yard, Odell watches Kenny, his thirteen-year-old son, rush out from behind the old cellar. A slender and handsome boy, Kenny looks even skinnier than he actually is under the tall, uncreased crown of his hat and western-style jeans so tight that he has barely fit a package of chewing tobacco into the hip pocket. Smiling, he opens a hand to show the nine horny rattles that he cut from the tail of a dark-brown rattlesnake. He must shift a large cud of tobacco into a jaw before he can speak. "Bunch of old roadrunners," he said, " 'em buggers done pecked 'at son-gun's eyes out and shook him to death. These the fourth rattles I got 'is year."

Odell shakes his head. "Believe 'at's more'n I got in a year when I was a boy."

The glider still screeching, long auburn hair swirling

around her shoulders, Jeanette, the fourteen-year-old daughter, rushes across the porch to open the door for Odell. Like Joyce, the shy, slim fifteen-year-old daughter, now turning off a transistor radio, Jeanette's high cheekbones and small smile accent their attractive features. "When they brought your horse in," she says, "we 'bout give you up for dead."

"Had to go half over the country looking for hands," Odell answers. "Might have a couple to help doctor calves 'at screwworms got to."

Rising from the sofa, its flowered seat covers freshly washed, Odell's wife Pauline walks into the kitchen to meet him. Neither her stretch slacks nor brown hair pinned atop her head helps to disguise the weight that she has gained in the sixteen years that she and Odell have been married. But she has lost none of her enthusiasm or loyalty. Dropping a large steak into the skillet as she talks, Pauline turns around to see Jeanette start into the bathroom. "Honey, let your daddy in first so he can wash up."

Odell, in no rush to remove his hat, sits down at a long table covered with a yellow oilcloth. " 'at's all right, I'm hungrier than I am dirty."

Kenny turns around a chair and wraps both arms over the back of it. "Billy Bob and Woody said you gonna be riding 'morrow. Want me to go too?"

Odell picks at his pinto beans and corn. "I'm gonna be huntin' up couple more hands first."

Undaunted, Kenny shakes his head. "When you do, I can ride good some 'em sorry old Mexicans you get."

"You can go when I go back out again," Odell says. "I'm gonna try to get the roundup goin' little early."

Pauline turns over the steak. "Warren don't know 'bout yet, does he?"

"He'll know when I tell'm what's goin' on."

Though Pauline's eyes remain on the steak, she quickly picks up the theme. " 'at's way your daddy is. I know when I married a cowboy 'at he wasn't gonna get off at four thirty — but he doesn't take nothing off anybody either."

Kenny straightens up. "Know what 'at new ag teacher at school said one time? Said you have go school more now 'cause ain't liable to be cowboy work someday way all feedlots fatten cattle quick now."

Pauline drops the steak into Odell's plate. "Aw, he was born in town somewheres like Dallas," she says, her voice rising quickly, "and just gone to Texas A. & M. and come out here smarting off. He probably won't know a real ranch from a hog trough."

Kenny smiles. "Know what old Jimmy said 'hind his back?"

"His daddy's a good cowboy," Pauline interjects. "Stay sober more and wasn't such a character."

"He said, 'They won't need any cowboys,' " Kenny continues, " 'time comes you learn scratch your hind end with your elbow.' "

Pauline motions toward Odell's steak. "Or time comes people don't want to eat no more beef. Steak."

"You can't hardly blame young boys teaching like 'at," Odell says, drawing total attention. "When 'ey come outta 'em big towns like Amarillo, 'bout all 'ey see is feedlots 'side the highway where they got fifty thousand head at a time. 'en you listen 'em Panhandle boys talk about machines pouring out the sweet feed and 'em running 'round in their old airplanes. And you get to half believing him. But there's only one way I know of to get a steer to fatten up in the first place. And 'at's having a cow in a pasture 'at can have a calf."

Pauline looks impressed. "You wait and see. Them feedlot people don't pull the wool over your daddy's eyes."

2. The Horses / Wild and Wonderful

THE STUBS of scrub oak branches sizzling beside him, a quarter moon clinging to the ash gray sky behind him, Pancho pushes a dried fence post into the fire. Sparks rise above the open metal pot boiling with coffee. Then, like the eight other men gathering in the chilled mountainous air of late September, he turns the back of his legs so close to the fire that the pants seem ready to ignite.

Squatting on his right knee, Odell wraps a leather glove around the handle of the pot and tilts it toward his tin cup. Each of the cowboys working full-time at the Double Diamond Ranch, along with Frosty and Sammie, who started two weeks ago, returns to the pot. Still, after all that remains in the pot is dregs thick with coarse grounds, it is only 6:30 A.M. by the Central Standard Time that is used in West Texas. With the Mountain Time Zone beginning only a few ridges to the west, it will be another hour before the barest light reaches the basin below the Rim Rock area of the ranch, where the men wait. Restive now that the preliminary searching for cooks and extra cowboys is finished and awaiting the fall roundup that is to start at Echo Canyon in only three days, Odell looks up thoughtfully. He turns toward the eastern horizon, as if hoping for signs that sunlight will arrive early. Ignoring the joking among the men, he is obviously engrossed in planning the job awaiting him today: Locate and catch approximately 170 horses that will be used to round up the cattle.

None of these men has seen horses for a roundup on a large ranch supplied in any other manner. With scarcely enough grass for their cattle, small cowmen usually find it simpler to buy horses at the auctions held in the fall by either large cattle ranches or those raising only horses. But with the need for a steady supply of horses about as great as ever, the huge ranches continue to raise hundreds of their own distinct type of horse that veteran cowboys learn to appreciate. Though Virgil has never ridden a horse from the Pitchfork Ranch, located near Guthrie, Texas, he is not hesitant to compliment the ranch on the techniques that help develop versatile horses. "They got a separate foreman and couple boys who don't do nothin' but take care the horses," he says. "Buddy, 'ey got good horses 'at'll do any kinda work you want out of 'em — 'specially light gray ones." Despite hearing that the wages might not match those he receives around Big Bend, Frosty has been tempted to work on the vast Waggoner Ranch, which owns 875 horses for breeding and working, because of its reputation among some cowboys for having "the wildest cattle and the fastest horses to catch 'em with."

Similarly, to raise what he insists are dependable horses, Odell keeps just enough of the Double Diamond's fillies to replenish the aging broodmares. As always, only gelded male horses are trusted to have the stamina and temperament to carry a cowboy alone through these twisting mountains and canyons where, if thrown or injured, he could die before he is found. Moreover, because they are reared in the steep, rocky pastures, most of the Double Diamond's horses are also known to be particularly suited for gathering cattle in rugged mountainous terrain.

Equally important, Virgil is quick to emphasize, a ranch's own horses help dispel the enduring suspicion among cowboys that horses purchased from a cowman have a concealed weakness or grudge. Gazing at the nearest men, Virgil stretches out a hand. "Yeah, wasn't for workin' for an outfit with good-count horses like 'is, I'll tell you one thing — my age I wouldn't ride no horse out'n 'is big old country less I knowed him since he's 'is high. Get one's been mistreated when he's young colt and he'll just wait for the chance to leave you layin' off on the ground som'er's."

"Yeah, it's like my daddy always told me," Frosty says, snapping his head for emphasis. "Rolled 'is own cigarettes to smoke and he wouldn't eat no sausage you bought. 'You gotta know what's inside somethin' 'fore you get 'volved in it,' 'at's what he'd say."

Smiling, Pancho pulls a fresh pinch of snuff away from his nose. "But his boy listen good, don't he?" he says, mixing Tex-Mex and accented English. His thumb points toward Frosty. "He go stick it in a knothole if it hot."

"Never found one big 'nough for me," Frosty replies.

Rising to his feet, Odell feels the need to remind the men that, as dependable as many of the older horses have seemed in the past, they won't want to be caught today. Since the drought caused part of the spring roundup to be canceled, many of these spirited horses haven't been ridden in nearly a year. The broodmares, almost never in captivity during the three to twelve years that they roamed these mountains, have become wild. Some are

about as defiant as the 17,000 surviving mustangs, the un-
tamed descendants of ranch, cavalry, and wild horses that
still range forbidding public lands of Nevada, Wyoming,
Idaho, and six other western states.

Though ostensibly speaking to the two men whom he
recently hired, Odell subtly reminds all of them how to
treat the horses. "You fellows, I want to tell you how we
go 'bout 'is," he says, scratching the stubble on a cheek.
"We want to catch ever'thing up 'ere but the mares with
little colts 'at's 'bout weaned. These old mares ain't
hardly been caught since we branded 'em as yearlings, so
'ey gonna be wild as all hell and gone. You let 'em slip
back through if you can do it without lettin' anything else
get away. But don't fight 'em if 'ey want to get with the
whole bunch. They get all excited and lose their babies
'ey carrying and cause their colts to stove themselves up
on the rocks. 'Em young fillies we sell off and those ball-
bearing colts 'at ain't never been caught before — 'ey get
all worked up like shithouse rats. So just try to keep 'em
headed down this way, fairly slow if you can."

Odell's facial expression turns smirky. "Now 'em two
studs — a big old bay and a sorrel — got a memory like an
old Indian woman," he continues. "They first see us, 'ey
gonna act like the big boss showin' all the mares how to
get way. But when 'ey get so far along 'ey gonna 'member
'at 'ey goin' back to their winter pasture and it'll be a good
six months before 'ey see a mare again. They'll try to
double back on you and get 'way if you don't pay attention ever minute. And 'at little slick-hipped palomino 'at
thinks he's king the mountain. He's 'bout four now and
we ain't never caught him yet. He ain't mean enough to
beat out the old studs for no mare except ones 'ey cut out
and 'ey come and take most those 'way from him. But 'at
little long-tail son-bitch gets 'way from us ever' time. So if
you can get close enough, knock his butt off good."

Several horses stirring inside the trailer kick the slats, bringing J.J. to his feet. "Whoa," he hollers, then, lowering his voice: "Sounds like one's done getting his butt knocked off."

Hearing the commotion, Odell opens the gate on the narrow trailer that is attached to his pickup truck. "Yeah, we'll head on out now," he says, grabbing the halter on Biscuit. "It ought to be light enough time we get up 'ere."

Everyone except Virgil saddles his horse. As in past years, when the sun illuminates the box-shaped canyon behind him, he will search it alone to chase any older horses he finds into the main group the other men bring down from the mountain. Barring an accident, he should finish in time to then water and drive the nine afternoon horses, now being hobbled and tied outside the trailers, on to meet the other men.

Like the negative of a photograph, little more than a murky outline of the nearest horse is visible to the men. As they ride across land, still slick with dew, only their own horses — by snorting and shortening their steps — can warn the men when they approach any ditch or creek bed. A half-hour later, the grayness of the sky still seems unchanged. But the men can see the barbed wire stretching across the entrance to a pasture enclosed on all other sides by the majestic red rocks towering, in places, a thousand feet above them. Everyone, waiting until Billy Bob drags open a sagging gate, follows Odell around an immense depression that resembles an ancient crater. Stopping near a rounded boulder, Odell points to the left. "J.J., you and Pancho want to take Frosty and Billy Bob up 'at left side 'ere," he says slowly. "And we'll meet up with you by 'em old sharp rocks where we did last year."

Turning toward the right, Odell weaves the three other men around the ledge below a ridge until settling on a faint path. Mile after mile the only sound is that of a heavy iron horseshoe scraping the rocks. Suddenly, though it brings no visible reaction from the men, the calmness is pierced by a sad, pleading cry of "Eeenn, eennn, eennn." As the men have often heard, a jack rabbit slowed down in the rocky terrain has been caught by either a coyote or bobcat. As it is eaten alive, the rabbit's cry quickly builds to a loud, hysterical "Eeennn! Eeennn! Eeennn!" Within twenty seconds the cry fades into a soft, helpless squeal of "Eeennn, eeenn," a tone suggesting the rabbit is resigned to its death. Now, less than a minute after the screams began, there is again silence.

Finally, as the shade of the eastern horizon turns salmon pink, the men expect horses to begin to wake from what is usually their longest nap of the night, the one between 4:00 A.M. and dawn. At a squat hill, Odell's arm thrusts down toward two mares, isolated and apparently rejected by a stallion, ambling across a draw. A brown mare, losing sight of the other, whinnies. "Yeah, neither one 'ere don't have no colt," he says, his neck stretching. "You never know whether it's the mares' fault or the stud's fault 'at 'ey don't have none. You can't figure out some stud's system he's got worked out. He'll go wear hisself out chasing some of 'em wild mares over and over. Practically kill hisself and the mare both to catch 'em sometimes. Then he'll cut out three or four 'at he don't want and, hell, he won't touch 'em even if 'ey shake it in his face."

Unnoticed by the mares, the men advance along the slope until they reach a wide clearing. Now, with the sun beginning to spill over the mountains, illuminating even the gullies, Odell puts Biscuit into a canter. He barely glances to see why a horse is screaming between the rocks to his left. Rearing, an older black horse and a gray colt attack each other with their front hooves. The gray colt wheels and bites the black horse's neck, seemingly winning the fight. But, spinning at blurring speed, the older horse kicks his hind hooves with such force that the gray colt is staggered. Backing away, the colt clearly withdraws from the fight.

With the mountain that seals off the pasture now little more than two miles away, Odell looks back at the other men. "Chili, you want to clean out 'at little old canyon 'ere," he says, speaking in the Tex-Mex dialect. "Now watch when you think you're at the head of it. You go round a bunch of 'em old red rocks and there's a little flat where there's pretty good grass." He switches back to English. "Woody, you and Sammie want to take 'em old draws little farther up there? Be sure'n wait outside when you finish to keep anything from sneakin' back in."

Approaching the peak, Odell locates J.J., his big sorrel in sharp contrast with the darker rocks, standing below the rim of the pasture. Squinting, while turning into the sun, he looks down the pasture which, in the two hours that he has ridden, has been transformed from almost total blackness to burning brightness. He waits until he sees Woody chase a roan and a golden dun horse out of a draw. Then, swinging his hat from hip to hip, Odell starts the men, spread so far apart that they see only the men on each side of them, sweeping down the entire pasture.

Zigzagging, either to allow a mare or yearling to slip past them, or to block frightened colts trying to escape, the men search more than an hour to locate eleven horses. As the horses trot down the pasture a smoky gray gelding, grazing toward the wind, perks up his ears. He moves warily for about 100 yards, snatching at sprigs of grass as he moves. Suddenly, as his eyes turn toward J.J., he lays back his ears and breaks into a gallop. Seeing the gray, the other horses fall in behind him. Each time another horse is chased from the brush or dry washes, the group of horses continues southward behind the high rocks and hills seemingly convinced that they have eluded the men. Reaching a clearing, the group of horses comes within sight of about twenty mares scattered for perhaps a half mile. A few mares, cocking their ears toward the approaching horses, spread in opposite directions.

Nickering, perhaps his command, a muscular sorrel stallion trots haughtily around the nearest mares. His instincts are unwittingly helping the cowboys. Unlike bulls, which claim a territory, a stallion feels, as Odell maintains, " 'at any mare 'at he can see is as good as having his brand on her." Now, seeing that other mares in his group have scattered, the stallion wheels and snorts fiercely. Laying back his ears, he sprints toward three mares drifting to the left until they gallop back toward the largest group of mares. Running at his maximum speed, hurdling creek beds and washes, he circles all of the mares in such an intimidating manner that he proves as efficient as three or four cowboys in clustering them.

But, in gazing at the mares, trying to reassert his authority, the stallion fails to see three yearling fillies fleeing over a distant ridge. By the time he notices the fillies, and now four weanlings desperate to gain the sanctuary of the remuda, a few mares move uneasily to the east. His ears erect, his nostrils expanding, the stallion starts angrily toward what appear to be the rebellious mares, but he turns quickly toward the muted hoofbeats. To his surprise, at least forty horses now galloping over the distant hills, ahead of the cowboys, pull together as they see the mares. Unable to intimidate either the mares or advancing horses, the stallion blends into the group running two or three abreast but, losing none of his proudness, soon sprints to the front of them.

Rather than maneuver closer to the stallion, most of the

horses have, with some exceptions, aligned themselves with those of the nearest age and color. Of the five gray horses and mares in this group, four of them are bunched together and the other, only a few yards behind, is running alongside a palomino and a roan. Two paints are following three duns. Behind them, eight of the next nine horses are either chestnut, bay, or brown — all weaving to block several younger colts struggling to go ahead of them.

As the morning passes, the sun intensifying as it rises, the one or two horses continuously chased from behind boulders and hills gallop far enough from the cowboys to force the main band of horses down the pasture. When the horses approach the bay stallion and mares, Odell gallops up behind them to merge the two groups. Relaying Odell's signal, all the men swing into a V-shaped formation that presses nearly 150 horses into a manageable bunch. Trotting down the slope, the horses stay comfortably ahead of the men. But each rebellious horse straying more than twenty-five yards away from either side of the group finds a cowboy galloping toward his path well before he can build up enough speed to draw others behind him.

Typically, on the right side, a nervous brown filly swerves. But Billy Bob, the youngest cowboy at the Double Diamond, does not see her until she begins to gallop. Flailing excitedly, he turns across the valley at an angle and pace that should just allow him to intercept her. Suddenly, finding speed born of fear, eight other colts and fillies break in the same direction.

Astonished by the speed of the filly, Billy Bob rakes both spurs across his horse's rib cage. Along a slope, the top speed of his horse brings Billy Bob into a position to chase the runaway fillies and colts back toward the remuda. But with Billy Bob's zone left unguarded, two closely bunched groups of horses veer away and, in turn, force Pancho to block them. Alertly, as the horses spread, Billy Bob delays the first group until Pancho can gallop out and encircle them. Then, looking fearless, he plunges toward the onrushing horses with such zest that all of them seem to turn back. But a palomino horse, white tail extending as he increases speed, suddenly feints and swerves around him. Billy Bob sees that there is not a brand on his left hip. In the confusion, as he later complains, he uses a couple of seconds to realize: " 'at's the son-bitching horse 'at always gets away."

Jerking his horse, again slapping and spurring, Billy Bob charges across the slope after the palomino, frantically untying the rope from his saddle. He does not throw the rope. In a continuous motion, the horse's front legs suddenly fold, pitching Billy Bob over his head; then the horse falls, violently, atop his legs.

Cursing in Spanish, Pancho realizes that there is no chance for him to catch the palomino before he escapes into the mountains, and, unless Odell wants to take everyone away from the remuda, he will have eluded them until the next roundup. He turns and, after waving for someone to move into his zone, gallops toward Billy Bob. By the time Pancho reaches him, Billy Bob rises up to lean on an elbow. But his horse, now limping excitedly, tries to run. Slowly, Pancho approaches the horse from the opposite side and, spurting forward with the loop on his rope swirling, arches it perfectly around the horse's neck. Leading him back to Billy Bob, the scuffed dry land tells Pancho that the horse stepped into a hole concealed by a dark weed. "You O.K.?" he hollers.

Holding his right ankle, Billy Bob looks down apologetically. "I ain't never been like 'is 'fore, I can't get up on 'is leg yet."

"Where he fall on you? Your leg?"

"Yeah, right where the saddle is came down here," he answers, pausing to breathe deeply. " 'at's where he fell on my foot, it felt like. You just wait a minute. I'm gonna walk 'is son-bitch off when it quits hurtin' a little more. Just help me kinda get up, would ya?"

Pancho twists both bridles around his left wrist, leading the horses foward, as he reaches his right arm under Billy Bob's shoulder. He raises Billy Bob to his uninjured leg. "Think you can put any weight on it?" he says, backing away.

Biting his lower lip, Billy Bob cautiously lowers his right foot. He screams, then falls onto his hands.

Startled by the sound, Billy Bob's horse rears so suddenly that he jerks Pancho backward. Though stumbling, Pancho's calloused hands cling stubbornly to both bridles. "Whoa! Whoa!" he hollers. Yet the force of two horses, 2200 pounds, pull the bay's reins from his fingers.

Hopping on his left leg, Billy Bob leaps forward, throwing himself against the horse's neck and clutching the bridle with both hands. "Whoa, you old son-bitch," he says, hanging from the halter. "Whoa!"

As soon as he regains control of his own horse, Pancho rushes over to grab the bay horse's bridle. "Your leg pretty bad off?"

Billy Bob breathes deeply. "Yeah, it feels like 'ere ain't nothin' down in the bottom of the boot," he answers.

"You just hold him there and I'll look," Pancho says. Dropping to one knee, he slowly slides a hand down Billy Bob's boot until he hears him sucking air. "Bone or something stick out. Your ankle broke probably."

Billy Bob shakes his head.

Having lost sight of the other men, even before reaching Billy Bob, Pancho decides not to ride for help. Taking the bay horse's bridle, he positions him beside Billy Bob. "You get hold the bridle good?" he asks as he squats. "O.K., now you sit on my shoulder here. When I raise you, grab other side of the saddle. Got hold? O.K., hang on and I'll stick your good leg in the stirrup. That's it."

Billy Bob lies across the saddle. "Oh, damn, shit, son-bitch!"

"Put your weight down on stirrup," Pancho says quietly, "and kinda raise up and I'll put your broke leg over. Rough, I know. Leave it right there. I'll put it in the stirrup for you."

Pancho picks up Billy Bob's hat, blown against a bush, and shakes the dust from it. "Time you get back to the gap," he says. "I'll go find the boss so somebody can get you to the doctor."

Billy Bob looks into Pancho's eyes. "I bet it's broke bad, don't you?"

Pancho shakes his head. "Not too."

Galloping back about one and a half miles, Pancho sees that by now Odell and the other men are no more than 150 yards apart.

As the men converge, yelping and swinging coiled ropes, they press the horses into a crescent-shaped indentation in the towering red cliff that they use to prevent the excitable weanlings, yearlings, and broodmares, when they are sorted, from cutting themselves trying to escape over the barbed wire that usually forms a trap. Seeing the horses safely inside the rocks, a small, satisfied grin breaks across Odell's face. Then, as he turns, he notices Pancho shake his head. "What'd Billy Bob go off looking for?" he asks.

Pancho points to the ridge behind him. "Have a wreck chasing the palomino," he answers, speaking in hurried Tex-Mex. "I get him back on his horse and he come in slow out through there. Anklebone look more broke than the boy who get broke up one year ago."

"Damn, already, and I ain't even got all the hands together yet," Odell says, slapping a glove against a thigh. Exhaling, he turns to draw the attention of J.J. "I better go see 'bout him. Would you tell Virgil to wait here when he brings the horses to change?"

Billy Bob appears embarrassed when Odell gallops up, then turns to ride beside him. "I'm sorry, but 'at wild palomino son-bitch made my horse step in a hole on me. Ain't never been 'is way 'fore."

"Just take it slow till you get back to the truck," Odell says. "We'll get you to town."

"You know, 'is ain't gonna keep me from workin' the roundup," says Billy Bob. "No, buddy. Once I get 'is fixed up, you just wait."

"We'll worry 'bout 'at then," Odell replies. "You ought be glad you was working with somebody. Man gets hurt by hisself doctorin' cows up some 'ese canyons and 'ey's been couple days before 'ey ever find him — and 'at's with a whole bunch pitching in to help too." He sees Billy Bob grimace. "Hurting pretty bad?"

Billy Bob breathes deeply. "Feels like the ankle's practically comin' off. Does goin' up 'ese old hills."

Odell points between two windswept slopes. "Now right straight through 'ere's the shortest and flattest way back to the pass. Ain't too far and you can get to 'at gate where the fence is with no old hills. You 'member 'at, don't ya? I'll go on ahead and have the pickup brought up 'ere close. We'll get to the doctor real quick, you hear."

"Hell, I'll be all right."

Returning to the remuda, Odell removes the bridle and saddle from Biscuit and braces them against his right hip. Already the horse is wallowing in the dry grass to massage the part of his back bearing the wet, lathery imprint of the saddle pad.

Odell stands until Virgil leads up a fresh horse. "How many you catch back 'ere?"

"Seventeen and all fat," Virgil says with a smile.

Staring toward the canyon, Chili pretends to empty the water from a gallon jug covered in frayed burlap. "Oh," he snaps, feigning horror, then offering the jug.

" 'at's all right," Odell says. "I had couple beers at the restaurant up the road 'ere." Setting the jug on a rock, Odell leads his fresh horse up to the men spread across the entrance to the canyon. "You all want stay right 'ere," he says, "and me and Chili'll cut out the ones we don't want to take. Don't let 'em studs even get up close to 'ere without a rope on 'em."

Riding between the horses, Odell and Chili patiently maneuver each of the mares, weanlings, and yearling colts along the sheer wall of the canyon until they reach the opening that is left for them to escape back into the pasture. Finding the bay stallion, Odell motions for Chili to distract him. As he does, Odell eases between several older horses and, before the stallion's ears turn toward him, flips the rope over his neck. Quickly, as Odell yanks the rope, Chili gallops up and pulls a halter over the stallion's head.

Seeing this, the other stallion eases slowly toward the edge of the canyon. But, before he can start to run, J.J. rushes forward to drive him back into the remuda. Then, as the sorrel stallion rears, trying to shake Odell's rope from his neck, J.J. also pitches his lariat over his neck. "Listen to old pretty boy bawl and carry on, would ya?" says J.J., smiling as he pulls the rope. "Hell, you know you don't never get none for the road."

Once he buckles a halter on the stallion, Odell leads him out to the edge of the canyon. Clutching the stallion's shank with one hand, busily moving his fresh, frisky horse in a circle with the other, Odell wastes little time in instructing his men. "I'm gonna bring these studs back to the trailer with Virgil," he says. "Woody, I'll take your brown pickup and get Billy Bob to the doctor 'cause it's faster. So you and Frosty bring back my truck with the horses and the studs when you come on in tonight."

"He bad off?" asks J.J.

"Broke ankle, look like," Odell replies. "On account of 'at slick hip palomino. But 'ese two old studs out of 'is here bunch ought be quieted down. J.J., you want to see 'at we didn't leave no little old yearlings or mares in here. You all get 'is bunch together with the horses 'at Virgil caught and get 'em in the big trap for the night and call it a day. In the morning now, J.J. and Pancho and Woody, you all come on out and drive the whole bunch on into the corral. I'll see you all there."

Now, a day after they were driven into the fenced trap below the mountains nine miles to the north, the horses approach the series of fences that funnel them into the maroon corral, encircled by smaller pens, between the barns at the Little Hills Division. Lifting a long cloud of dust high above them, the horses show much the same reactions as when they were captured. Conditioned by past roundups, nearly all of the other horses in the remuda trot in an orderly manner through the lanes until they recognize the corral and then, ears rising slightly, gallop into it without further urging. The young colts and fillies are so tense that the first one to approach the chutes — then a dozen at a time — rear and try to escape back into the pasture. Several stumble onto their sides. But, hollering, kicking, and slapping their ropes, J.J., Pancho, and Woody force the young horses through the gate, then quickly close it behind them.

Hearing the rumble of the horses, the other men idling around the shady side of the tack room amble toward them. A cowboy who will be receiving Workman's Compensation, not wages, for riding on a roundup, Billy Bob seems to feel that he must keep pace with the men. He hurries toward the corral, his encased right ankle swaying under the new crutches. Turning around, he angrily punches his left crutch into the ground. "Damn if I couldn't be breaking one of 'em if 'is hadn't happened," he scowls.

Barely noticing the youthful anger, Virgil's eyes linger on one of his favorite cutting horses, an alert eight-year-old sorrel, already looking at the row of saddles draped atop the main corral. "Old Preacher's done fired up to get after 'em mean little old calves," he says, exposing teeth darkened by tobacco juice. "Fool with'm and he'll bite their ear off."

Preacher's spirited temperament led him to resist capture only yesterday and the right side of his neck reveals the scars of a vicious fight on the range. The horse does not project the image of domesticity. But the enthusiasm that Preacher now shows for chasing calves is routinely expected from his breed. Considered superior to any horse used by the original cowboy, the contemporary cow pony has evolved as a mixture of the descendants of the sturdy mustangs, or Andalusians, brought to the Southwest by the Spanish conquistadors, the Colonists' sleek English thoroughbreds, and agreeable Kentucky saddle horses developed by both cowboys and cavalrymen. As their agility and durability proved useful in outmaneuvering cattle, mature mustangs and saddle horses were bred to the faster thoroughbreds, predominantly at the King Ranch on the southeast coast of Texas, until a new breed of quarter horse was recognized. In retaining many characteristics of the mustang, a quarter horse's 1100 to 1300 pounds give him the strength to absorb assaults from cattle and to carry a man for an entire day. His combination of short, widely spaced forelegs and thickly muscled haunches enables him to maintain his balance as he turns or starts or stops quickly. With his thoroughbred lineage, a quarter horse can gain the confidence that he can outrun any calf bolting away from a herd — a fact that few Texas cowmen seem hesitant to remind anyone. For many years, a feature at the annual quarter horse races and re-union in Gladewater, Texas, was a 220-yard race between a quarter horse, liberally infused with thoroughbred blood, and a late model Cadillac. The race was finally canceled, Virgil remembers, after the horse won just about every year.

As physically endowed as this kind of horse may be, most large cowmen continue to hone his ability to help the cowboy gather aggressive cattle. Seeking what Odell calls "Army remount horses with good cow sense," the Double Diamond has strengthened its remuda with broodmares carrying the genes of Little Joe, considered the Man o' War of the cow horses, and several stallions from the bloodline of cutting horses that seemingly would kill themselves rather than allow a particular calf to es-cape. Though the freedom of their youth fosters wild in-stincts, most of the Double Diamond's horses eventually show the inherent spirit veteran cowboys have come to appreciate. His toe pressed between planks of the corral, Frosty looks admiringly at the horses as he speaks. "Way 'ese horses belly down on a calf sure musta changed from old days," he says. "Big outfits sure got better breeded horses now'days, huh?"

The opinion brings a bemused smile to Virgil's face. "Yeah, 'ey good. But you too young to 'member how Joe's Last loved to work cattle."

"Who's he?"

"Joe Reed's last colt," he says. "Lord, be end of the day and 'is mouth be all bleeding and 'is sides and belly be all bloodied up. He be down on 'is knees and you'd think he couldn't do no more. But he just be waitin' for an old cow or calf to make her move either way. He'd get 'er too."

" 'Course, if 'ese still ain't broke out right when 'ey colts," says Frosty, pausing to glance at a chestnut filly rearing on her hind legs, "you might as well be riding a stick."

"They'll find out who the boss 'fore they're broke out," snaps Odell. Swinging the gate to a man behind him, he walks into the center of the circular corral, still thick with dust, and gazes at several colts, about thirty months old, known as "long two-year-olds." "Soon as we cut out 'ese filly colts we sell off," he says, "I want to get 'ese boys to gentling some of 'ese ball-bearing colts we gonna take on the roundup. Work 'em while 'ey ain't so full of piss and vinegar after all 'at runnin'.'"

Virgil's eyes radiate his enthusiasm for testing a certain compact little colt with an intelligent head. "Ain't 'at short-eared chestnut a good-boned thing, huh?"

"Looks real broad 'tween the eyes, too," Odell replies, nodding approvingly. "Want to catch'm and see how much sense he's got?"

As Virgil eases slowly toward the rounded corner of the corral, dragging his large noose behind him, the colt attempts to hide between several other young horses rushing back and forth to avoid being caught. But, showing the finesse that characterizes older cowboys, Virgil simply pushes his right arm upward like someone flipping a basketball over a taller opponent. The front of his loop drops cleanly over seven other horses and around the colt's neck. Pulling gently, Virgil leads the colt until he sticks his toes in the ground. Rather than tug on the rope, he takes a second rope from his left shoulder and fastens the loop under the colt's tail and over his back. Feeling ropes pull against both his neck and thighs, the colt decides to follow Virgil to a smaller wooden pen.

Frosty strolls over to hold the rope as Virgil, mumbling in a low, inaudible tone, finally fits a limp hackamore over his head and ties him to a post. Though the colt jerks frantically on the rope, Virgil knows that if he is similarly tied and left another five or six times, he usually can be considered halter broken. "You start to get a nose on you," he says, as if conversing with the colt, "and I'll come back and see you in 'bout a hour."

Walking past another pen, Frosty seems intrigued by the way Chili tries to lift a saddle onto a brown colt that about two weeks earlier was brought in from a smaller pasture and since taught to wear a halter. Wary but not frightened, the colt offered only token resistance when someone laid a folded quilt over him to demonstrate the painlessness of having an object on his back. But now snorting and kicking, he refuses to allow either Chili, or Sammie, the young hand clutching his halter, to place the saddle on him.

"If you wanta jack up a leg," Frosty says, "I'll get ya your rope."

Sammie flicks his head. " 'at ought to take little the snort out of him."

With the young cowboy holding the halter, Chili waits until the colt kicks to tie a rope around his left rear hock. Quickly, he loops the other end of the rope over the colt's neck and, much like someone using a pulley, draws the foot about ten inches above the ground. Forced to balance himself on three legs, the colt can only shuffle his front feet nervously as a heavy saddle, cracked from age, is fitted on his back. The straps under his girth, left loose in order to minimize the colt's fear, will be gradually tightened during each of the subsequent five or six saddling lessons.

Sammie, the newest hand at the Double Diamond and anxious to gain stature among the older men, clears his voice as he leaves the corral, "If he was just saddle broke," he says, "I'd ride 'at old colt right now."

Odell, appreciating the enthusiasm, spins around before he answers. "After we get the roundup over with, you gonna be sittin' on a bunch more like him. But if your ass's itchy 'ere's a little brown colt in 'at second pen 'at's 'bout saddle broke."

Sammie trots into the tack room. Arms swinging, he returns in a pair of old limp boots with enough of the seams split to allow him to pull out his foot if he is thrown and entangled in a stirrup. He listens carefully as Odell recalls that, in the past month, the colt has gradually learned to wear a hackamore, saddle, and a metal noseband to familiarize him with the feel of the steel bit that he will later wear in his mouth. But, with Odell walking away from the pen, he knows that no cowboy tells another how to ride a horse that has never felt a human on his back. Moving slowly to avoid frightening the colt, he pats his left neck and shoulder as he unsnaps the shank. He stands, still petting him, until the colt turns to observe what he is doing. Then, in a simultaneous motion, he pulls back the left rein, tightens his right fingers around the saddle horn, and presses a boot into the left stirrup, swinging himself atop the colt.

Head shaking from shoulder to shoulder, nostrils and eye sockets seemingly enlarging, the colt digs his hooves into the dirt and twists his back. With violent suddenness, the colt's withers and hips spring upward, leaving the rider tilted, almost dangling, over his neck. Still Sammie manages to pull back the left rein. Pulling even harder, once he straightens his body, he forces the colt to move in a circle for nearly a minute, greatly reducing his ability to buck. Finally gaining some authority, Sammie balances his grip on both reins and allows the colt to trot directly across the pen. The colt moves calmly, but without the slightest warning, his spine gyrates with such force that the cowboy bounces. Jerking back the left rein, pinching his legs against the colt's ribs, the cowboy clings gamely atop him for an agonizingly long ten seconds before, as the colt rears, he is heaved against the wall of the pen.

Rolling over, oblivious to fresh manure under his knees, Sammie lunges, unsuccessfully, for the colt's hackamore. Anxious to conceal his pain, he walks with both arms extended until the colt is backed against the pen. The instant his rump touches the boards, the colt spurts forward. But Sammie grabs the reins and, shouting "Whoa! whoa!" maneuvers beside the colt's left stirrup. Showing no anger, no brutality that could be avenged in later years, he calmly remounts the colt and stays on the saddle until a sudden, defiant twist of the spine hurls him to the ground again. Once more he climbs back on the colt, only to be pressed against the boards. After fifteen minutes the perspiration that drenches both Sammie's brown shirt and the colt's brown hide underscores their fatigue. Still the cowboy has ridden the colt until demonstrating that he, and not the colt, has decided when he will dismount. Judging from the experiences of other cowboys, Sammie reasons that the colt will need only another six or seven sessions in the corral before he can be tested in a pasture. Yet, knowing that he made little progress in teaching the colt to obey his signals to turn, he walks toward the gate wearing a heavy frown. "Still got a cold mouth kinda," he says.

"We got some medicine to cure 'at," Odell replies. Quickly he ties the reins to the horn on the saddle, pinning the colt's head against his left shoulder. "If 'bout an hour of 'at don't learn him to turn the way you want him to," he says dryly, "then holler and we'll tie the other side back for an hour. He'll take a rein then."

Regardless of when the colt accepts the reins, he and other two-year-olds will receive considerable seasoning for another three spring and fall roundups before working cowboys trust them. To orient the colt to his job, he will be taken on the roundup to observe how the experienced horses follow orders, stay with the remuda, and herd cattle. During the winter, after the pressure of the roundup ends, the colt will be ridden almost every day until he is considered "saddle broke," and then, after adapting to a pencil-thick steel bit under his tongue, needs to feel only the slightest tug of a rein for him to change directions. Next year, along with the other three-year-old colts, he will be taught to canter in sharp circles and to separate spunky calves from their mothers without disturbing the remainder of a herd. To preserve his interest in these jobs, immune to the distractions of the brood-mares, he will then be immobilized in a collapsible chute and castrated. By contrast, an outstanding thoroughbred colt competes in the Kentucky Derby, the most famous of all horse races, when he is three years old and usually reaches the peak of his career during his fourth year. But, when four years old, this colt will participate on a roundup only as a substitute for experienced horses that become lame and, even then, only to drive cattle across relatively open terrain. Simply, few veteran cowboys ever feel that a horse has the maturity for the work demanded of him until he is about six years old. "Shaping up a cow pony is lot like *good* whiskey," Odell insists; "takes 'bout as long to get enough clinkers out to keep you out of trouble when you all working together."

In looking at the current four-year-olds to evaluate their previous training, Odell voices doubts on some of them as replacements for older horses. " 'at 'ere brown and black ones will do all right for green horses on the roundup," he says, turning to the men behind him. " 'at chestnut, 'at gray, and 'em two duns there 'about ninety percent broke out. You want to get the cat backs outta something, 'em's the ones to work on first."

Moving across the corral, Odell cocks his head toward a large, haughty bay gelding that has been trained just as meticulously as these four-year-olds after the past two roundups. But, unlike them, the bay horse still has not permitted anyone to ride him for more than a few seconds. "You think you got a cocklebur stuck to your old ass," Odell says. Glancing behind him, he flicks his head. "Pitching son-bitch."

His lips twisting into a cocky smile, Frosty glances at the gelding. "Well, I'm gonna be your old pal 'fore it winters up," he volunteers. "Or you gonna get your hind end whipped one 'nother."

Odell welcomes the challenge. "Winter nothing! His old butt's gonna straighten out some 'is time or he ain't goin' on no roundup. He's going ridin' on the truck."

Pinching off a fresh chaw, as if it is his fuel, Frosty eases toward the horse only to see him spurt to the other end of the corral before he can lift his rope. Noticing this, Chili walks over to maneuver him along a side of the corral. Shrewdly, by the time he lopes past Frosty, the bay is wedged between two other horses. But arching his rope over one horse, Frosty lands the noose behind the bay's ears with such precision that it falls over the nose. As the horse runs across the corral, Frosty clings to the rope, digging his large heels into the dirt to slow him down. Calmly, Odell tosses his rope around the bay's neck and jerks it to the right. Though lunging against Odell's rope, the horse feels both Frosty and Chili pull so tightly on their ropes that he is forced to stand. "Better take him to 'at pen away over 'ere," Odell says, "so he don't put no more ideas in 'em young colts' heads."

Rough but never punishing, Frosty throws his right arm around the horse's neck, swinging his body from it, and hurriedly fits on a halter. As the gelding slaps his head, knocking away the bridle, Odell steps into the pen and, in a single practiced motion, snaps a shank onto the halter and ties it to a solid post. As the horse is distracted, Frosty buckles leather hobbles around his forelegs. Rearing and shaking his feet, lifting Frosty with him, the horse falls onto his right side. He has little chance to rise up. Rolling against the horse's stifle, Frosty binds both hind legs with a soft cotton rope. One cowboy pushes a curved bit, known as a "sweetwater" bit, into the horse's mouth. Another, holding a saddle on the horse's back, waits until the rope is pulled from his ankles; then, as the horse rises to his feet, he reaches under his girth and tightens the straps on the saddle. Finally equipped with a saddle and bridle, the horse is freed of the hobbles and allowed to trot about the pen until he appears calm.

Barely snorting, the horse looks back submissively as Frosty plants his weight on the left stirrup and raises himself into the saddle. He trots quietly across the pen. Suddenly, the horse's forelegs drop, as if he intends to squat. His spine arches. Repeating "Whoa!" Frosty draws back on the rein to keep the horse moving in a circle, away from the wall of the pen that can be used to crush his legs. Thighs thumping against the saddle, nostrils dilating, Frosty clings to the saddle until the horse, glancing back, seems resigned to carrying a rider. He takes a few steps and, while his head is low and shaking, dips his forelegs to throw Frosty over his neck and onto the ground. Rearing high, the horse brings his front hoofs directly toward Frosty's stomach. Instinctively, as Frosty twists his body between the horse's feet, he shoves the horse's ankle so hard that the horse falls away from him.

Bouncing to his feet, Frosty pulls back on the left rein and, before even resettling in the saddle, rakes a spur across the horse's left ribs. Forced to move in a small circle, the horse's eyes glint with anger as he fails to shake Frosty from his back. Finally, after turning the horse for a minute, Frosty allows him to trot across the pen. He reaches the opposite side calmly. But, as the horse turns, he rears so high that he staggers backward. Feeling the horse lose his balance, Frosty pulls both boots from the stirrups in time to fall away before he is crushed.

"You son-bitch," Odell yells, rushing into the pen. He twirls his rope twice to open the loop; then, with a deft underhanded motion, jettisons the lasso over the colt's neck. His eyes glancing to see that Frosty's face reveals no pain, Odell digs his heels into the soil, cursing louder than the horse snickers until he can grab the halter. "You old son-bitch," he scowls, "you got worst kinks in your old back then last year."

Walking toward Frosty, Odell shakes his head as he talks. "Naw, I know you could break'm if you want to. But ain't no sense fooling with'm no more. He ain't gonna do us no good."

Already on his feet, Frosty accepts his spill with a philosophic smile. "Know what 'at fellow 'round Valentine I used to work for would do with sorry ones like 'is?" he says, fanning himself with a crushed beige hat. "I seen him sell off three almost as ornery and swear 'at none of 'em hadn't pitched nobody for a year. Fellow gets pitched on his butt right off and comes back askin' about 'is promise. 'Yeah,' I said, ' 'ey ain't pitched nobody in over a year,' he told him, 'but you didn't ask if they'd been rode in a year either.' "

Training temperamental horses is left to specialists or small cowmen. On large ranches, the fate is preordained for almost any horse that is irascible, or, though otherwise gentle, learns how to rotate his body to dislodge a rider for pure amusement. Considered too eccentric to risk riding in mountains, even if he is eventually broken, the bay gelding will be sold at a price, depending on how stylistically he bucks during a demonstration, to a trader whose search for such horses brings him to the Double Diamond after each roundup. His life then will be either very brief or very long. In a common method of deciding an excitable horse's future, he and hundreds of others are taken to a sale much like the Bucking Horse Auction that is held each spring and fall in the Custer County Fairgrounds in Miles City, Montana. Then, with more than 7000 people filling the grandstand, about 125 cowboys or sons of cowboys and cowmen take turns riding what are called "old misfits." Ironically, such a horse is treated as a misfit only if his moderate bucking indicates that, with some patient training, he might soon allow himself to be ridden. Except for an occasional "misfit" that is purchased by a cowboy confident that he can train a rejected horse, this type of horse seldom is sold for more than sixty dollars, and at that only to a cannery which will grind his carcass into food for cats and dogs. But men who supply livestock for rodeos often bid up to seven hundred dollars for a horse demonstrating either a nasty temper or a rhythmic twisting motion that will sufficiently bounce a rider to entertain an audience.

If any purpose was served, say cowboys at the Double Diamond, the most aggressive horse probably could be ridden until he scarcely bucked. Without any riders attempting to break a rodeo bronc, many such bucking horses become so conditioned to riders and audiences that the ostensible wildness is perpetuated by gadgets and a good portion of ham. At a professional rodeo in Odessa, Texas, for example, Frosty studied the reaction of an unsaddled "bucking bronc" as a young rider settled atop him. He still chuckles at the recollection: " 'at ol' horse looked around all calm like he figures, 'Boy, we all in 'is thing together!' "

The horse was introduced to the spectators as another wild, untamable "outlaw" — unwilling to tolerate any human on his back. At the same time, a man jerked a belt that tightened the compulsory sheepskin-lined "flank strap" encircling the horse's stomach and testicles; then, a split second before the chute opened, a man used a "powerized" cattle prod to send enough electrical shocks through the horse's hips, tail, and rectum to encourage him to buck. Unlike an unbroken colt, the bronc made no attempt to crush the rider against the wall. Heading for the middle of the arena, as programmed, the bronc rotated his rump violently, it appeared, to throw off the rider. Actually, he wanted to free himself from the irritating flank strap on his testicles. With the attention focused on the rodeo cowboy, Frosty was one of the few spectators who noticed that this and any other bucking bronc continued to buck even after the rider had either been thrown or, after riding him the required ten seconds, had leaped onto a pickup man's horse. When the other pickup man pulled off the flank strap, then the horse stopped bucking.

Compared to the unmistakably wild horses that these men break, the rodeo broncs hold no more status with them than do the men represented as rodeo cowboys. Hearing that Odell will sell the bay gelding as a bucking horse, J.J.'s reaction perhaps typifies the working cowboy's opinion of professional rodeo cowboys. "Chili, 'ey tickle you 'tween the legs like 'at with a flank strap," he smiles, pointing at him, "and you'll buck worse'n a bareback bronc, right?"

"Pitch ever'body," Chili says, trying to look serious.

Frosty turns toward Chili. "Let's me and you go show 'is bay son-bitch who's the boss, huh?"

Odell's face tightens. "Naw, one boy already hurt 'is close to the roundup is enough," he says. Pausing, he looks around for the four cowboys who live on remote divisions of the ranch. "Chili, why don't you go find Pancho and 'en you and J.J. and Virgil here take off for home and get rested up? I'll see you all here for supper 'morrow night when we get all the hands together for the roundup."

Grinning, Chili presses both gloves into a hip pocket. "J.J., one night to go, you get plenty of sleep, huh."

J.J. flicks an arm good-naturedly. "If I have to send somebody to town lookin' for you 'morrow, want him to look first at the jail? Or Juanita's?"

"One way lookin' at it," Odell smiles, walking toward his house. "Least we'll get the lead outta some pencils 'fore we get started."

3. The Hands / The Hardest Roundup

CURLEY, ONE OF THE MEN hired for the roundup, arrives at the Double Diamond's Little Hills division just before 5:00 P.M. Driving up in an old black Ford, its rear end sloping near the ground, its hood ornamented with a statue of a long-horned steer, the cowhand parks in the sparse brown weeds beside the tack room. A lean and lanky man wearing a large belt buckle that accents his slim stomach, he slings a dark, heavy saddle atop the saddling pens that encircle the corral. Turning, he walks toward Odell with a hand outstretched.

Odell greets him with a boyish smile. "See your old lady's anxious to get rid of you for a month."

Curley pushes back the brim on his black hat that is curled almost to the crown. "Naw, I told her I'd just be gone few days. Get to thinkin' you're dead or gone for good and 'preciate you more when you do get back in a month."

Odell smiles. "Why don't you get over to the barn and get your bed picked out 'fore others get all the good ones?"

Having worked on another roundup at the Double Diamond, Curley knows that the regular or older cowboys have taken all nine beds in the bunkhouse. Instead, claiming an airy area in the barn, he spreads out a musty green tarpaulin and two small faded mattresses that he will use as a bed during the entire roundup. On top of them, he drops his tightly rolled blanket and a knotted cloth bag containing a razor, shirt and pair of pants, and two pint bottles of bourbon.

Steadily, for the next two hours, men drive up, often in pairs, in old Chevrolets and newer pickup trucks that will be returned to their homes later in the evening by either girl friends or wives with an affinity for loose slacks or toreador pants, tight Orlon blouses, and bouffant hair styles. With no wife or girl friend, one man arrives in a dirty Ford pickup truck, which a bright-eyed boy, no more than thirteen years old, promises to "get back home even if I have to kick the gas to it if Texas Rangers think 'ey gonna catch me for no driver's license." Others, with no automobile or truck of their own, are driven to the ranch by men, often bringing along a companion, in return for the chance to eat supper at the ranch.

Seeing the men and women crowded around the cooking shed, a large sheet of corrugated tin attached to four tall posts, few of the last cowboys to arrive bother to unroll their bedding. Pausing only to speak to Odell, or fake a punch to the stomach of an acquaintance, the men each pick up a tin plate and fall into line. Bending over the blackened kettles, the men heap their plates with slabs of steamed beef, pan-fried steak, chili meat, chili peppers, pinto beans, fried potatoes, corn bread, and peach cobbler. To find a place to sit they must move past those filling the benches, the wooden boxes, and the pile of weathered lumber.

By the time a kettle is nearly emptied of chili, a

chubby, dark-complexioned man, claiming that he is waiting for a cowboy named "Cricket Collins," returns to it again. Unlike his previous two trips, he turns his soulful eyes toward Odell before dipping into the kettle.

Odell nods. " 'at's O.K. We throw out more to dogs than most people even cook."

Hunched over a cup of black coffee, Virgil gazes toward a man wiping his plate with a piece of corn bread. "I tell you, Odell," he says, "big supper sure brings 'em out like flies on a horse turd, don't it?"

"Comin' out of caves or som'er's," Odell answers, as his brow furrows. "But not all the right ones."

The problem causes Odell to mingle among the men again. To supplement the able-bodied cowboys already working for the Double Diamond, he has located twenty-five men spread over four counties in Texas and three towns in Mexico who have promised to work for the entire roundup. He never expected more than twenty of them to actually appear at the ranch. But now, the night before he moves his crew into the mountains for the roundup, he has found only sixteen of the men. And the sun, lost behind the high, irregular peaks to the west, reminds him that he will not see any of the missing men this evening. "Yeah, if a man's goin' to work," Odell says, looking across the corral, "you figure on'm being early. One old boy is 'bout all I figure to be in half hung over 'bout time Cookie starts the coffee in the morning. He's got'm a bottle and a woman right now and tryin' to get enough of both to do'm for the month he's gonna be gone."

Woody, the man nearest to him, feigns a move toward a truck. "Ain't no bad idea."

"Little more'n I'd go with you," Odell says with a wry smile. Rising, exchanging small talk as he moves, he saunters toward two of his regular men.

Watching Odell from a long wooden table where she and her two daughters have lingered after supper, Pauline senses that her husband, the only man she has really known, is annoyed. "Betcha I know why your daddy's burned up," she says.

Joyce rises from the bench. "I'll go get him for you," she says buoyantly.

Pauline shakes her head. Though unaccustomed to seeing visitors around the ranch, her eagerness to watch the assembling roundup crew has not allowed her to forget the cowboy's reputation for befriending young women. As usual, she keeps both daughters a comfortable distance from all but the elderly men. "Your brother'll go get him," she replies.

Odell stares vacantly as he sits on the extreme edge of the bench.

"Left you short-handed, didn't they?" Pauline says.

"Least five men."

Kenny hurriedly shifts a chaw of tobacco that seems larger than any chewed by the adults. "I can ride as good as any 'em old sorry ones you gonna get."

Pauline responds sharply. "Working in the summer and a roundup is two different things," she says, her head shaking from shoulder to shoulder. "Times changing like this, you can't quit school now'days till you're sixteen. 'sides, your daddy didn't quit till 'bout then anyway. School people get the law out for you now."

"I ain't quitting," Kenny responds adamantly. "I'll go back after the roundup."

Pauline continues to shake her head. "You don't go to school for a month and 'ey'll send the law after your daddy worse'n if you shot somebody. 'sides, it's good for you."

Odell's tone settles the question. "Time you're sixteen

and finish up school, you won't have a bit trouble gettin' on some big outfit. If you do, you still won't have to go no further'n right here if you want to cowboy."

From past experience, Odell suspects that he need not leave the ranch to replace some of the missing men. For all the loneliness of the cattle country, an isolation so complete that an approaching stranger may be initially viewed as a problem requiring a rifle, the roundup season always brings a motley collection of men and women to the large ranches. Including the ranches where he has worked, Odell has seen roundup time draw Mexican aliens willing to work for five dollars a day; hungry drifters seeking only a meal; wanderlust cowboys and petty cattle thieves; older, hard-drinking men who might once have been capable cowboys; and younger romantics wanting to either become cowboys or compensate for their disappointment in school or another job.

In studying the men now milling around the cooking shed, Odell does not expect to discover any competent cowboys. To hear him curse, he obviously anticipates none of the luck enjoyed by Buzz Nichols, the foreman of the 06 Ranch in Southwest Texas, when five stout men in their early forties drove up the night before a spring roundup in two Chevrolets with the tops covered with saddles and bedrolls. Each of the men represented himself as an experienced cowboy from Cimarron, New Mexico, who had drifted into jobs as extras for western movies but, being unemployed for the previous three months, wanted to "get back to real cowboying." Nichols' suspicion ended the minute that he saw the men lasso several horses. All proved to be first-rate cowhands throughout the roundup. But, on the other hand, Odell does not expect to find himself being misled as he was the evening before the start of the previous fall roundup when he felt that a tall, husky man pulling an empty one-horse trailer behind his automobile could make a capable cowhand. After eating supper, though, the man volunteered in a direct but thick Texas accent that he was not a prospective employee, but a preacher asking the ranch to "donate a beef to help the Lord's work."

From their appearance, Odell has been moderately impressed with two youthful but rugged-looking men arriving together in an old Mercury with fenders that have been repainted with a shade of blue that doesn't match the original color. To learn something of the men's background, he motions for J.J. to meet him beside the barn. "Old car looks like a bull's ass sewed up with a long chain, don't it," says Odell, managing a smile. "But it got'm here."

J.J. nods. "Yeah, 'ey wantin' to work and might make decent hands if we short-handed. Said 'ey had all kinds of experience. Got bedrolls, both of 'em. Big old gawky one 'ere got old saddle 'at's been rode a lot."

Walking away, Odell calls aside the tall, slope-shouldered young man, whose previous employment on a sheep ranch has already brought him the nickname of "Sheep." Looking around, Odell asks: "Where's your buddy you drove out with?"

"I never knowed him till he caught a ride off me back in town," replies Sheep, a modest man with close-cropped blond hair. "But I'll get him." Hustling toward the corral, he waves for someone to join him.

Wiping a bone-handled knife against his fringed chaps, a wiry man barely in his twenties swaggers toward Odell, exuding the confidence of a bantam rooster. In his incongruity, he is an intriguing figure. His black Derringer-style hat has a low, flat crown and Apache headband that differs from those worn by the other men. But the unbuttoned blue shirt, held in place by the loops on a buckskin vest, and doughty smile that twists his thinly bearded face make him look tougher than any other man — almost like the stereotyped villain in cowboy movies.

Remembering his own youthful anxieties that he might not be hired, Odell looks sympathetically toward both of the men. "I heard you've rode 'is kinda country workin' sheep," he says. "But now, where's it you worked cattle some?"

"Couple, three years working my way up from San Antone," the tough-looking young man replies. "Up in the Panhandle. Little places around the Diamond Tail. Seven X. But I wanted to work for a real big outfit."

"That Weymouth, Bevins-Coldwater, other outfits run awful lot cattle 'round their part country," replies Odell. "Them ranches wasn't big enough for you, guess."

The young man shrugs his shoulders. "Real wild cattle is what I wanted to work. Break few horses, maybe, after the roundup."

Odell looks at the young man's calloused palms as he answers: " 'at sleeping bag you brought — 'at's your bedroll, right? But you ain't got a saddle?"

"Naw. But it don't make no never mind with me. I'll take what's left over."

"I'm gonna put you both on for the same pay as ever'body else — at eleven and a half a day and chuck," says Odell. Pausing, he shows them a crooked finger. "But I want to warn you 'fore we start why we payin' so high. End the second night after we pull outta here, you gonna be too far up in the rough country to change your mind then 'bout quittin' off. Break a little finger or something like 'at don't matter much. You have to be hurt pretty bad to get brought in to the doctor. You all understand 'at 'fore you start now."

"I didn't come all way out here, shit, to quit," the young man answers, looking amused. "I want to work cattle."

Pulling a black notebook from a shirt pocket, Odell writes down the names and Social Security numbers given by the young men. "Glad you all came out," he says.

"That makes eighteen extras for sure not countin' the cooks, don't it?" J.J. asks.

"Eighteen right now," replies Odell. "But ain't morning yet."

Nearly two hours before the dawn of Sunday, Odell tints his coffee with canned milk and warms the back of his legs against the burning oak limbs. With the fire and dangling 100-watt bulb illuminating a small area outside the cook's shed, Odell recognizes a fleshy, black-haired cowboy whose fondness for life, far more than his Mexican mother, has brought him the good-natured nickname of "Half Breed" any time acquaintances see him near a bottle of whiskey or a woman.

A diluted cup of coffee in his left hand, a warm can of Coors beer tucked between the boards that he is resting against, Half Breed greets Odell with a handshake that looks weaker than his forced smile. "Start this morning, right?"

Odell nods. "Knock off somethin' pretty good?"

"Seemed like it the time."

"Right up where cook keeps the pepper and stuff," Odell says, " 'ere's aspirins and 'em little mints you chew up for bad stomach."

Half Breed takes a small sip of coffee as he nods.

Having gained one man during the night, Odell is anxious to learn if he has lost any of those having second thoughts about working a month on the roundup. He looks past the men either eating pancakes and bacon or walking a few feet to take a leak or empty the coarse coffee grounds settling in their tin cups. Uneasy, Odell sets his cup on the shelf and walks away to see that only three men are still sleeping on the mattresses and cots spread outside the barn. Pouring more coffee, he remembers that Rio took the two young men with him when he left an hour earlier to gather the horses from the fenced trap behind the corral. But, for the moment, he can only account for fifteen of the eighteen extra men who were present last night. Turning toward J.J., he asks if anyone has seen two Mexican-Americans, claiming to be related, any time this morning.

"Naw," J.J. answers, "but Pancho knows 'em I think."

"Pancho, you seen either one 'em skinny cousins from over by the railroad tracks, the Santa Fe, 'is morning?"

"No, I never see them sleep nowhere," replies Pancho. "They eat supper and go 'way at night probably."

"No probably about 'em boys eating," Odell answers sarcastically. "Way 'ey were goin' back for more supper — you'd think 'ey were putting it in their pocket."

Virgil unfolds his arms. "Pancho, tell'm why 'ey couldn't put nothin' else in their pocket."

Pancho garbles his words as he giggles. "Their pockets already full cigarettes they take off truck."

"They ones I'm thinking of," says Virgil, "their uncle I worked with wasn't much count either."

Throwing out an arm, pursing his lips, Odell walks toward the trucks and automobiles. When he returns, he is seething over the discovery that a short Anglo cowboy also left during the night. "Any you all see 'at little Danny Ray take his bedroll outta 'at old car of his?" he asks, barely waiting for an answer. " 'at little son-bitch — he give a hard-up story and got thirty dollars pay off me in advance so 'at woman who brought him out have somethin' to eat on while he's on roundup. I didn't pay no attention to see if he was in the car when she drove off. You all, huh? Betcha he didn't even take his bedroll outta 'at car."

A cowboy spears a small pancake from the edge of a skillet. "They won't have to spend none 'at money to eat on. Eat enough meat last night to last 'em half the winter."

"Yeah, 'at old woman of his," Odell snaps. "Her old belly's like filling up a washtub. Naw, you catch him, he'll just say 'is wife got sick."

In his frustration, as he walks toward the tack room, Odell broods over his inability to replace such men as simply as many foremen, wagon bosses, and cattlemen across South Texas. With proven cowboys in the strategic positions, these men fill the lesser jobs from among the tough Mexican aliens, locally known as "wetbacks" or "wets," who either for economic necessity or adventure cross the unfenced Rio Grande River at night and cower behind mesquite and rocks during the day until they reach a friendly ranch or an area where they feel safe from the federal Border Patrol. The wets are always much safer on certain ranches than others. Some cowmen, by courting particular members of the Border Patrol, continue to have their Mexican-American cowboys haul experienced wetbacks to their ranches. When such a cowman is occasionally challenged by an unfriendly or strict inspector, he merely insists that he thought the wets were the fourth- or fifth-generation Mexican-Americans whose population dominate southwestern border towns.

Many cowmen offer little pretense on how many wetback cowboys work for them, particularly during roundups. Recently, at a large cowman's backyard cookout, a smaller rancher exemplified the truce that such men enjoy. "With the way prices and people are now'days," he volunteered, swirling the melting ice in his bourbon, "I'd have to have my wife out ropin' and me doing half the branding." Turning around, he purposely caught the eye of a Border Patrol inspector refilling his plate with biscuits and charcoal-grilled steak. "Isn't that right, huh?" he continued, pressing a heel in the soil for emphasis. "You fellows know we couldn't get by without working some wets. You all fair about it, ain't ya?" The inspector, pretending that his mouth was too full to speak, answered with a faint, expressionless nod that seemed to convey: "Do we have to talk about it like this?"

Similarly, Warren, the owner of the Double Diamond ranch, has no reservations about filling late vacancies on a roundup crew with wetbacks. But, for reasons that Odell can only interpret as either aloofness or laziness, he refuses to befriend the Border Patrol. "Picked up your wets again, huh?" he will shrug. "Well, guess you'll have to go out and get some more." As a result, if he wants to keep wetbacks for any reasonable length of time, Odell has to hide them far from his house. Looking around, he is visibly anxious to hear about the status of the two Mexican cowboys, both aliens, recommended by Frosty. But he finds that, for all his enthusiasm, Frosty is one of the last cowboys to rise and about the only Anglo to shave in the morning. When Frosty finally ambles toward the tack room, Odell meets him with a question: "'em Mexican boys show up where you expected?"

Frosty shakes his head. "No trouble," he says, sounding enthused. "They brought themselfs plenty beer and I took 'em out some steak meat and bread and 'ey way back off the road over by gate sixty-three. I'll show where to pick 'em up when truck comes through tonight."

"Way Border Patrol's cracking down over some big shot popping off," Odell replies, "I'll need 'ese boys too much for 'em to get caught."

Frosty laughs. "Catch 'ese boys running? Hell, Border Patrol catch deer 'fore 'ese old boys."

Returning to the tack room, where he opens cartons of new horseshoes, Odell fails to notice the pair of lights breaking through the murky grayness to the south. The first to see the lights, Frosty points with mock excitement at Chili, a Mexican-American, born in Texas. "Better run, you damn old wetback. Here comes the Border Patrol. *Chotas.* Run! Damnit, run!"

Walking up, J.J. chuckles as he speaks. "Either the Border Patrol — or Danny Ray and 'is old woman's comin' back for breakfast 'is time."

The laughter brings Odell out of the tack room. "Naw," he says slowly, "Border Patrol ain't apt to come out while it's still dark enough to hide wets on 'em. And old Danny Ray's done already eating at 'nother place som'er's."

When Odell recognizes the rusted Ford, a narrow trailer bouncing behind it, he correctly guesses the driver: Cecil, a white-haired, sixty-nine-year-old cowhand with only one eye and no apparent fear of losing the other. A sage cowboy, trusting only a horse that he has raised and broken, Cecil no longer agrees to work for more than two days at a time. But, as he leads his horse toward the saddling pen, he cannot hide his enthusiasm for going on still another roundup. "Help you all shoeing today," he says, "but brung my horse and bedroll case things ain't no better then 'ey were."

"Get little worse off ever' year," Odell answers. "You gonna need a jacket, too, 'fore you finish up with us."

"I brung 'at too," Cecil replies.

Remembering Cecil from another roundup, Chili stares into his eyes. "You going to leave that horse to me when you die?"

"Shoot, people's always wanting to buy him off me,"

Cecil replies, exposing teeth liberally studded with gold. "I know 'im better anybody and I'd be afoot sure without him."

Frowning, Frosty looks toward Chili. "Be more like you leaving your old saddle and woman to Cecil. He's shacked up with more widow women than you and all your relatives ever have. Still better shape than you are, I bet."

Cecil smiles. "Ain't worrying 'bout being in bad shape," he says. "I can tell you 'at. Went to the government office 'ey had and 'is girl said man my age could get a medicine card. Told 'em I didn't need one. Never been sick. I been mashed, stoved up, fell on. Kicked and stepped on and bit. But 'ere ain't no germs in 'is high country to get you sick."

"Why'n you tell 'em to give you the money?" Woody asks.

"The girl asked me how much I made in year's time and said I'm in poverty," he replies. "But 'ey never heard of me 'cept for Social Security. Census never took my name, guess." He pauses to stroke a paunch that is accented by tight blue denim pants which seem to have been a size too small even before they shrank. "Poverty, I tell her," he continues, voice rising in amusement. "Don't look like I'm starving, does it?"

"If you gonna feed your belly any breakfast 'is morning," Odell interjects, "you better hurry over 'ere and beat the dogs to what's left."

Within a few minutes, Cecil saunters back from the cooking shed with two pancakes wrapped around several pieces of thick, hand-sliced bacon in much the same fashion that a bun covers a frankfurter. Trimming off small chunks of the pancake with a pocketknife, he squats to watch the men sitting in the dirt or on the dried lumber stacked against the tack room.

With an hour elapsing before the horses are even expected, most of the men remain busy between the conversations. Time after time, many of the Anglo cowboys, their denim pants hanging over their boots, reach for chaws of Mail Pouch tobacco; the Mexicans, their pants tucked inside their high, stitched boots, pull smaller portions of tobacco from packages labeled "Conwood." Looking for weaknesses in their equipment, the Anglos fidget with their bridles, the Mexicans with the girth straps on their saddles. Whirling, the younger cowboys pitch their thirty-three-foot nylon ropes against each other's ankles; several Mexicans do the same with forty-foot ropes.

His eyes narrowing, Odell continues to watch Willie, a lean, lithe Mexican with the largest spurs, chaps, and brim of all these men, carefully massage every inch of an aged, forty-five-foot rope. An infectiously happy man, with a continuous glint in his eyes, Willie already has been nicknamed "Big Mex" by those seeing him for the first time. But few really suspect, judging from the way his rope creates a zinging sound when he snaps it, that Willie is, at seventy-three, the oldest member of the roundup.

Winking, Odell taps Willie on an elbow. "Go take 'at new rope laying back behind 'at old sack in 'ere," he says in Spanish. "You keep it and get it all broke in for next year."

Looking as self-assured as ever, the wiry, thinly mustachioed young man has not stirred from the steel post that he plopped against an hour earlier. Breaking off the filter tip of a cigarette, then lighting the ragged end, he continues to study the habits of the older men. Willie, intriguing him more than the others, sharpens both blades of a long pocketknife. Then, as a lubricant, he rubs fat trimmed from a beef kidney on the embossed leather skirt of his saddle.

Noticing the young man's interest, Odell lowers his voice. "Right 'ere's one reason 'em older ones always make the best cowboys," he says. "I've seen it and my daddy seen it. Don't make no difference if they white or Mexican. Old ones smart enough to know 'at they can always learn something out in 'is country. They always ready to know 'ey never know ever'thing 'ere is to know about cowboying."

The young man nods. "Much obliged."

About seven o'clock, well before the remuda is visible to them, the men hear the rumble of the hooves and, a minute or so later, the wrangler yelling "do wa." Suddenly, the horses burst over a slope, all 164 of them strung out two and three abreast.

The young man, though looking around, speaks to no one in particular. "You all feed 'em first?"

J.J. seems amused. "They had all summer to eat. They'll fart loud enough without no feed."

Noticing the ranch's regular cowboys pick up their ropes, Billy Bob angrily stabs a crutch into the dirt. "Damn, if I could find 'at old palomino 'at caused me to break a leg and miss all 'is — I'd shoot'm. I would! Yeah, I would!"

"I got a good job for you," Odell says, pointing toward the tack room. "Go cut off a big piece of cardboard off 'at old box in 'ere and get 'at pencil stuck up in the wall."

The regular cowboys following closely, Odell walks into the center of the corral, unmindful of the rising dust and decomposed manure that choke the air. In the spawning daylight, he needs to see only the slightest variation in the color or physique of any of the 164 horses to remember each of their personalities, names, or ages. Once Billy Bob prints all twenty-six of the cowboys' names on the cardboard, Odell begins selecting for each man the five horses that he will use throughout the roundup. Neither Odell nor J.J., as his top assistant, offers any pretense of allowing equity or charity to influence his decisions. Having chosen their own spare horses, the two men follow the century-old tradition: Assign the smartest, sturdiest, and gentlest horses to the full-time cowboys; then, match up the other horses in the order that they evaluate the competence of the men.

With typical decisiveness, as a closely bunched group of horses circles past him, Odell studies an alert chestnut gelding for less than ten seconds. His arm swivels toward the cardboard that Billy Bob has braced against a crutch. "Give old Cactus 'ere to Chili."

Writing only "CA," Billy Bob frowns as he turns toward the nearest cowboy. "How you spell cactus? C what? C-A-T. Wait a minute. I-S. Hell, I ain't supposed to be no pencil man nohow."

Odell's right arm continues to follow the horse that, to avoid being caught, squeezes between taller horses running from one end of the corral to the other. "Chili, you take 'at chestnut — old Cactus 'ere," he says, sounding enthused. "You warm his butt up good and he's got more cow sense'n half the people you can hire now'days."

Before Chili even pitches his rope toward the chestnut horse, Odell has pointed Frosty toward a muscular gray gelding. "Hey, grab old Smokey 'ere. He's smart and tough to boot. He's one of the few you won't have to even shoe less you overwork'm up in the rocks."

Billy Bob sounds frustrated. "Frosty gets Smokey — right? Huh?"

Moving slowly, winding his rope, Frosty thrusts his loop through the air with an elegant grace. Still, the noose lands behind the horse's ears, then falls to the dust. "Damn if 'is rope ain't stiffer'n my prick was when I woke up 'is morning."

Obligingly, J.J. points toward a stitched saddle atop the

nearest saddling pen. "Use 'at extra rope of mine 'ere if you want to. It's real limber."

" 'Course it is," Frosty jests, walking toward the rope. "You're used to ever'thing being limber."

Cursing, J.J. moves into the center of the corral. "Hey, cut out old Chigger for old hard-on over 'ere."

Stretching his neck as he looks, Odell locates a spirited brown horse with three white stockings and a small white patch on his belly. "Frosty gets old Chigger 'ere too."

Frosty smiles good-naturedly. "What's his problem?"

"He'll have you scratchin' after a good drive," Odell says, with a smile.

Waiting until Billy Bob writes "Chigger," Odell also shows the same forethought in assigning the skittish or rankest horses to the unproven cowboys. Though his voice is lowered, it hardens as he stares at a calm black gelding. "Give old Black Jack 'ere to Curley," he says. "Be perfect fit. I rode 'at son-bitch last fall and he never did a thing. Got 'at?"

Quickly, no sooner than pointing out Black Jack to Curley, Odell seems pleased by the sight of a reddish sorrel horse loping past him. "Hold it. Sheep — 'at old gawky boy — he's big enough to ride Dandy 'ere real good. Always prancing round with his head up like he's in some parade. You can't hardly see over him 'less you as tall as him."

By this time, the saddling pens outside the corral begin to fill with men shoeing each of the horses assigned to them. As a young cowboy holds a yellowish dun horse's halter, Virgil rubs a hand down the entire hind leg to alert him that he is about to lift it. After allowing the horse to kick, he grabs the foot so tightly that it cannot be wiggled loose. Arching his back toward the horse's head, Virgil squeezes the ankle between his thighs and calmly scrapes the dirt from the frog, a V-shaped shock absorber, that is

centered in the hoof. Without Virgil's experience, this
stance could cost him his testicles. But, in a few minutes,
Virgil's thighs feel the tenseness in the horse's leg that
precedes a violent kick. Suddenly, yelling "Ho-a! Ho-
a!" he drops the foot in time to avoid being savagely
kicked.

With long strokes from a rasp, Virgil files away the
cracked, horny rim of the hoof but still leaves enough of
the white hoof to hold nails. He chooses a number two
shoe, the correct size of the plain, fifteen-ounce steel shoe
that is more than thrice as thick and heavy as the alumi-
num plates worn by racehorses. As with any such shoe,
though, he still must hammer it on the anvil, hold it
against the hoof twice, then tediously expand it in two
places to fit the hoof. If a shoe is too narrow, he knows
enough hoof will grow around it to cause complications
that must be corrected later. Taking flat nails from between his teeth, he drives them at an angle that passes
through enough horny hoof to hold, but leaves the end of
a nail protruding outside the hoof instead of striking, and
thereby infecting, the sensitive tissue.

Just as Virgil lifts another hind leg, somebody yells
above the rumbling and nickering, "You damn old
wreck!" Virgil glances back as a light bay horse, so restive that his front legs already have been hobbled, rears
high in an effort to shake loose the straps. When the
horse falls backward, leaving all four legs pointing sky-
ward, he causes several younger cowboys to scramble in
all directions. Anticipating where the horse will fall,
Virgil doesn't even bother to shift more than a step. Only
his own horse, unnerved by those trying to break away,
tempts him to move outside the pen. Laughing, trading
jokes, but never hurrying, he takes nearly an hour to shoe
three hooves.

Exemplifying the camaraderie among the cowboys, as well as their respect for age, Frosty walks up to take the rasp from Virgil. "I watched the kind of women you screw in 'em awful old houses," he says with a frown. "You too old for work like 'is."

Shaking his head, Virgil smiles until he exposes his gold tooth. "Naw, I ain't been in 'em places in Ojinaga or Juarez in pretty near six year."

"Then you're six years worse off for 'is kind of work than I thought," Frosty snaps as he continues to nail on the fourth shoe.

Leading the horse back into the corral, Virgil is hopeful that the shoes will stay on for the entire roundup. But, past experiences tell him, he will be lucky if only two shoes are pulled or kicked away. Within two months, on the average, all of the shoes will be gone.

Walking away, Frosty asks: "Wanta get coffeed up?"

Virgil shakes his head as he packs dark tobacco into his mouth. " 'is time a day I wouldn't give one good chew," he replies, beginning to space out his words, "for three cups of coffee."

Hearing this, Odell flicks an eye toward Rio, a stocky Mexican hired for the job of wrangler, busily shoeing one of the spare horses. "Right 'bout sundown and old Rio over 'ere," he says, grinning slightly, "wouldn't trade you what he drinks for 'is whole ranch."

Though wranglers of earlier eras were the lowest ranked members of a roundup, an assistant with little more status than the equipment manager on a football team, Odell so highly values Rio's ability to handle the remuda that he tolerates his fondness for liquor. During past roundups, Odell has taken his crew to the places where other wranglers were told to bring the fresh horses at noon only to find that they had mistakenly been driven to a site three or four miles away. But, as Odell has learned to appreciate, Rio not only has the remuda waiting at the correct place at the right time, but he also has reshod any first-rate horse that has lost a shoe.

To encourage him, Odell drops a hand on his left shoulder as he gazes down at a shoe being nailed to a hoof. "Old Pistol's the one who had the bad cracked hoof," he says, speaking in Tex-Mex dialect. "You sure pulled 'at together real good."

Rio nods appreciatively.

Walking around the pen, Odell sees Virgil waiting with a question: "His breath smell like whiskey or tequila?"

"More like vanilla extract'n anything," says Odell dryly. " 'Course, 'at's got more alcohol in it than lots old stuff."

"Wonder if he hides it down in his boot."

Odell chuckles. "Betcha you'll never see him take one drink. Right? But suppertime ever' night he's all bug-eyed and gets a little drunker ever'day. Day 'fore we topped out on Two Mile Mesa last fall, he'd go up to a gate and try to open the wrong end."

"You can't never say he didn't hang in 'ere all the way."

"Like old alarm clock," Odell replies, "next to last day he's so loaded 'at damn if he didn't have a hind shoe on backwards on Coffee, 'at brown horse. When we finished, 'member 'em young boys talking 'bout going to get some tail and whiskey. Here's old Rio done passed out complete. Way he laid 'ere, wonder old buzzards didn't want to check him out."

Virgil chuckles as Billy Bob shuffles up beside them. "You was to find Rio's bottle and Odell'll put one of 'em tight Mexican girls on you."

"I find it," Billy Bob says. "I'll take a leak right in it."

Odell smiles. " 'at'll just make him think he's got more left to drink than he thought. Naw, you find his bottle 'fore the roundup's half over and I'll sic Maxine on you."

"He's gonna be up 'ere high and dry," Billy Bob replies puckishly. " 'Cause I'm gonna get it."

Walking for another set of shoes, Odell begins to suspect the thinly mustachioed young man in the open shirt could present far more problems than Rio. With that confident smile seemingly frozen on his face, he still looks tougher than anyone hired just for the roundup. But his awkwardness in flinging his rope soon tells Odell, beyond any doubt, that he only hopes to become a cowboy.

On four consecutive tosses, the loop of his rope collapses before it even reaches a chestnut horse. Embarrassed, the young man pretends to loosen the new rope. Before he cocks his arm again, though, Billy Bob motions for him to drive the horse slowly past his right side. Shifting his weight onto his left crutch, Billy Bob pitches his loop over the horse's head without disturbing him. Anxious to disguise his inexperience, the young man excitedly tosses his rope only to see the loop bounce off the horse's neck, then slide under a foreleg. Surprised to have caught a leg, he jerks the rope quickly. The horse stumbles, pulling Billy Bob away from his crutches and sending startled colts crashing against the rails. Doggedly, the novice clings to his rope.

"Let go 'fore you break leg," yells Pancho. He rushes to pick up the rope that is dangling from the horse's neck. "Whoa, boy," he says in a settling tone. "Whoa, whoa, whoa."

Odell waits until the young man leads the horse to a saddling pen, away from the other men, before confronting him. "What's name couple the bosses you worked for 'round San Antone — Abilene?" he says. "I probably know 'em."

"Little closer to Fort Worth maybe," the young man replies, dropping a hand to his waist. "Hell, I been around cows since I was this high."

Odell's voice remains calm. "What's name the big ranch where you gathered cattle like 'is? Where you worked the longest?"

"More sorta a mixed place," the young man answers hesitantly. "Had little everything. Bulls. Sold off few calves. Lot of dairy cattle."

"Dairy? 'at's where you worked?" says Odell, his mouth opening.

The young man nods.

Odell's voice bristles. "Boy, 'ese wild bitches in the mountains ain't like old Jersey milk cows. They'll hook ya!"

"Yeah, but I can work a roundup good as anybody if I get a chance to get some experience."

"I tell ya, if you'd done this when I was startin' out on the ranch," Odell says, with a quick shake of the head, "they'd just hauled ya out to the road right then and let ya go. I'm goin' let you see if you can be a pretty good hand. But you gotta pay attention all the time and don't cause no trouble. O.K., you can go get your horses shoed."

Sauntering back from the cooking shed, Chili notices Odell's facial expression. "Worry," he smiles, twirling a finger toward an ear.

Frosty drops his hammer. " 'at worrying sure something 'at don't never pay," he comments, splattering tobacco juice on the ground. "I might cuss like hell but I ain't gonna worry about it. You can't go through life biting your fingers and getting all constipated. If you worry or don't worry, it all turns out the same, you know."

Unlike the carefree men, Odell's discovery that "Dairy" is only an apprentice cowboy serves to increase his worries about the entire roundup. Walking beside the barn, coughing deeply, he laments the risks of an inexperienced man's impulsive decisions around a herd of cattle.

"See 'at dairy boy," he says, eyes glinting. "He couldn't rope hisself."

"If we didn't need somebody to make a shadow," J.J. interjects, "I'd done hauled him to town and dumped him."

"Naw, hell, least we done know he's an idiot," Odell says, his voice hardening. "Thing I'm 'fraid of most is we don't find out how many more idiots like 'is we got along till one goes sleep and spills a big bunch cattle."

J.J. scratches the ground with a toe. "Let 'em get to stampeding all to hell — and what'll 'ey lose — ten, twelve pounds apiece."

"Maybe fifteen pounds a head in 'is weather. You weren't here time we spilled, were you? Worse part is way it spoils ever' head. Cattle learn once 'ey can get away from being caught and from then on — it's hell to pay to get anywhere on time. They'll fight ya all the rest of the way tryin' to break out of the bunch."

But even as a cowboy now burdened with managerial pressures, Odell quickly regains his composure. Having shod a spotted brown horse, which he favors on hills, he locks his eyes on an approaching vehicle. He is soon relieved, once the blue color of the vehicle is discernible, that it is not a minibus used by the Border Patrol, but the new pickup truck that Warren, the owner of the Double Diamond, uses to drive out to the accessible parts of the ranch. "Bounce off couple of 'em rails, boys," he says gingerly. "Here comes the head nigger."

"*El Uno Grande*," Chili comments.

Taking Odell's message literally, Sheep saunters into the corral and, fingering a rope nervously, times his toss to drop over a roan horse's neck just after Warren steps out of the truck.

A relatively tall, heavy, and contented-looking man

wearing freshly pressed gabardine slacks, Warren marches up to the corral and plants an unmarked boot on an overturned five-gallon bucket. Smiling, he pushes back his gray hat just enough to uncover a forehead that seems nearly as pale as his cream- and pink-checkered shirt. Like many large, comfortable cattlemen or cattle-women, far removed from the daily operations of a ranch, he is eager to put a personal approval on the general logistics of a roundup. "Well, Odell," he asks in a friendly tone, "you scrounge up enough old cowboys to make out all right, you think?"

Odell's voice is cheerful. "Only trouble is hands show-ing up at practically noontime like 'is and expectin' a day's pay and dinner besides."

"Not gonna talk me outta this chuck." Warren's forefin-ger dances as he counts the men stirring around the corral and pens. "Got seventeen extras at least, huh?"

Odell snaps his head. "We was sure short-handed as shit last time I talked to ya. But even got couple more hid out now and 'at gives us twenty-six altogether — not countin' the boy who's hurt. Don't know if we got twenty-six cowboys or not. But we gonna start out with twenty-six saddles filled up. 'Course . . ."

Warren raises his right hand like someone taking an oath. "I don't know nothing about hiring any wets," he says, his foot dropping from the bucket. He winks. With Odell following, Warren walks far enough to keep the other men from hearing his comments. Removing a crisp hundred-dollar bill, which he periodically replaces as a marker, he reads from a red leather notebook. Though Odell initially planned the order in which cattle would be gathered from certain pastures, he reviews each of the dates — and waits for Odell's comment — that the salable cattle must be driven to the trailer trucks that will be waiting along the county road. Then, after both men cover their plates with beef, chili peppers, and pinto beans, Warren strolls to the nearest tree to reiterate how much time he wants to allot each group of cattle to refill themselves with water before they are driven onto a scale.

"Don't you worry about your cows," Odell says, raising his voice. "If 'ey don't drink twice much as 'ey piss, 'ey ain't done with me."

When he and Odell return to the corral, Warren stops beside a slim Mexican cowboy, whose large spurs clink with each step, leading a roan horse that has just been shod. "Poke, poke," Warren says to the cowboy and points to the ground. Facing Odell, he adds: "You have to tell Mexicans to slow down, you know. All them Mexicans work cattle too fast."

"Ain't no worse'n some of 'em young white ones nowadays," Odell replies. " 'at'n there's a roping son-bitch. He'll put 'at rope over ten horses and still get one you want."

Warren eases toward his truck as he answers. "I sure hope you don't have too many who learned how to work cattle watching picture shows on TV," he says, looking into his side mirror. "Ones playing cowboy in them old shows now'days make 'em young ones think all you got to do is jump off a box and rope cows for a roundup. Now, Odell, they'll run all the meat off these cattle if you let 'em think this is like some old rodeo."

"They try 'at and I'll run the damn meat off of 'em," Odell answers sharply. " 'Course, I wanta lay the cards right out on table. Some sorry ones in 'is bunch, I 'spect."

"If you didn't have some ornery ones like that," Warren says dryly, as he shuts his door, "then that'd really be something new for a roundup."

By midafternoon, as the men prepare to leave for the camp at Echo Canyon, the continuity of the makeup of a large cattle crew comes into clearer focus. His enthusiasm for attempted humor undaunted, the cook presses his horn before he and his assistant drive away in a covered pickup truck and customized trailer that opens into a workbench. "Have to get there early," he says loudly, "so I can shoot a rabbit for supper."

Dropping the saddle that he is carrying, Chili tries to answer before the cook leaves the yard. "Run over extra one with truck," he chortles. "Gringo love rabbits."

Seeing all the men gathering their equipment, Odell calls aside two young Anglos and one Mexican. "After you fellows throw your stuff on the truck," he says, "you want to help Rio drive the horses." Walking over to Rio, he faces the mountain pass, obscured by distance, where the men will drive the remuda to reach the fenced trap below Echo Canyon. "'em three old idiots over 'ere gonna go with you," Odell says. "Least you'll have somebody open 'at old gate for you."

The other men, who will ride over thirty-three miles of county and dirt roads to reach the camp, look for space in either the three empty pickup trucks or behind the canned and dried food that fills nearly half a large truck. Moving leisurely in the heat, stopping to strap on their chaps rather than carry them, the men take more than an hour to load onto the trucks their saddles, bridles, tightly rolled mattresses or bedding, slickers, insulated jackets, and either cotton bags or small satchels.

Crowded around the trucks, picking a place where they will ride, the men form a diverse group: degrees of competence ranging from storied to hazardous, physiques that are willowish to barrelish, ages from a possible twenty years old to a proud seventy-three, and education, with admitted allowances for "a little lying," from first grade to high school. Moreover, the men's nationalities, roughly divided between Anglo-American and either full or half-breed Mexican, may contradict the popular picture of cowboys driving cattle through the West. But the characteristics of these men, recall older cowboys, are not all that different from those rounding up cattle in earlier eras. Whittling a wooden match into a toothpick as he talks, Cecil needs little prompting to compare the racial makeup of current and past crews. "My daddy's days, they'd want to get all the good white boys 'ey could for roundup too," he says, growing thoughtful. "You had more young boys back 'en for sure. But it was kinda like it is now: 'bout always took the meanest son-bitches you could find and don't care if part of 'em is Mexican boys, or nigger fellows, or Indians."

If Cecil's grandfather were alive for similar reflections, he could enumerate the skills of the Mexican, Indian, or Negro cowboys. Earlier Mexicans were not simply hired for roundups but were the genesis of the cowboy in North America. For all his flair, the American cowboy, born in the triangular area bounded by the present cities of San Antonio, Laredo, and Corpus Christi, Texas, was an idea copied from privileged Mexicans found to have a novel concept of raising beef cattle. First, they allowed the hardiest Andalusian, the red, black, or white Moorish cattle that the Spanish brought to their missions in Mexico, to multiply into a lanky, often multicolored breed with curved horns sometimes measuring four feet from point to point. Second, instead of keeping only as many cattle as could be fenced, these rancheros employed mounted Indian or Mexican *vaqueros* to tend, round up, and brand thousands of longhorns ranging freely over open ranchos on both sides of the Rio Grande.

Subsequently, 300 Anglo-American families, many owning slaves, received an opportunity to begin ranches after Moses Austin, banker, merchant, and lead miner, arranged for the young Republic of Mexico to allow them to settle a fertile portion of her state of Coahuila, now East Texas, as a means of strengthening her declaration of independence from Spain. Except for Stephen Austin, the son, who took 65,000 acres, each settler received up to 177 acres to farm, or 13,000 acres to raise cattle. But Mexico's eventual restrictions against both slavery and further immigration, born from suspicions of "land thieves," collided with the irrepressible visions of personal empires. Quickly, just nine years after the first families arrived in Texas, the more numerous, vociferous, and influential Anglo-Saxons formed a provisional legislature to take a decisive gamble. Vowing loyalty to the constitution, the legislature declared that Texas was an independent nation — as well as the 100,000 unbranded cattle in the area being "public property" — and drew a band of adventurous followers into a victorious battle with an element of the Mexican army already overextended by revolutions, banditry, and the Spaniards.

Patriotism brought many opportunities to become cattle kings during the dramatic sequence of events that followed. Maintaining that "dead prisoners never shoot you," one Mexican brigade, led by General Antonio López de Santa Anna, killed all 187 Texas-American volunteers barricaded in the Alamo mission in San Antonio, and another shot to death a reported 300 Texans in a battle that became known as a rallying Massacre of Goliad. Yet, all the time that cattlemen expanded, both while Texas was a separate republic and particularly after gaining statehood, an obvious pattern prevailed. In winning all but one battle in the United States–Mexican War of 1846–1848, precipitated in part by advancing the border of Texas to the Rio Grande, the United States military forces were so dominant that, despite suicidal resistance, they drove into the capital, Mexico City. Conquered and occupied, Mexico was forced to sell to the United

States territory that now is California, New Mexico, Nevada, Wyoming, and portions of Colorado, Utah, and Texas.

Still, to further advance the independence of Texas, before and after the war, many new cattle kings hired as cowhunters both Mexican-Americans and, increasingly, Anglo-Americans who often had a court case or debt pending back east that ended with the notation "GTT" (Gone To Texas). The mission of many such cowhunters: Drive away all cattle or horses from the "enemy" even if they belonged to Mexicans who had fought on the side of the Texans or were living in Mexico. Mostly young southerners, proficient with horses and guns, these cowhunters eventually developed into excellent replicas of the *vaqueros*. So complete was the Texans' imitation of the Mexican cowboy that it included even his equipment — from large spurs to wide-brimmed hats, from leather chaps to adding the horn and deep-vented seat on an English saddle, and the Mexican vocabulary, from *corral* to *bronc*, from *rodeo* to *lasso*.

Using the Mexican longhorns as the foundation stock, the cattlemen who moved into the watered grasslands of Central and West Texas vacated by the Kiowa, Comanche, and Apache often considered themselves fortunate to be able to hire full or half-breed Indians. With their intimate knowledge of the terrain, some Indian cowboys were so adept in teaching Anglo cowhands the art of following trails that, in time, few Texans cared to drive cattle a long distance without them. Indicative of the Indians' contribution as cowhands, it was a half-breed Cherokee cowboy trader and guide, Jesse Chisholm, whose tracks opened the famous 700-mile-long Chisholm Trail. With this path, subsequent cowboys were able to drive three million Texas longhorns to the railhead of the Kansas Pacific Railroad station in Abilene, Kansas, and, as a result, help develop a national market for beef cattle and enable the Texas cowboy, just as he had learned from Mexicans, to move on and teach the new trade to men in the Great Plains and Rockies.

Finding the western cattle country far more integrated than the east, the one or two Negroes who nearly always worked on trail crews, or for such historic ranches as the XIT, Pitchfork, and JJ, were far from forerunners of a quota system. In a notable example, Charles Goodnight, one of the earliest cowmen in the Texas Panhandle and co-founder of the Goodnight–Loving Trail through New Mexico, Colorado, and Wyoming, remembered Bose Ikard, a Negro, as a "top hand . . . the most devoted man to me that I ever had . . . [he] also was my detective and banker when going through the wild country . . . for a thief would never think of robbing him — never looking in a Negro's bed for money."

Like the Mexicans or Indians, many Negro cowboys distinguished themselves in the jobs often too dirty or risky for Anglo cowboys. One was Bill Pickett (of Choctaw and Negro lineage) whom Zack Miller, one of three brothers operating the 101 Ranch in Oklahoma, called "the greatest sweat-and-dirt cowhand who ever lived." As the originator of the sport of steer wrestling, an act that he enlivened by biting the steer's upper lip and nose, Pickett was featured in advertisements for rodeos as "The Wonderful Negro Pickett — Throwing a Wild Steer by the Nose with His Teeth." He is an honoree in the rodeo room of the National Cowboy Hall of Fame in Oklahoma City, Oklahoma. Except for feeling unwelcome at the white whorehouses in most cattle towns, perhaps contributing to his absence from cowboy folklore, the Negro cowhand also shared much of his Anglo counterpart's prejudice against Indians and zest for the prevailing way of life. Starting with "Tex," a Negro who became the first cowhand shot to death outside Dodge City's infamous saloons, the black cowboy went on to participate in the settling West as noted cattle rustler, gunman, bronc rider, outlaw, and card swindler.

Still, some animosities are too innate to die naturally. Emulating their ancestors, some of today's third- and fourth-generation cowboys convey an obligation to reiterate that neither Mexicans nor Indians may have shed all traces of vengeance. Regardless of his age, many a cowboy raised in Southwest Texas seldom forgets that, during the Mexican bandit raids continuing into the nineteen twenties, a relative or acquaintance was in Columbus, New Mexico, the March day that 400 men rode in with Pancho Villa, the most elusive bandit of all, to kill sixteen Anglos and burn all the businesses that they considered guilty of injustice. Or, at the least, they know a relative or acquaintance of one of the eighteen persons killed in a gunfight on the Christmas Day when Mexican bandits entered the large Brite Ranch in the mountains outside Valentine, Texas. Drawing on more recent experiences, Cecil and Virgil are quick to recall the time they fired a .30-.30 rifle across the Rio Grande at what appeared to be Mexican cattle thieves or that they paid ten dollars to one Mexican cowhand to resteal a horse that another had stolen from their employer.

The cowboys are not always unfair about these views but, it seems, believe only what they see. An older cowboy always recognizes an individual Mexican *vaquero*'s skills and trust, even to the extent of mentioning that "Old Willie's probably the fourth or fifth best hand in this bunch" at the Double Diamond. At the same time, he is prone to generalize, until proven otherwise, that about all other Mexicans are motivated by the type of unpredictable philosophy exemplified during an earlier roundup season. On that moonlit evening, for example, an inspector for the U.S. Border Patrol excused himself in order to hide near a certain culvert. "Yeah, got to pick up another load of wets coming across Rio Bravo and get me 'nother fifteen apprehensions," he said with a wry smile.

"How," he was asked, "do you know there will be fifteen in this load?"

"Informer we got on the payroll tipped us off," he said. "This Mexican's bringing fifteen wets across for about twelve pesos apiece and letting 'em out certain place on the road at eleven thirty tonight."

Asked if the informer's details were reliable, the agent jerked the unlit cigar away from his mouth. "Hell, he's the one who's bringing 'em across."

"He doesn't mind taking money from you and the wets both?"

"Christ sakes, he's a Mexican!" the inspector replied, obviously considering the question as naive. "Your heart's where the deal is."

Against this background, Cecil grows thoughtful about the Mexicans around him. Staring appraisingly, his hazel eyes follow the last of the *vaqueros*, feet dangling over the truck, riding away from the Double Diamond's Little Hills Division. "Odell," he says slowly, "you handled 'is many Mexicans 'fore, ain't you?"

Odell answers immediately, "Enough to know they're done thinking of how to get the upper hand. You know well as anybody you got to be thinkin' two steps 'head of ever'body to keep things from gettin' out of hand on a roundup. And Mexican boys'll talk real nice. But only one thing a Mexican is thinkin' in spot like 'is: 'Fuck the gringo.' "

When Odell arrives at Echo Canyon, more than an hour after the remainder of the crew, he still has not forgotten to watch the Mexican cowboys. Eyes wandering in all directions, he gazes suspiciously at the Mexicans either slumping around their beds or fidgeting with saddles. Seeing that Rio is asleep, he walks around the red boulders and looks into the old wooden corral. "He got the morning horses put up again," he says, seeming relieved. "But can't be too careful till all his old bottle's gone."

Turning toward the chuck tent, Odell pauses to nod admiringly at the way Willie crafts soft, tiny rope into a saddle girth as evenly as any woven with a machine. "See why Willie's got fingers to pitch rope way he does over a horse, huh?" he says to the nearest men.

Cecil nods. " 'at's Old Mexico. My brother had him Mexican saddle 'at was made in the penitentiary. Lasted him all his life."

Kneeling beside the dying ashes, Odell finds only two kettles are still warm.

Frosty walks up behind Odell. " 'em two wets I hid out," he says. "You ought to see the beeline 'ey both made for 'is chuck."

Odell glares toward the Mexican men who, he knows, must be the wetbacks, leaning against the fender of a truck. "They'd better beeline it 'way from my truck."

As Odell eats hurriedly, dunking each bite of bread into the soupy mixture of beef, beans, and chili, both wetbacks demonstrate that they enjoyed hiding in the pasture. Carlos, a short, dark-complexioned Indian, points to the sky and hunches his bulky arms to demonstrate how he hid when a Border Patrol plane flew through the valley. Luke, a smaller, light-complexioned mestizo, is anxious to relate the sense of adventure that has brought him to the roundup. Since the Mexican government does not allow female cattle to be exported, Luke explains, he has helped rancheros sneak cows across the Rio Grande. The practice, with the price of cows considerably higher in Texas, is not uncommon. But Luke claims to have a ruse that prevents a ranchero from having a single cow confiscated by the U.S. Bureau of Customs. Even when two agents caught him gathering sixteen heifer yearlings in Texas, he waved and hollered to show that he was only trying to help a thirteen-year-old boy, standing on the Mexican side of the Rio Grande, recover cattle that had strayed away from him. Still, Luke adds with a shrug, the fact that he is now known to customs agents and a river rider keeps him from being hired to "chase wetback cows."

In response to a question, Luke agrees that he could avoid such a problem if he tended cattle for 400 pesos ($32) a month and board at one of the immense ranches in the states of Chihuahua or Sonora. The tropical terrain and walled headquarters with gun portals, he acknowledges, convey an air of mystery that even attracts an occasional Anglo cowboy. "But running from Border Patrol is more better excitement," he says in stilted Tex-Mex. "See, Mexican police think it is his duty to punish you good. If they arrest you, two things happen almost. You do not never hardly get nothing to eat and the police will always get a confession about something. Border Patrol, they only think about how many wetbacks they catch for their records. Sometimes, Border Patrol wait for you to get your money from the boss before they take you back. If they put you in jail, you eat good and rest. If you not get caught, you get gringo cowboy dollars."

When Odell leaves the chuck tent, Cookie angles around his truck to stop him. "Rest the meat hung in the shade," he says, shaking his head, "but if it sure don't cool off tomorrow, it'll spoil on you."

Unconcerned, Odell walks on to his pickup truck. "Just have to cook up enough supper meat early. 'en we'll kill 'nother beef if we have to."

Recognizing the glint in Odell's blue eyes, Frosty has the foresight to carry a cup, hidden against a hip, as he saunters toward Odell's truck. "Done had your worm medicine for the night?" he says glibly.

Odell twists an arm under the seat to pull out a fifth of Early Times bourbon.

J.J. decides to put a rope into Odell's truck. "You done worked off rest 'at old fifth left over?"

"Yeah, you gotta keep 'head 'em Mexican boys," Odell says dryly, pausing to slice the bottle's seal with a thumbnail. "You gotta see what 'ey up to ever' minute."

Frosty, noticing Odell flick the bottle toward him, sets his cup on the floor of the truck. "I got little put 'way, too, case it gets cold and wet some night."

"Never knowed it not to get cold and wet," Odell replies.

Seeing Odell study his notebook, Frosty follows J.J. to the far side of the truck. "You know, you can't take a drink like 'is with Mexicans," he says softly. "No different from 'em Indian boys I worked with up in Arizona. If you was to get drunk or go get piece pussy with 'em — 'ey just can't forget 'bout it and go back work in the morning like white boys. They'll figure I'm in good with the boss and I'll screw off good now."

Showing the confidence that gives the status of head Mexican-American cowboy, Chili soon waddles up to the truck wearing an artificial frown. "Wetbacks' morale very low," he says, holding out his cup.

Odell pushes the bottle toward him. "Want to get my morale built up too?"

Chili, looking slightly surprised, nods.

"Well, 'fore I go to sleep," Odell says, "I want you to make sure ain't none the keys left in 'ese pickups for anybody who gets no ideas."

"Hell, I never not make it back in 'fore sunup," J.J. replies, his words turning into a giggle. "Huh?"

"I don't want to cut it 'at close again," Odell says, "not as early as we movin' out in the morning."

4. Gathering / Ride, Rope, and Cuss

IN SILHOUETTE against the gray sky as they begin the roundup, the men follow Odell away from the camp beside Echo Canyon. Quickly spreading out, many of the cowboys wisely allow their fleshy horses to gallop at a pace that will release some of the energy which has accumulated during their many months on the range and is now accentuated by the deceptive coolness of dawn. Slightly more spirited than the others, or perhaps sensing his young rider's inexperience, a bay horse repeatedly arches his spine and swings his head from shoulder to shoulder. As he bounces the young cowboy, the horse passes enough gas for most of the men to hear him.

A smile creasing his face, Chili breaks wind just as loudly.

" 'atta way to talk back!" somebody hollers.

"Hook'm, daddy," another man chortles.

"Naw, naw, keep bending him to the left," Odell snaps, pausing until the young man regains control of his horse. " 'at's way to quiet him down. You new boys, too, you all want to keep your spurs out of 'em till 'ey've worked a little the pitch out. Else back up 'at old pasture, hitchhiking ain't too good."

Passing between two windswept hills to an enormous area known as Backbone Country, a name owed to the rippled rocks towering over its south end, Odell offers no advice on how to gather the cattle. By motioning to only five of the men he is able to divide them all into two groups that are roughly balanced with Anglos and Mexicans, the proven and unproven cowboys. Then, before leading one group to the right side of the pasture, he reminds J.J., in a lowered voice, how he wants the men positioned across the other side of it: "Willie, there, get him next to one the new white boys. And be sure you put a good one in between ever'one the idiots."

Skilled or unskilled, each man soon finds himself riding alone. Collectively, these men are sweeping through the pasture to ideally find every cow, calf, and bull in it. But so great is the space between the cowboys that each works for long periods in a solitary stillness that is broken, only if he stops to listen carefully, by the clicking of bloated crickets and spotted grasshoppers bouncing away from his horse's hooves.

Woody's style typifies the routine. As one of the Double Diamond's full-time cowboys, reasonably familiar with its terrain, Woody is positioned on a flank that requires him to search the dim gullies and draws which overhanging rocks continue to seal from the sun. Keeping his chestnut horse in a rhythmic lope, winding back and forth across his zone, he looks into each of the cavities in the rocky, folding land. Quickly, the number of places to search multiplies. And with little difference in the reddish brown color of the cattle and the rock outcroppings, Woody moves to the crest of the highest hill to survey the land ahead of him. Near several yucca, about

200 yards to his left, he sees three cows grazing beside their calves.

Approaching the depression where the cows were seen, Woody is not surprised to find that just the sound of his horse's hooves has already sent the cows and calves retreating toward the south. With this herd's genes, the cows are expected to flee. Since the railroads reached the cattle country, eliminating the need to raise the spare longhorns able to walk long distances without water, the continuous search for hardy but increasingly heavier beef cattle has resulted in more than 20 types of them from both pure- and cross-breeding of such established favorites as England's brick and white Herefords; Scotland's black Angus; India's humped Brahman; and France's white Charolais. Yet, of all breeds introduced to Texas, the most numerous, these white-faced Herefords, have also evolved into mountain strains that sometimes approach the self-sufficiency of the native wild animals among them. Strong breeders and mothers, ranging far and high to find water or sparse natural vegetation, most of these Herefords have adapted to drought, heat, snow, or the mountain lions and bobcats that emerge from the rocky caves at night. Knowing that these Herefords also would run "like buggers" if he came much closer, Woody finds it easy to follow the strategy of roundup: Whenever possible, just quietly drive any cow, calf, or bull that is seen toward the south; then, by sundown, if all goes well, the cattle will reach the strip of barbed wire and a huge, impassable bluff, forming an L-shaped trap, that forces them into a corner of the pasture.

But, with his disposition, Woody does not seem to mind the additional labor of stopping a cow determined to lead her calf in the opposite direction. Though otherwise an easy-tempered young man, unruffled at even the possibility of injuring himself, Woody thrives on an attitude that

leaves little margin for compromise. "If no old contrary
son-bitch don't tell me what to do," he contends, "then I
ain't gonna take nothing off nothing I find out riding a
horse or pickup." He is not hesitant to reconfirm this feature of his life. With decided zest, he spins toward the
glimpse of something that disappears behind an embed-
ded boulder. Galloping closer, he sees that he only located four pronghorn antelopes. Lips curling, he pauses
to curse them, as if that rectifies being misled.

Continuing across a ridge, dipping snuff as he rides, he
chooses to enlarge his responsibility. Periodically, he
slants far toward his right to see that no cattle sneak past
the new hand who occasionally comes into view. In
doing so, he pauses to see if the man drives on the cow
and calf standing motionless in the crease between two
slopes. When the man bears in the opposite direction,
Woody knows that he either has missed the cow or mistakenly left her to him. He encircles the cow and calf,
sending them both trotting southward. Before returning
to his own position, he notices a calf bounding northward
through a gully far in the distance. Slapping his horse, he
gallops at a pace that should enable him to intercept the
calf. Unexpectedly, two cows and a calf emerge from a
deeper draw much farther north. Seeing them, the lone
calf scrambles up the bank and begins to run. Within a
few seconds, both of the cows and their calves break into
what seems to be their fastest speed. Spurs raking his
horse's ribs, Woody finally draws near the cattle. But, apparently desperate to escape into the scrub oak covering
the slope ahead of them, all of the cows and calves scatter
so far apart that he has no chance to encircle them.

Woody's reaction is instinctive. Isolating the heifer calf
that is farthest from him, tying his nylon rope to the saddle horn as he rides, Woody soon draws close enough to
pitch the loop toward the calf's neck. Hearing the sound

of the rope, the horse stops, turns, and braces his haunches. Running at his maximum speed, the calf is flipped backward the instant that she reaches the end of the rope. Bouncing down from his horse, Woody crosses the calf's forelegs, binding them with a soft manila rope, or "piggin string," before she begins to regain her balance. Confident that the mother will return to the calf, Woody canters up to a slope that provides him a view into the crevices and depressions in the terrain for a radius of nearly a half mile. Waiting, he knows that, in the rising heat, the other calf and mother will need to stop. Finally, he sees that they are reunited and walking slowly along the foot of a hill.

He circles wide, hiding himself from the cow and calf, until he broaches a hill well to the north of them. Then, trotting slowly toward the pair, he allows them time to realize that their path to the mountains is blocked. But once they turn, Woody yells and charges directly at them. As the cow leads the calf to the south, the direction that he needs to drive them, Woody canters along behind for about 100 yards. Riding back toward the calf that he found, he sights her mother watching, rather impatiently, from the crease between two small hills to the north. Swerving back and forth, he finally maneuvers the cow toward a depression on the south side of the calf. Quickly, before the cow moves from that place, Woody gallops up to the calf, whose eyes are watering and rolling from fear, at an angle that causes her to hobble in the opposite direction. As planned, the calf sees the cow. Woody pulls the rope from the calf's forelegs, then slaps it across her tail. He chases the calf and her mother, forcing them to run, until he is convinced that they are too frightened to turn back toward the land where the calf was born. Woody chuckles to himself as he realizes how Warren, or any other cowman, would be exasperated at the sight of a calf being chased or tied and, thus, losing weight. But, Woody tells himself, Warren should appreciate his ability to lasso cattle. On at least three occasions, none noticeably warmer than today, he or the man riding with him has chased a cow or calf so long that the cow later died from heat prostration.

Cantering at an easy pace, enabling his horse to regain his breath, Woody rides for about half a mile without seeing another cow or calf. No doubt, the cattle he has chased have, in turn, caused any other cows in the area to drift southward. When a cow appears, Woody yields little to the punishing vegetation that, as cowmen like to tell visitors to South Texas, "either sticks, stinks, or stings." As he nears a butte rising dramatically from the grayish soil, a cow suddenly leads her calf diagonally across the range, bearing northward. Swerving, rushing at an angle that will take him comfortably in front of the cow, his chaps, wrists, and sometimes his horse's shoulders thread through the high, thorny mesquite and sharp leaves, known as Spanish dagger, protruding from the yucca. Catching the cow and calf, he chases them in the opposite direction.

His satisfaction is short-lived. Galloping nearer the middle of his zone, he glances by habit into a long gully that he already found empty of cattle. Stopping, he notices what appears to be a young cow at the north tip of the gully. He gallops his horse in that direction, only to realize that he has seen a bull calf, one without the Double Diamond's brand or its earmarks — a "slick-eared" calf. A year ago he was just another calf that was either missed or able to elude everyone on the roundup. But the bull's slyness, developed from 20 months of freedom, has already taken him far ahead of Woody. Routinely, perhaps not even thinking, Woody sprints toward the yearling bull. But the bull's speed and instincts, already widening the large space between him and Woody, underscore the price of trying to intercept him. With numerous places to hide in the terrain ahead, Woody realizes that he would certainly exhaust his horse, already darkened with sweat, if he chased the yearling until he caught him. He turns southward. Yet his decision, exemplifying why large cowmen contend that roundup crews miss about 5 to 10 percent of all cattle in mountain regions, does not escape comment from Woody. "Adios, you son-bitch." He scowls at the calf. "Next time, I'll be laying for you."

The chances lessen of finding every calf. Crossing the floor of a valley, weaving between the thickening vegetation, Woody no longer expects to even see many cattle. His eyes strain for any clues to where a cow or calf may have hidden in the mesquite or sagebrush. Sometimes, when the sun penetrates the brush, he has a glimpse of a cow's red body or white feet. Most of the time, he depends upon his or the horse's intuition. Typically, when his horse snorts warily, he pivots toward a clump of brush, which, in a few seconds, begins swaying from the movements of a small animal. He gallops around the brush, expecting to intercept a frightened calf. Instead, a squat javelina (collared peccary) sow, bristles on her back already rising, scrambles into the open, cracked bed of a creek. Her curiosity and nearsightedness bring her within ten feet of the horse. With practiced calmness, as the sow grunts menacingly, Woody pulls a rock about the size of an egg from his saddlebag. He throws it hard and straight, striking the flab under the javelina's eye. Spinning around, the sow retreats toward the five pigs in the herd that have emerged from the brush. But once again, the javelina tightens her haunches, angrily threatening to drive both tusks into the cowboy or horse. Though interpreting the sow's movements as a bluff, Woody chooses to throw another rock that lands between her front legs. He waits until the javelina backs farther away, then in a mocking tone says, "You ain't gonna whip nobody."

Continuing across the strip of bottom land, occasionally yelping to frighten calves from a thicket, he knows not to complain about the difficulties of finding cattle in this brush. Even for a cowboy with his brief experience, the range is considered relatively open. In valley after valley of New Mexico to the west or in the infinite brush country of South Texas to the east, a hardened breed of cowboy is needed just to penetrate the refuge of some cattle. For example, at the huge Callaghan Ranch, north of Laredo, Texas, the *vaqueros* never lose when they bet that a drifting cowboy from the brushless areas of Oklahoma, Kansas, Colorado, and Wyoming will not work more than two months. "It takes a long time to know how to handle the brush," says one. "By then, the brush has done got him good."

Cowboys who remain on other brushy ranches have long found a cowdog almost as necessary as a horse. But the dogs must be skilled. Time after time, along the Rio Grande, cowboys have sent pairs of trained barking cowdogs to bring wild cattle from the thick mesquite that often is higher than a horse and matted with black brush, guajillo, granjeno, and prickly pear. When the dogs emerged, they often were alone, or bleeding. Since the cattle would not otherwise be found, many a cowboy or small cowman such as "Hot Dog" Dawson, a friendly man favoring exceptionally wide-brimmed hats, has been hired to bring his four cowdogs on a roundup. Though Dawson followed other members of a roundup crew, crisscrossing land that had already been searched, he and his dogs averaged, each day, prodding from the brush, seven cows and their calves.

When the vegetation thins, the land offers little relief to

Woody's horse. As the morning drones on, the heavy, dripping sweat that has worked into a white lather coating his horse's neck and shoulders underscores why a cowboy needs at least two or three horses each day of a roundup. Finally, atop a slope, where huge outcroppings of rocks narrow the pasture, Woody notices six men coming into view. One, wearing a blue shirt, waits on the hill to block any cattle drifting back to the places where they prefer to graze. Woody sees Odell lead five men across the pasture and motion for him to join them as they gallop swiftly down to the fenced pass where the remuda is supposed to have been driven. The faint sound of a horse, nickering for his missing companion, tells the men that the remuda is waiting in the place that Odell had selected.

The men find that Rio, moving his buckskin horse with leisurely confidence, has the remuda penned in a corner where rusted barbed wire intersects with high red rocks.

Perched low against a flat boulder, shielding him from the sun, Billy Bob also discourages any restive horse from stirring more than a dozen or so yards from the other horses. Grabbing one of the small, rounded rocks that he has piled beside him, he throws it under the stomach of a three-year-old colt easing farther toward the left. "Get back here," he hollers: "You ain't boss nothing."

The older horses are equally quick to demonstrate to the colt how he ranks in the social organization of the remuda. When the colt starts to drink, a tall black horse knocks his head away from the water. Waiting until the black horse has drunk, the colt then walks back to the water. But, taking turns nudging or snapping, each of four other older horses in the group will not allow the colt to touch the water until all of them have finished or pretended to drink. Then, as soon as the colt settles in a grassy spot about 15 yards away, two of the same older horses decide that, of all the space surrounding them, this is the precise place where they want to stand. Snapping fiercely at his neck, the two horses push the colt away from his space.

Every horse in the remuda backs up protectively when Odell, Woody, and the other men start to remove the saddles from their horses. Slapping at a mosquito with his right hand and scratching inside his thighs with the other, Odell walks immediately toward the remuda to lasso and saddle Trails, a sturdy roan horse he wants to ride for the remainder of the day. As he ties Trails's reins to a fence post, then binds his forelegs with a leather hobble, Odell watches to see which of the two water jugs is used by a Mexican cowboy. After sucking water from the other jug, he pulls two slabs of fried steak from the cleaned syrup bucket.

Woody settles beside Odell. "I didn't see none with screwworm bad enough to get close to."

"I roped and doctored one little old calf with a bad case," Odell replies. "Left him up there. Wasn't no shape to drive 'is far."

"They'll be plenty we get to Backbone," says Woody.

"You bet," Odell answers, speaking with his mouth full. "And soon you get finished eating, want to show couple 'ese new boys way to get back and you go work 'at flank on other side."

The sun peaks overhead before the last six men arrive to change horses. Aware that the roundup will not resume until their group returns, J.J. and Frosty hurriedly saddle fresh horses and bite into their steak before the less experienced men with them even catch their horses. But, leaning on the shady side of a large rock, neither man notices that Dairy, first needing help from Rio just to lasso and saddle a spirited black horse, has given no thought to hobbling his forelegs. Showing the nonchalance of a fictionalized cowboy approaching a saloon, Dairy ties the black horse's reins to a fence post and walks jauntily to a water jug. All the other horses are also pulling on their shanks. But, without hobbles, the black horse is able to alternately rear and brace his legs stiffly as he tugs on the reins. Suddenly, before he is even noticed, Dairy's horse tears his reins away from the post. Wheeling, he sprints so recklessly between the horses being saddled by two new Mexican cowboys that they rear simultaneously and, in turn, excite much of the remuda into scrambling for an opening past Rio.

With the reins already wrapped around a wrist, the light-complexioned Mexican cowboy clings stubbornly to his horse. The younger man, just starting to push the bit into a brown horse's mouth, is knocked backward. Still, showing no fear of the horse's pounding forefeet, he lunges for, but misses, the dangling rope. With Rio facing the remuda, the brown horse escapes across a flat section, seemingly trying to reach the black horse.

Cursing loudly and flinging his steak, J.J. runs to his horse and loosens the hobbles and reins. Frosty quickly follows. Not even the determination etched on their faces, though, seems to reduce the odds against J.J. and Frosty's catching either horse. Angling wide to the right, hoping to trap the runaway horses against a low bluff, J.J. and Frosty press their spurs into their horses until both run at what must be maximum speed. But already at least 200 yards ahead, and carrying only an empty saddle instead of a man, each runaway horse disappears quickly from the sight of everyone standing around the remuda. Needing only about two minutes to calm the remuda, then leaving it attended by the other men, Rio sprints toward the path presumed to have been taken by the runaway horses. But unable to locate either the horses, J.J., or Frosty, he soon returns.

"If 'ey had some more saddles here," Billy Bob says

quizzically, " 'ey could just let 'em old horses go, huh?"

Rio is careful to look away from Dairy, his eyes still conveying his embarrassment, as he speaks in a stilted nasal tone of English. "J.J., no stop. Odell be one who be hot as hell. Stop roundup, he get mad good."

When an hour passes and neither J.J. nor Frosty returns, Rio and Billy Bob reason that Odell should be told what has happened so that, if he wishes, he can resume the roundup without the missing men. After Rio points out the trail, the two members of J.J.'s group who have saddles gallop back toward the pasture where the roundup crew waits.

Billy Bob, as he nods to Dairy, picks up the cardboard listing the horses assigned to each man. "If I was you all," he says, shaking his head, "I'd go 'head and catch my third horse now so you all won't get J.J. no madder'n he gets back."

After helping Dairy and the slight Mexican lasso and hobble their fresh horses, Rio then catches a calm sorrel horse that is listed as J.J.'s third choice.

J.J. needs him. When he and Frosty finally reappear, far apart on a ridge, each has a runaway horse on the end of his rope. But, with the horse he is riding now staggering, J.J. waves for someone to meet him. Before Rio can gallop out to him, J.J.'s horse stumbles. J.J. jumps from him and kicks the dirt. Seriously overheated and dehydrated from running more than an hour, the horse falls onto his front knees. He is panting heavily. His veins seem to enlarge each time they pulsate. To help the horse breathe, J.J. quickly pulls off the saddle and bridle. As Rio holds the runaway horse, J.J. saddles the sorrel. Still his concern remains with his overheated horse. "I hope he'll be O.K.," he says, frowning deeply. "Don't let him drink for a while, you hear. It'll clot his blood up and kill him if he does 'fore he cools off. It'll kill him sure, you hear."

Rio shakes his head. "No drink."

J.J.'s anger has not diminished after he leads the runaway horse to the remuda to be unsaddled. "You old wild son-of-a-bitch. If I had a thirty-thirty, I'd just shot him and took the saddle and been done with it long time 'go. Be better than ruin that good horse over you."

Billy Bob, while shuffling to block a nervous horse, nods at the slight Mexican. "He'd shoot'm, too. No shit, he would."

Taking hurried, gulping drinks from the jug, J.J. turns toward the hazy mountains as he speaks. But he plainly wants Dairy to hear his warning. "If he loses his horse again," he says, voice rising, "don't give'm 'nother one. Just take the saddle back to Echo Canyon and haul him out to the road and leave him." Barely glancing back to see Frosty tighten his girth strap, J.J. gallops at once toward the hills where he left the roundup crew.

The two young men, still saddling their frisky horses, must gallop much faster to get close to Frosty. When the time comes to spread across the pasture both young men are told, in a minimum number of words, to ride southward until sighting someone and then to slant toward the space between him and the nearest man.

With the hills immediately ahead already searched, J.J. gallops at a pace that advances him toward the cowboys now crisscrossing zones widened by his and the other men's absence. He stops only to chase from behind some mesquite an orphan calf, stunted from fending for herself too early in life, that eventually will be taken to the dogie pen and fed grain. Then, during the next half-hour, he does not move from his course until he sees a black horse descending from a large mesa. Back in position, realigned with the crew, he searches for a solitary cow and calf. With increasing frequency, though, he must sprint to block groups of calves turning back toward the mountains. But, at the least, many of the cattle are closer to each other. With the crew having ridden over six miles of the pasture, driving about 400 cows and their calves ahead of it, he begins to find cows clustering together. Once, seeing about twenty cows trot away from a cowboy faintly visible on his right, he maneuvers his own bunch onto a course that merges all of them.

With the cattle following a trail around a hill, he canters up to the crest of it to view the land lying ahead of him. Far to the left, a bull stands on the shady side of a low butte. When the cowboy comes into sight, the reaction is consistent with that of a range bull finding his territory invaded for no apparent reason. Muscles tightening, ears turned toward the rider, the bull bellows loudly — piercing the still air about every ten seconds. Head down, he scrapes the ground angrily, lifting grass and dirt over his shoulder. He growls in a deeper tone, then waits for a reply. Hearing a distant sound from the cattle, one possibly interpreted as a challenge from another bull, his anger intensifies. The bull cocks his head toward the path of the oncoming cattle. There he sees, for the first time, a bull loping ahead of the bunch. Head lowered further, he brandishes his thick, curved horns — ones with only the tips cut — in the same way that he uses them to fight. Seeming enraged, the bull surges forward a few steps to reinforce his threats. But when he sees the entire group of cattle approach, J.J. knows, his mood will change markedly.

Each of these fertile bulls, from a lineage with the heritable ability to gain weight rapidly, has flaunted his aggressiveness from the minute that he was turned into the pasture during the previous March. Released at the rate of one for every twenty cows, or one per seventeen cows in the rougher ranges, each bull has been obsessed with searching for cows in their breeding period.

In mating about four times a day, five when in peak condition, each of these bulls has always caught every lighter unbred heifer running from sheer fear. He has knocked away, or at least scuffled with, many a bull already mounting a cow rather than wait his turn, then, rejuvenated by the coolness of dusk, has stalked his territory to find if he possibly missed a cow in heat. Now, after more than six months in this range, the bull ahead of J.J. typically realizes that a roundup is occurring. Welcoming the chance to return to his winter pasture, the bull needs no prompting from J.J. He lumbers southward, sides bouncing with each step, to join the five other bulls that have trotted aloofly ahead of the cows and calves. Neither he nor any of the other bulls shows interest in a lone "bulling" cow, later chased into the bunch, being ridden by bull calves too small to mate with her.

Advancing mile after mile, virtually ignoring the swelling numbers of cows behind them, the bulls move much like scouts on a trail they know leads to the corner of the pasture. Sometimes the bulls get so far ahead of the cows that they stop. Yet, even when eleven bulls congregate, their temperament is the antithesis of that of the uneasy cows and calves continually trying to escape into the mountains. These bulls' orderliness, as J.J. is well aware, is owed to the series of earlier fights that decided the ranking among them. Another cowboy is quick to observe this trait as he later drives four bulls near those ahead of J.J. "Much 'ey like to fight," he says, " 'ey sure done found out who the boss bull is, ain't 'ey?"

J.J. knows that, in another day or two, the bulls will again turn belligerent. "Yeah, but wait till 'ese old fuckers get put in with 'em new bulls from up in the Two

Bar Country 'at 'ey ain't seen before. 'ey'll start finding
out who can whip who damn quick. Ground be all shaking."

After advancing another two miles, bringing all thirty-
seven of them in the pasture within sight of each other,
the bulls blend into one group. Two older bulls, which
none of the others attempt to pass, periodically raise their
heads as if looking for landmarks to guide them. Skirting
a long hill, the two bulls gaze across a basin stretching to
a corner of the pasture. Apparently recognizing it, the
older bulls begin to trot, bringing the others closer to
them. All the bulls stop and mill around the connecting
red gates that lead from the pasture. Only one cowboy is
sent to wait behind the bulls in the event that their thirst,
or impatience, might tempt them to drift back into the
pasture. But all the other men, now converging into a
mile-wide wall, must swerve, dart, and yell to keep the
1400 cows and calves in front of them. One by one, the
men chase cows and calves probing for places to escape.
As the men press closer toward Backbone Cliff, they try to
avoid overheating the cattle, already panting and irritable,
they have driven at least eight miles from the opposite
end of the pasture. Yet, complicating the men's work,
about 200 cows and their calves already reaching the wall
of jagged rock have turned around and seemingly are determined to wedge their way northward. With cattle
moving in three directions, the basin is entangled with
cows and calves filling the air with a continuous, deafen-
ing chorus of bawls and bleats. Encircling the herd, a
growing number of black sparrows and brown-headed
cowbirds race to land on the fresh manure.

Seeing Odell's right arm rise, the men pause until the
cows begin to turn away from the wind. Facing the herd,
but staying at least fifty yards from it, the men have the
space to shift into the path of any cow or calf trying to

ease between them. Now they must avoid any commotion. The sprinting and yelping that enabled the men to drive the cattle can, now that the cows and calves are herded together, start a reaction among the skittish that could cause all of the herd to stampede. But, the men are reminded, they never know what can disturb some cows. Cursing in a low voice, J.J. glances at the clear blue sky that, throughout much of the day, has seemed unmarked by even a vulture. Now, a few miles to the left, the faint roar from a silvery two-passenger plane, the size flown by cattle buyers from the Oklahoma or Texas Panhandles, stirs much of the herd. Anticipating where many cows will dash, the men contain the herd with only one calf escaping them. Then, just when the herd seems calm, two calves suddenly bolt between Pancho and Sheep. Hunched over their horses, spurs raking the rib cages, the two men sprint toward the calves.

Leaning forward, arms pointing in all directions, Odell quietly selects either cows that need to be treated for screwworms or calves born late in the spring that are still too small to be sold.

On the other flank of the herd, a young Mexican, slack with fatigue, fails to notice four cows amble toward him. Their calves follow just as slowly. Heads lifted, the cows pause to await his reaction. Apparently dozing, the young man slumps forward in the saddle until his brim touches the mane of his horse. Seeing this, five more cows follow those advancing toward him. Then, all of them trot three or four steps and, without stopping, begin to run. Another cowboy, turning toward the young Mexican, yells out a warning. But, before he can move his horse, the cows are already parallel with him and, doubtlessly motivated by the unguarded land lying ahead, sprint excitedly. Instantly, three other cowboys charge after the cows. But men must move laterally, kicking or swinging ropes, to stop about 150 cows rushing toward the places vacated by the Mexican and, in turn, the three cowboys helping him. The men are still working to settle the herd when the runaway cows return.

As the sun slowly recedes, coppering the sea of cattle before them, nearly all of the men continue to keep their horses pointed toward the herd. Finally, Odell is told that the two men he sent to drive the bulls to another pasture are well beyond the sight of the cows. Now the herd can be driven along the wing. As the point man, riding directly in front of the herd to keep it from stampeding, he moves slowly. The cowboy nearest him waves a tan windbreaker as the signal to drive the cattle toward the gate.

Seeing several cows jostle, Dairy cups a hand against his mouth. "Ones that get in front," he asks, raising his voice above the bawls, "they the lead cows, ain't they?"

Cecil flings an arm toward the ground. "Old craziest son-bitches ones 'at 'bout always get up front or on outside some ways."

A young cow running along the outside of the herd supports Cecil's opinion. Typical of those resisting all the time that they are driven, she nudges a calf in front of her and sprints toward a gully dividing two slopes. Instantly, about ten calves follow her. But three of the men riding on that flank veer in front of the cattle.

Conversely, hundreds of cows wedged in the middle of the herd, sticking their hooves into the ground, hold stubbornly to their positions. Other cows and calves move forward only because of the sheer weight of the cattle being pressed behind them. To move them, all of the seventeen men positioned around the rear of the herd yell or wave ropes, hats, or sticks. Bracing a handcrafted, rawhide whip against his stiff forefinger, Willie snaps it with such force that the sound frightens several cows, which wedge themselves forward. But many cows still balk. Seeing someone swirl an arm, a signal that the herd has stopped, J.J. plunges between cows. For the next twenty minutes, he kicks cows and calves in the tail to send them crashing into other cattle and, in time, create a forward momentum.

At the front of the herd, a quarter of a mile away, cattle eight and ten abreast hug the barbed wire, occasionally nicking their ribs, as cowboys press them through the gates. Some cows are calm. Many others, wheeling around, sling their horns and fight desperately for places to escape. Once chased through the gates, though, the cattle trot toward either the pond or the concrete tank of water that an old windmill sucked up from the earth; then, heads erect, the cows amble around with a renewed sense of freedom. But the cattle are in a trap, a holding pasture so large that none of the other barbed wire boundaries is visible, and this eliminates the need for cowboys to hold them in a place during the night. The men can return to camp.

At dawn, now a day later, the crew spreads out along the borders of the trap. Though the 700 acres of it dwarf many a large farm, the pasture is so small that the men need only an hour to collect all 1384 cows and calves in it against the barbed wire. Three men canter beside the cattle, turning them toward a buckled valley. Moving closer, J.J. shakes his rope at some cows at the front of the herd. One by one, cattle turn into a moving line, stretching more than a half mile between Odell, riding ahead of the herd as the point man, and the youngest of the new men crowding the laggard, confused, or stubborn in the thickening dust at the rear. As the horizon lightens, Odell leads the herd straight ahead, away from the barbed wire that continues toward a peak. Now, as the experienced cowboys move along both sides of them, the cattle advance across a corridor that is broken only by yucca or cat's-claw. Looking much like an ancient caravan, the cattle plod along at a pace interrupted only intermittently when an excited calf is chased back into the column. An hour passes. Then two. Then still another. Around 11:30 A.M., almost four hours after leaving the holding pasture, Odell turns to stop the cattle near him. With the other cattle spreading out as they stop, the cowboys encircle them. The newly hired men stay in their positions to hold the herd in a slight depression in the land. Taking Frosty and Willie with them, the Double Diamond's full-time cowboys gallop to the remuda, awaiting nearby, to change to fresh cutting horses.

The men could scarcely sort cattle in the open pasture without these sensitive cutting horses. Working in silent unison with their horses, seldom noticed by more than six other cows, Odell, J.J., Chili, and Virgil begin a tedious job: Separate each steer calf from his mother. Staring straight ahead, J.J. points his bay horse toward a calf about eight months old. He eases between the calf and his mother and, before either realizes what is occurring, spreads them at least twenty yards apart. When the calf retreats, looking for a space to dash back toward his mother, Woody and Pancho move in from behind and force him and two other calves into the largest compartment of a weathered wooden corral.

Both the men and horses seem well prepared, sometimes eager, to engage the most spirited calves or cows. After cutting out another calf, Odell hurriedly spurs his horse to avoid being bumped from the side by an angry young cow fighting to elude Chili. Annoyed by the cow, he quickly faces her. "All 'em first-calf heifers like a woman with her first baby," he says, voice turning raspy. " 'at wild bitch don't want to give her calf up."

Loosening his grip, Odell demonstrates why he chose

to ride Runt, a short, muscular gray horse speckled by black hair, with an aggressive personality that he considers "a whole lot of cow sense." Improved by years of breeding, any first-rate cutting horse inherently grasps his training to subtly separate a particular calf or cow from the herd without disturbing the other cattle — a skill leaving the rider to feel, as one points out, that "you're on a horse with power steering." But after he has been cued to this calf, Runt works with such enthusiasm that Odell really doesn't need to guide him. In one continuous motion, Runt charges toward the calf's ribs — forcing him to jump away from his path — and pivots as he skids to a stop. Now, positioned between the cow and calf, Runt bends his head and haunches in opposite directions to block any path the calf chooses. His eyes and nostrils both dilating, his snorts growing fiercer, Runt manifests how intensively he wants to defeat his opponent. Each time the calf feints, Runt merely shifts. Then, head and knees lowered almost to the ground, he anticipates where the calf starts to turn.

Suddenly, without the slightest warning, the mother cow charges toward Runt's blind side. Her left horn stabs savagely for his abdomen. Reacting to the signal from Odell's right spur, Runt swirls with the grace of a matador; then he slants his body just enough for the cow's horn, thrust too forcibly to change the angle, to miss him by about six inches. The calf dashes toward his mother. Spinning once again, Runt lunges toward the calf and, as his head swings aside, bites viciously into the cow's neck. Ignoring her own position and concentrating only on the horse and calf, the cow is swept back into the herd by the weight of closely bunched cattle trotting past her. Losing sight of her calf, the cow bawls out short, hurried messages to him. In his desperation to reach his mother, the calf feints and charges under the horse's neck. He is met by a swipe from Runt's teeth. Seemingly defying gravity, the horse shuffles so easily in front of the calf, preparing for the next move, that his legs slant in one direction, Odell in the other. But little more than a minute after the contest began, it ends. Just as the calf retreats two steps, Odell sends Runt charging forward to scare him farther from the herd. Another cowboy, moving over to jab a stick against the calf's neck, chases him into the pen with the calves already separated. His head erect, reflecting his sense of triumph, Runt awaits the next adversary.

One by one, as the afternoon lengthens, Runt and the other cutting horses follow their cues with tireless dedication. By the time every bull calf is cut from the herd, each horse bears the price of his zest. Steel bits and spurs, digging each time a horse is spun, have left their mark on every horse's mouth and sides; blood oozes slightly from three horses. Yet, after resting only while the men count the steer calves, the horses gaze toward the herd with no less enthusiasm.

Planting an elbow between the planks of the corral, Odell looks quizzically at the men around him. "I counted three hundred and thirty-nine bull calves."

J.J. answers quickly, "Three thirty-seven."

"Pretty good," Virgil drawls. "Times I worked for old boy who couldn't count no higher'n fifty. He'd get a bunch up to fifty and have you hold 'em and he'd start all over till he got 'nother fifty put together."

"Some I've seen," J.J. snaps, "I wouldn't want to try up to fifty."

Odell continues to write in his notebook, damp with perspiration. He decides that he will need 165 heifer calves to fulfill the ranch's contract with a cattle feeder to deliver a minimum of 500 calves from the Backbone pasture. Before selecting the heifer calves, though, Odell and the other men begin to remove about 150 of the most

handsomely formed calves, which they will keep to replenish the ranch's older brood cows. As they choose the
heifer calves to be sold, the men first cut out the few that
seem slighter, ill, or simply less desirable. Knowing the
owner's prejudice against any cow that might mar the uni-
form appearance of his herd, Odell eases toward an
evenly proportioned heifer with the white strip of hair
jutting back from her head not stopping, as most do, midway above her shoulders. Thus he maneuvers her into
the corral, along with the steer calves, for being what is
considered an undesirable "line back." Spinning his
horse, Odell then points out to Chili a heifer calf with a
swatch of reddish hair on her chest instead of entirely
white hair, as preferred, extending all the way from her
face to the other end of her belly. "Hey, cut out 'at old
red neck 'ere," he hollers. "One with her hind end
turned toward you."

Now Odell begins to cull both the remaining cows and
calves. Leaning over his horse, eyes glaring, he studies
each cow as she and her calf are driven past him. Somebody, warning him about the condition of an excited cow,
hollers: "Bad-eyed'n on the left." But afterward, Odell
needs no more than five or six seconds to yell "keep" at a
cow that he wants returned to the herd or "cut" because a
cow has a slightly wide mouth or ringed horns, indicating
that she is about twelve years old, or is occasionally bar-
ren or suffering from cancer, pinked eye, or screwworms.
Each time that he hollers "cut," three men rotate in chasing the cow into another part of the corral. Inside, two
other men, wielding heavy sticks, force each cow into an
adjoining compartment, separating her from the calf.

After resting a few minutes, the men again point their
cutting horses toward the remaining calves until they
have, in separate compartments, between 500 and 503
calves that will be sold to the operator of a feedlot, ninety-

one mother cows that will be sent to the auction at the stockyards in San Angelo, Texas, and all the heifer calves that will be driven to another pasture and bred once they reach sufficient age.

Virgil and Pancho position the twelve men chosen to help them drive the choice mother cows, their low, long bawls now saturating the air, back to the pasture where they and their calves were rounded up yesterday.

Dairy looks surprised to hear that the cows will be returned to the same pasture. "How come we didn't just cut the calves out when we're up in Backbone Country?"

Cecil spits out enough tobacco juice to allow him to smile. "You couldn't get the calves to come way down here with 'em knowing their mothers back in the pasture behind 'em. They wouldn't go a-tall without their mother."

As the cows are driven toward the Backbone Country, each of their series of three or four bawls seems to grow longer; the cows stop only long enough to await a reply from their calves. Finally, beyond the sound of the calves, the cows' bawls become heavy with grief.

Sheep swerves in front of a young cow fighting to return to the corral. "They gonna be all tired out 'fore they get back there," he says, looking at the nearest man, "and here they gonna be walking the fence line all night lookin' for their calf."

Woody shakes his head. "Silly old bitch mooin' and worryin' for nothing," he says, waving an arm. "Next time we see 'em again, they'll have 'nother calf."

5. An Evening /
Beef and Bull

THE SMILE that is seemingly frozen on Cookie's face expands once again, stretching into his heavy jowls and uncovering three gold teeth. His words spill out in the same cheerful tone that rarely differs whether he talks to himself or to another cowboy who strolls up to pour some coffee. "Nobody eats no better than cowboys," he says.

The experience of cooking at twenty-three spring or fall roundups — six of them at the Double Diamond Ranch — has not diminished Cookie's enthusiasm for upholding this tradition. Settling under the raveled ten-by-ten-foot tarpaulin, which he has stretched over four metal posts anchored in the earth, he looks carefully at each handful of dried pinto beans that he scoops from a burlap bag labeled "Grown at 7,000 feet." Flinging aside every pebble and broken bean, he drops the approved beans into a blackened kettle of water and seasons them with a slab of sugar-cured bacon.

Pausing only to wipe his hands on his apron, then tilting a stained hemp cap toward the sun, he stands wondering if he should cook more beef. Already at the edge of the tent, a dented pan is heaped with slabs of chicken-fried steak, left from the noontime meal, for anyone wanting to snack before supper. To his right, Dub, the chubby, easygoing assistant cook, saws off pound-size pieces of a calf's rib that he holds across a folding chair. Still, deciding to prepare stew, Cookie whittles off the hind leg of beef, studies each piece for any fat, then drops it into a deep kettle containing potatoes, onions, and garlic.

Hobbling up, Billy Bob leans on the left crutch. "Think you fixed enough meat, huh?"

"Chi-lee," Cookie answers. "Cowboys always have chi-lee." To start the chili, he patiently dices a large section of top round steak over a skillet and drops almost every visible piece of fat into the fold of his apron. He walks less than ten yards, shakes the fat into the dust, and returns to watch the cubes of meat turn brown over the fire. Drawing back the skillet, he stirs in enough seasoning to completely coat the beef. But to satisfy the men preferring still spicier chili, he also chops small white onions and green chili peppers into an enameled pan.

Rinsing out his cup, Billy Bob gazes toward Cookie. " 'em old peppers 'bout halfway burnin' my nose way up here."

Cookie smiles as he points a raw chili pepper toward his nose. "Verde good for you," he says, nodding. "Forty-one years 'round a ranch and chili peppers, and I ain't never had no bad cold."

Taking a bucket, Dub walks across the grass to dip out water that a windmill pumps into a concrete cattle tank now greened with moss. Pouring through a screen, he fills both the fifteen-gallon cream can, containing the drinking water, and the large kettle that is kept at the end of the fire for washing dishes and hands.

Cookie removes the white apron, smudged with blood and grease, and reverses it to leave the cleaner side visible. Working from tiered shelves, unfolding from the end of a pickup truck and small trailer much like those on the old mule-drawn chuck wagon, he continues his leisurely but unending pace throughout the afternoon. He blends Clabber Girl baking powder into a batter of dough and Buffalo Brand tomato purée into a sauce. Then, picking up a long spoon, he bends over to stir each of the four kettles hanging from an iron bar. The burning scrub oak and pine branches, which two cowboys had piled here and at all other satellite camps before the roundup began, keep the food boiling evenly. Nonetheless Cookie prefers that it barely simmer. With Dub's assistance, he carries each of the kettles to a shallow earthen pit crackling with red coals. One minute he shovels more coals, taken from the main fire, on top of the white embers. Another minute he uses a hook to lift the rimmed cover of a heavy Dutch oven, coated with gray coals, and darkens the crust of the peach cobbler with cinnamon. "You cook it slow," he announces in his customary drawl, "you cook it good."

He cooks the food essentially the same way it is prepared during roundups on most large ranches. In the two to seven weeks that the men gather cattle, sometimes fifty miles from the nearest electricity or refrigerator, the method of cooking for them has scarcely changed in all the years that have passed since provisions were carried on a horse-drawn wagon instead of a truck. Except for using more canned vegetables and fruit, the cowboys passing through the Double Diamond in recent years often strain to remember any substantial variations in the styles of contemporary chuck wagons. One restless cowboy recalled that when crossing portions of five counties of rolling prairies in Texas that comprise the Waggoner Ranch, he found much the same food prepared on wood-burning stoves, but, depending on the intensity of the sun, it was sometimes served under a huge tent. Another tall man sounded impressed with the method used by the Mescalero tribe of Apaches in gathering cattle from their 520,000 acres in South Central New Mexico. Two cooks, working from what the crew called "The Greasy Wheels," a kitchen and two butane-fueled stoves built onto a truck, met the cowboys at mealtime as they drove nearly 9000 cows and calves from the slopes of the towering Sierra Blanca to the piny valleys, where the cooks often surprised them by catching, and baking, brown trout. But vast tracts of some ranches are not yet ready for trucks: a pockmarked cowboy insisted that, when he gathered cattle, two mules were used to pull his chuck wagon into the high corners of the Marble Ranch in mountainous Nevada.

As the food barely simmers, sometimes hour after hour, Dub shows that he is not as partial to work as Cookie. Folding a Navajo blanket behind his head, he slumps down against the shady side of the pickup truck and falls asleep.

With no food left to stir or season, Cookie carries his new fly sprayer, a Hot Shot model, around the edge of the tent and pumps the handle vigorously.

"Damn if your eyes ain't better'n mine," Billy Bob says, squinting slightly. "Damn if I saw no old flies."

"Flies like cowboys." Cookie smiles, aiming the spray toward Billy Bob's cast. "Have to head 'em off at the pass."

Cookie's sense of timing matches his spirit. Just when the first group of cowboys gallop back to camp, a fresh pot of coffee hangs at the edge of the fire. As the men sip coffee or rinse their faces, Cookie and Dub arrange skillets on tin cans and pull kettles to the rim of the pit. Though standing amid the men, Cookie chooses to yell: "Come and get it 'fore I throw it out."

As they have done during most meals, three young Mexicans, waiting near the stack of tin plates, lead everyone past the food, which looks as appetizing as it smells. Carlos, the slightest man, scoops up both the fresh, steaming pinto beans and those left from another meal that have been refried into a Mexican delicacy. Moving quickly, he fills the remainder of his plate with the thick, saucy chili and drops on about half a spoonful of green chili peppers. From the next kettle he adds some beef and potato stew. With his plate completely filled, he passes the kettle of canned corn flavored with shredded red pepper, but he piles on a slab of the prime rib. Plate in one hand, a chunk of golden corn bread in the other, he walks away to lean against a stack of aged fence posts.

Seldom rushed to eat, Virgil breaks off a piece of the sourdough bread that resembles a large biscuit. By the time he finally eases toward the beef, Carlos has already returned for more chili and, again, for peach cobbler.

The food, as much as their physical condition, keeps the men in a jocular mood that obscures any sign of fatigue. Typical of the experienced cowboys, Odell's lips twist into a grin between bites of steak. "Pancho, hey," he says loudly, "you think you could get a steak supper like 'at in some café som'er's for seven and a half, huh?"

"Be no better," Pancho answers. Setting his plate on the grass, he fingers an unused hole in a belt embossed with his name. "This much on roundup I gain."

A sharpened matchstick jutting from his mouth, Woody glares at Chili. "You old son-bitch, you never wash your hands 'fore you eat, do you?"

Balancing his plate on a knee, Chili pats the ragged gloves that hang from his hip pocket. "Have gloves on all day. No way to get 'em dirty."

When Odell squats down to eat, Frosty backs away from him to feign horror. He flicks his thick eyebrows, gaining an audience, as he watches Odell slice the long blade of his pocketknife through the prime rib and then swab the beef through his beans. "Uh, uh," he says, repeatedly clearing his voice. "Ain't 'at the same blade you used to poke 'at medicine up 'at old cow?"

"Hell, medicine 'at's strong enough to kill screw-worms," Odell replies. "You know it just tears 'em little germs you can't see all to hell." Waiting until he chews up another piece of beef, Odell allows a disarming smile to spread across his face as he looks around, first at J.J. and Chili, and then at Cookie. "When the hands start pickin' on the old studs 'stead of the cook," he says, " 'at's sure bragging on the cookin' good, ain't it?"

His mouth already filled, J.J. nods in agreement; then, chewing hurriedly, he mumbles: "Especially after last fall, right?"

Odell frowns until his brow is wrinkled. "Fat old thing I had to get when Cookie got hired off on me last year," he begins. "Way he was half tight all the time — you could see why he got fired at some old Mexican restaurant for not comin' in on Saturdays. He'd do pretty good for while and 'en you know 'em two-pound coffee cans 'ey make now where you can put the top back on? He had bunch of 'em filled with pints of old white-looking wine. Give 'at old Mexican credit, though. He was pretty clean. But he'd be drinkin' and he'd think you couldn't tell when he spilled a big bunch of nutmeg in the chili 'stead of chili powder. Things like 'at ever' day."

"No wonder, pretty country like 'is," J.J. comments, looking terribly serious. "Don't know why if you could be a cowboy you'd want to be a cook nohow. Half crazy, I guess."

Cecil drops his bread into a plate. " 'at's it," he says.

"I knowed of ones who'd go off and forget the flour and salt or 'bout half wreck the pickup in a ditch someplace. Go back a few years, I can 'member some real good ones and plenty 'at I could tell you 'bout I know's crazy."

And he could. A variety of recollections about the caliber of both cooks' food and sanity, whether originating from fact or caricature, awaits virtually any willing listener around a contemporary chuck wagon. But one of the most poignant testaments remains in the weakening concrete marker, lying near Geronimo Pass on a ranch in Hidalgo County, New Mexico, which cattle now mistakenly lick for a block of salt. Crafted by Bernard (Deafy) Whiting, a wrangler for the Hatchet Ranch, the tombstone expresses a cook's role in the death of a cowboy, only a few yards from the Mexican border:

FRANK EVANS, BORN JUNE 12, 1865,
KILLED HERE MAY 1, 1907, BY A CRAZY COOK.
MURDER IN COLD BLOOD WITH A AX.
MARK BY DEAFY, AUG. 6, 1947. WITNESS
BY LOHNIE FREEMAN, FRANK W. ASGOOD,
AGOOD MASSEY . . .

Even if they compromise their standards, many foremen find that the search for a cook remains unending. "I've been working right on this ranch for thirty years," recalls Jiggs Porter, the cattle foreman for the CS Ranch near Cimarron, New Mexico. He pauses to slap the dust from his black hat. "And seems like half the time's gone looking for a rain cloud and a cook, and I'll probably be looking till I die off."

For the ranches that keep outstanding cooks, though, many cowboys are equally adamant in their praise. For example, the cowboys at the Pitchfork Ranch usually can ride in pickup trucks over the rolling flinty plains of Texas to eat at the central cookhouse operated by R. J. Bell and his wife Rita. But on some roundups, nobody has complained about the food prepared by Richard Bolt, the son of a camp cook for the well-known 33D, Triangle, and 6666 ranches in Texas, who now seems equally skilled as a cowboy, Baptist preacher, and cook. As cowboys travel, enough of them compliment Bolt's cooking to bring him letters asking for his recipes.

During a long roundup, moreover, a foreman or wagon boss is not hesitant to emphasize the value of a competent cook. At a larger ranch, the 06 in Brewster and Jeff Davis counties of Texas, where the horse-drawn chuck wagon remains in a barn, the foreman, Buzz Nichols, courted a satisfied smile as he watched his cook season frijoles simmering over an oak fire. "Here's an old cowhand who got all his bones broke," he says. "But we got a helluva good cook because of it."

Hearing this, the cook, Ramon Hornette, pointed instantly toward a rolling pasture. His other hand clasped a knee. "Right back there thirty years this February the ninth a wild old steer hooked me," he volunteered. "Hooked me good and tore up my knee. Been operated on and ever'thing. Thirty years, I've been havin' cowboys bring their plates back for more. Keeps morale up."

To raise the morale even further, after his roundup crew ate supper one night, Nichols persuaded three mariachis, members of a Mexican band that plays at cowmen's barbecues and weddings, to follow the winding dirt road to their camp at the ranch's Willow Springs division. Hour after hour, as they washed down leftover steaks with cups of bourbon, the three short, bouncy men sang, swayed, and stroked either Spanish guitars or a Japanese bass fiddle just about as large as any of them. Yet not one of the cowboys showed any loss of enthusiasm. Several snapped their thumbs or drawled "aw-haw" no matter how many times they heard, in a twangy dialect of border

Spanish, the mariachis' complete repertoire of "Beautiful Sky," "San Antonio Rose," "El Rancho Grande," or "Three Days Since I've Seen a Woman."

"Goin' to be three more weeks," the cook said, with a typical shake of the head, " 'fore these boys see no woman."

Nichols' reply sounded confident. "Yeah, but if some of the people in Alpine who wouldn't even work saw the kind of cooking and music we got," he said, turning toward a cowboy wearing uneven spurs, "what'd they do now?"

"Work for nothing practically," snapped the cowboy.

"On a roundup, you keep your hands' bellies full of food that's good and clean," Nichols said. "Then you keep the morale up and all the arguing and fighting down."

"Aw-haw! San Antone," somebody yelled.

Any time that the roundup crew eats at the Double Diamond, the men know that both the food and dishes are clean. Following the tone set earlier by Odell and J.J., two cowboys pick up the gray towels and carefully dry the tin dishes as soon as Dub washes them.

Odell moves over to the gully where Cookie empties onto the grass all the remaining food except the beef, bread, and cobbler that is saved for snacks. Cookie points toward the twenty or so slabs of beef piled in a kettle. "All's the meat 'at's left," he says. "Couldn't come no closer'n 'at, huh?"

"You gonna have to find shade for more meat 'an you know what do with," Odell replies. "Pretty damn quick too."

True to character, Odell is equally demanding in his choice of the beef that is cooked during a roundup. For the moment he has a friendly smile when Dub introduces his brother-in-law, a short man with a plaid shirt flopping in the breeze who has driven out in an old Ford to butcher the calf that will be slaughtered. "Get yourself 'nough supper?" he asks. "Plenty meat left over."

The man pats his stomach. "Too much."

Though knowing why the man volunteered to work without pay, Odell quickly puts him at ease. " 'sides all the kidneys and things 'at just go to waste out here," he says, "be sure'n take yourself good piece of steak meat back home. Cool weather don't blow in here pretty damn soon, I ought to have you take a side of beef into the freeze box at headquarters for us."

Turning toward the barbed wire, Rio holds up three fingers to indicate that he has three husky calves in the corral.

"You can get my thirty-thirty out the truck if you want to shoot 'em," Odell says. "But I want to go with you. I want the fattest son-bitch I can find."

"Ones 'at's got some fire in 'em too," comments Virgil, joining the men following Odell and Rio. "They make the best meat."

"Least you know you gettin' good meat," Frosty adds. "Most of 'em big feedlots get cattle so full of medicine and dope and all to make 'em fat quicker. Hell, you don't never know what you liable be eating, you know."

Virgil chuckles. " 'at ain't the worse of it. I rode with old boy 'at hauled load all way to El Paso one time. Couple old dry cows so sick I didn't think 'ey gonna make it. But 'ey stagger through the main door, 'ey somebody's supper pretty quick."

Odell points to the corner of the pen. "Want to shoot 'at old red neck on the left there," he says. Walking back a few steps, Odell motions for Cookie to join the men. He suppresses a smile with a hardened expression. "Now you don't see 'at son-bitch right over 'ere," Odell says, pointing to the calf. "You don't see'm eatin' no garlic, do you?"

Bemused by Odell's dislike of garlic, Cookie jiggles his thick eyebrows in anticipation of the answer. "No," he says, chuckling. "But I think he likes chili peppers pretty good."

"Now if I wanted 'at meat to taste like old garlic," Odell says, "I'd be feeding him garlic to eat. O.K.?"

Rio unlocks the safety on the rifle.

Virgil speaks quickly in Tex-Mex. "Don't you butcher'm where you can hang 'em side truck to cool out?"

Odell, already walking toward the fire, stops and turns around. "You shoot 'em there, and he ain't gonna get way over 'ere less a bunch of you lug him."

The men maneuver the calf within thirty yards of the truck only to have him attempt to run toward the rocks. "Get 'hind him, Frosty," somebody jests, " 'fore he tries take off. Hurry up."

"And get my ass shot off," Frosty replies, grabbing his groin.

With a quick, deft flip, Willie throws a rope around the calf's neck and, as two other men grab the tail, force him to a level place above a long ditch. Both men back away, leaving the calf to tug on the rope.

"Be a better place to gut 'em," Cookie says.

Squatting on his right knee, Rio aims the rifle. He waits until the calf faces him. Then, as someone whistles between his teeth, the calf turns his head. Rio pulls the trigger, sending the bullet between the calf's eyes.

When the calf wheels, Willie rushes forward so quickly that he is in a position to remove his lariat by the time the calf falls. Pinching the rope under his left armpit, he pulls back on the calf's chin to tighten the vein in its neck. Using short jerking motions, Dub's brother-in-law slashes a butcher knife across the calf's throat until blood covers his wrist.

As the blood pours from the calf, reddening the brown grass around him, all but three men saunter back toward the fire or their bed. But, gradually, several of them return to watch or offer assistance during the time that Dub and his brother-in-law disembowel, skin, rinse, and, finally, split the carcass. With the men's assistance, the two sides of the calf are hung on the rack of the truck to cool during the evening.

Slouching around the cook's tent, now illuminated by a low fire and a hanging gasoline lantern, the experienced cowboys seldom lapse into silence. Following a conversation about the merits of beer brewed in Texas or Colorado, Frosty picks up an empty burlap bag lying under the cooking shelf. He walks to the edge of the tent to offer the bag to Dairy. "Here's you a pallet to sleep on tonight," he says. "I had 'em haul 'at old mattress of yours back to headquarters so you could find out way 'ey'd sleep 'em old days of cowboys. Thought 'at'd be way you'd want it."

Dairy looks slightly embarrassed.

"This way 'ey did in 'em picture shows," Frosty continues. "Don't you think 'at's way you'd sleep?"

The remark inspires the only comparison, in the month that the men are together, of the way that the working cowboy is depicted in movies or television.

"You know the thing 'at galls my ass 'bout the old days?" Odell asks, but not waiting for an answer. " 'em old picture shows on TV like 'at Matt Dillon telling the rookie to go do this or 'at other old thing saying to work cattle 'is way or 'at. See how silly 'at is, right? I was to ever catch 'at Dillon son-bitch walking down a street som'er's, I'd haul off and knock the hell out of'm."

"You'd have to beat me to'm," J.J. says. "Way 'ey practically have somebody sitting behind rock ever' mile or two waving at ya. Now how many people you ever run into out workin' cattle, right?"

" 'ey's all kinda funny to me," Frosty interjects. "Ever see a show where some old cowboy is shakin' the last drop out his canteen in the desert and 'ey have old turkey buzzards cruisin' round all winkin' and pissin' and gittin' ready to eat'm minute he lays down?"

A perplexed expression spreads across Billy Bob's face. "Buzzards don't eat nothin' till it's done dead couple days and got good and soft."

Another voice, rising quickly, dissolves into a cackle. "Have to be all stinkin'. Maggots and flies all over it first."

" 'at's the whole point," Frosty answers. "Anybody who's ever worked cattle or been 'round a desert knows 'at. I see 'at kinda old show — I turn 'at son-bitch right off."

Anxious to comment, Virgil must raise his voice to be understood. On the opposite side of the fire, Luke, the spirited wetback, continues to draw the younger Mexican cowboys around him with his version of an adventure with a woman. Chuckles grow louder. Young men slap their knees in amusement at the reconstructed dialogue that supposedly follows when he is threatened by the woman's former husband. Arms gesturing, he continues to speak in animated border Spanish, punctuated about every fifteen words with "shit" spoken in English.

Virgil turns away from the Mexicans. "Know what I betcha causes all 'at thinkin' you work cattle fallin' off your horse, things like 'at? 'em old professional rodeos like 'ey have over Odessa and 'em big cities. San Antone, Dallas, you know. Oklahoma City. Houston. All over where 'ey have little old calves trained to run certain way in a ring, 'en you drop rope over'm and jump off your horse. Yeah, and 'ey got 'nother old boy right 'bout two feet on other side the steer so he don't swerve outta the way of the man after him."

Billy Bob throws down a match. "You ain't been Dallas, all 'em places, have ya? Ain't been no farther'n Odessa or El Paso, I bet."

"Naw, but I worked over New Mexico, old Mexico both. Even Oklahoma."

"You pretty well know 'xactly where rodeo cattle's gonna move," Odell says quickly. "Out in a pasture, you never know what 'ese wild son-bitches wanta do next."

No one on the roundup seems to harbor any unfulfilled aspirations of succeeding in a professional rodeo. Some time during their lives, to satisfy themselves or to win a bet or a belt buckle, many of these men have wrestled a steer or roped and tied a calf within about fifteen seconds. Farther east, nearly 500 cowhands assemble to participate in the Texas Cowboy Reunion, a rodeo limited to cowhands working on ranches that is held each July in Stamford, Texas. Yet these cowboys give no thought to joining the 3300 men whose experiences with either cattle, horses, or rodeo clubs, or, increasingly, Little League, high school, or college rodeo teams have them seeking some of their livelihood as members of the touring Rodeo Cowboys Association, Inc. When told, none of the men at the Double Diamond seem to care, or really know, that professional rodeos have brought young East Texan Paul Lyne, a former national high school and college rodeo champion, the current status of the United States' "All-Around Champion Cowboy." Nor are the men any more aware of Larry Mahan, an agile man who sufficiently honed his rodeo skills working for an amateur roping club and competing in teen-age rodeos around Salem, Oregon, to gain recognition as "America's greatest cowboy" for the previous five years.

Not too many other occupations or events impress the roundup crew. Content with the Spartan natural beauty and life-style of their native region, these men allow themselves few regrets. Already isolated from the strife of crimes or cities, they seldom listen to a newscast on the transistor radio in the camp. At no time had anyone discussed current events occurring outside his region until J.J. was asked how cowboys view, say, politics. In response, he strained for an answer: "Sheriff we got, he don't supposed to lie none to you or put up with nothin' like smart alecks ever comin' through on a motorcycle. Altogether, I guess he's shot about dozen Mexicans on Saturday night to show he ain't gonna put up with all 'at gettin' drunk and talkin' 'bout shootin' each other, all 'at kinda stuff."

Sheep rakes a boot across some embers. "Whippin' shit outta couple Mexicans at a time is one thing," he says. "But shootin' 'em while 'ey all drunk and fightin' each other is somethin' else, you know."

Similarly, the pending election for President of the United States, a month away, has gained little more respect among most of these men. Pondering a question about it, Frosty replies that though cowboys "are pretty good voters," both candidates for President seem "too sorry to waste your gas on." Speaking slowly, as if weighing his words carefully, he elaborates: "I guess old Nixon's doin' best he can with what sense he's got. I guess. But 'at McGovern — I swear I couldn't vote for a man who's retarded, save the life of me."

"McGovern's mentally retarded?" he is asked.

"Yeah, retarded right up here," he replies firmly, pointing to his temple. "Practically nothin' much 'tween the horns — old saying goes."

"Where'd you hear that?"

"The radio one night," he says. "Some Fort Worth station had him talkin' and 'bout five minutes all time it took to figure out 'bout him. I know I'm not the smartest guy in the world. But he's sure's hell retarded. 'at has to be the only excuse 'at man's got for actin' way he does, you know."

Odell takes his notebook from a pocket. "Don't make hardly no difference which one 'em old things wins," he says. " 'fore we ever go out on spring roundup, one who gets in — he'll do somethin' crooked as dog's hind leg. You just wait'n see."

"Chili's big votin' man, ain't ya, you old wetback?" Woody asks.

Tobacco juice once again seeps from a corner of Chili's mouth as he replies. "They can't get a hard-on probably. They want people vote for 'em and make 'em big shot."

Sensing little enthusiasm for prolonging the conversation, Frosty looks around for a more relevant subject. His eyes settle on the deerskin boots that Woody treasures. "Hey, what's 'at you stepped in in 'em old boots?" he asks glibly.

Woody looks down hurriedly. "You old son-bitch. I give forty-eight dollars 'em boots."

"You send off for 'em?" Cecil asks.

"Damn right, I'm gonna have good boots I don't ever have nothin' else."

Predictably, for this time of evening, the stillness of the land is broken by the high, far-off wail of a coyote. No doubt perched on the edge of a rocky bluff, where he views the area below him, the coyote emits a quick, shrill bark — one almost sounding like a yelp — which then dissolves into a long howl: "Ki — yoo-ooo-ooo — ooo-ooo-ooo." Another coyote, answering the bark immediately, fills the air with an unbroken chorus of "Yooo-ooo-ooo-ooo-ooo."

Though not yet annoying, the howls soon grow louder.

Dairy, noticing that the experienced cowboys are unmoved by the coyotes, speaks to no one in particular: "Must be a whole pack of coyotes, huh?"

"Naw, 'at's just two of 'em over 'bove 'at creek," someone answers. "You get an old bitch and a dog together like 'at and 'ey carry on till two of 'em sound like two dozen. Make 'nough noise to hear 'em three, four miles away."

Seeming enlightened, Dairy turns an ear toward the direction where the coyotes wail. The howls continue, with only brief interruptions, for another ten minutes. By now, two men are irritated by the howls.

Noticing this, Billy Bob plants a hand on his right hip as he turns toward the rocks. Mimicking a coyote, he hollers, "Ooo-ooo-oooh!"

Chili motions toward Billy Bob's back. "It be O.K. now," he says. "Coyotes talk to gringo."

Billy Bob looks for a receptive face to direct his reply. "Ain't 'at right?" he says, eyes locking on Frosty. "Buzzards won't eat coyotes or Mexicans?"

Frosty's voice, rising above the wail, reveals little trace of his usual humor. "They keep hollering like 'is when I'm tryin' to sleep and there's gonna be two dead coyotes for the buzzards to look at anyhow."

"Then you gonna have better luck outsmarting 'em than I do," Odell interjects. "I betcha 'ere's only been four of 'em close enough for me to take a shot at in the last year. But you wait till I'm ridin' around som'er's without my Winchester. Hell, if a old pair don't come tippytoeing by — practically like 'ey know you can't shoot at 'em."

Odell's observation exemplifies the grudging respect that the bushy yellowish or gray coyote — a Spanish name meaning "clever one" — retains among veteran cowboys. Sprinkled with enough black hair to resemble small timber wolves and gifted with foxlike craftiness, pairs of coyotes that mate for years (though not life) have shown men that it's impractical to set traps for them: they never hunt anywhere near the concealed rabbit holes they enlarge into dens for their pups. Familiar with the cattle trails and creek beds in his area, the coyote ranges far to feed primarily on field mice, jack rabbits, or quail eggs, and an occasional antelope or weak deer that he either works in a group to ambush or finds left by a mountain lion. When pressured into a strange territory, coyotes have been known to kill a few lambs or calves. But, as scavengers, coyotes usually eat only calves or lambs that they find already dead, and then, leaving little question about their presence, they often urinate on the uneaten carcass to claim it. In all, a coyote's curious but sly mannerisms foster such an inherent hatred of him that an effective insult cast out in anger remains: "You damn old coyote!" By the time a boy is eight years old, he learns to say: "Just a sneaky old wild dog, that's all coyotes are. Old dirty dog."

Further exposed to steady announcements from sheepmen and cattlemen organizations claiming projected losses of livestock to coyotes or "these wolves," a cowhand needs a strong personal judgment to keep him from killing any coyote that he sees. For example, in *The Cattleman*, a trade magazine arriving at most large ranches in Texas, Odell recently noticed the intense reaction to the federal Environmental Protection Agency's recent decision to prohibit the interstate shipment, or use on public grazing lands, of cyanide, strychnine, "1080" (sodium monofluoroacetate), and gas ejected from a spring-activated "Humane Coyote Getter" — long used to kill coyotes and, many times, the other wildlife and birds in the area.

In one issue, a cowman feels impelled to share his secrets and photographs of a personal, fifty-year war on the coyote. Another month, Representative W. R. (Bob) Poage, a Texan who chairs the House's Committee on Agriculture, announced that he would hold hearings to encourage the enactment of his bill requiring the federal government to compensate ranchers and farmers for the estimated "10 million to 40 million dollars a year" that they will now suffer in losses to coyotes. Promising to help fight the government's "perpetuation of predators," Representative Poage emphasized that the public will need to be educated to the fact that "the population of coyotes in the United States is on the increase in spite of all we have been able to do." Or, in talking to other men, the cowboy hears that, altogether, about 100,000 coyotes are killed each year by sheepmen and some cattlemen, lacing carcasses of deer or calves with odorless poison; bounty-seekers, government trappers, and stockmen gather with increasing zest to hunt them from jeeps or small airplanes.

"I knowed a feller running cattle on old grass so poor 'ey's practically starving," Cecil recalls. "And 'stead of movin' 'is cattle 'round, he's out renting him a airplane on Sunday to ride up and down canyons hollering and shooting a shotgun at coyotes."

Twisting around, Pancho speaks softly. "One came up to screen door my house other night."

" 'at ain't like a coyote," J.J. says, " 'less he's got rabies."

"He had a screwworm in eye," Pancho says. "Way he rubbing against the screen he want me to help him."

"What'd you do?" Dairy asks.

"Why I shot him," Pancho replies quickly. "That what you supposed to do."

Yet, fittingly, a first-rate cowboy knows why the wily coyote — the sight and sound synonymous with the pioneer West — has expanded his territory instead of being completely driven from it like the buffalo and wolf. As usual, any time that he sees a young cowhand intrigued by a coyote's howl, Virgil's eyes glint appreciatively. "Yeah, 'ey's still runnin' down the coyote like 'ey did the Indians when I was a boy," he says reflectively. "Always sayin' how much faster an antelope is. Might be, but 'ey ain't never seen how one or two coyotes will go chase a jack rabbit or antelope right through some brush someplace where 'nother coyote or two is waiting to jump out and get 'em. Like I tell new boys ever' year — a coyote can stop and scratch fleas and still figure out a way to catch anything he wants to eat."

"Somebody else gonna be more'n scratchin' for fleas if he goes where I think," Odell says sarcastically. His eyes narrow as they watch a gaunt, older Mexican cowboy saunter toward his bed with a new roll of toilet tissue in one hand, a collapsible cot in the other. Noticing Odell's reaction, the regular cowboys turn quiet until the man finally unfolds the cot about twenty yards from the area occupied by the other new Mexican cowboys.

Cecil ends the silence. "He just wantin' to move his bed 'way from the side the truck where the new beef's hung up. Kinda likes sleepin' little off to hisself."

Odell snaps his head. "He don't like it no better'n I do."

Cecil's tone of voice is complimentary. "Shoot, he sure can work cattle though. Lotta ranches put'm on regular, 'ey seen him work."

"Work regular!" Odell says sharply. "Hell, he gets by all year on just what he makes off a roundup in spring and fall."

Cecil starts to speak. "Old Mexico, some of 'em know how to . . ."

" 'Course 'at's 'llowing some for little stealing in between," Odell interjects. "He must've found couple stray mavericks too close to the Rio Grande 'cause last spring roundup he didn't work a-tall. I go to Ojinaga looking for him, I make sure I wear dirtiest pair old pants I got so people don't think I'm the law or nothing."

Frosty draws back his shoulders and yawns. "He's got the right idea now — get some sleep."

"Yeah," J.J. mutters, throwing down a toothpick. He scoops up enough water from the enameled washpan to dampen his face; then, patting the dark stubble on a cheek, he walks away without shaving. "No sense makin' it easier for 'squitoes to work on you."

Few of the men need much more preparation to sleep. Three Mexicans and two Anglo cowboys shave. Another, Sheep, walks to the side of the cook's shelf and brushes his teeth.

Having little experience with a toothbrush, Chili stares quizzically at Sheep. "What you taking your temperature for?"

Sheep, assuming that Chili is joking, has no answer.

Two or three at a time, the men walk to either the cots or narrow mattresses spread irregularly across the grass. None needs a flashlight to find his bed or belongings. To the right, the moon begins to bathe the pasture. In any direction, the sky resembles a mammoth, overlighted planetarium that is congested with thousands and thousands of glowing stars — both large and small, dim and bright — that seem close to the earth.

Ignoring the sound of someone relieving himself, no more than three yards away, J.J. folds a plaid blanket to use as a pillow. He lays his boots and vest atop the bag and pulls the tail of his shirt from inside his pants. Turning his face away from the moon, he slides under a blanket covered with a quilted tarpaulin that reeks of alfalfa hay from the months it has been in the barn.

Noticing just one other man remove his pants, Frosty

looks for a receptive target. "Sure nice you, J.J.," he says slowly, trying to sound appreciative, "to take your boots off for us 'is way."

J.J. handles the comment with ease. "Yeah, you gotta let air get to your socks ever' now and 'en."

Frosty does not stand long. The air that bakes through clothing during the day now chills his bare legs. Suddenly, the wind ruffles the brush in Echo Canyon, and the temperature hints that it may fall still lower. But by the time Frosty wiggles into his sleeping bag, one of only three in camp, the breeze ends just as abruptly. The temperature remains around forty-three degrees throughout the evening.

As the sounds of the coyotes and men wane, everyone but a couple of the young men fall asleep in just minutes. Fully at ease in their surroundings, none of them stirs. Occasionally, the wind whistles for a minute or so through the canyon. Several older horses, alternately napping and grazing, mill closer and closer to the camp until about a dozen of those ridden throughout the year come within fifteen feet of the full-time cowboys and stare inquisitively. Even when the coyotes bark again, around 4:30 A.M., their wails are so muted, perhaps by distance, that no one is awakened.

Just before five o'clock, as if an alarm clock had rung, Cookie twists up from his cot. Pulling on his heavy shoes, but leaving them untied, he trudges to the earthen pit. He douses a pile of oak and cedar branches with enough kerosene to turn it into a blazing fire; then, after filling the pot with water, he pours in two cups of coffee and hangs it over the fire.

Hearing the fire crack, Dub rises from his two mattresses. He walks around the pickup truck to find Rio already shaking his boots, then slapping the sides of them to assure himself that neither a lizard nor a tarantula crawled in during the night.

Cup already in hand, J.J. watches Dub toss cold water into the coffee pot, now boiling, to drive most of the grounds to the bottom. Before he sips more than half a cup, eleven of the men have pushed back their blankets, damp with dew, and walked up to rinse their faces over the pan or stand just inches from the fire. By 5:45 A.M., when only a lone bright star remains visible, everyone except Odell and two young men stir around the cook's tent.

Nearly all seem as refreshed as Virgil. Holding the inside of his soft, patched chaps against the fire, he needs no prompting to resume an account, begun last night, of a cowboy who lives in deserted line camps. " 'nother time he talked a woman into coming back and staying with him," Virgil says.

Odell walks up buttoning his vest. "She must've been a real pistol," he comments, "to come back after seeing way 'at old fart lived out 'ere."

"Yeah, he went to town and told her he'd fixed up the old place," replies Virgil, his smile widening. "Then she gets back out 'ere agin and all 'at nasty old thing's done was put up screen door to keep some flies out."

"Didn't 'at turn out be little too fancy for'm," Odell says, stirring his coffee with a finger. "Wouldn't surprise me to see him out old cave som'er's."

"Oh, you knowed 'at's where he'd go off to sometimes," Virgil continues, "living in caves and doin' little government trapping."

Cookie strikes a spoon across a kettle. "Oats for the babies." He smiles. Men surround him as they help themselves to mounds of scrambled eggs, yellow pancakes, and thick bacon.

Odell notices Lester, the man better known as Half

Breed, fidgeting with the bottle of aspirin atop the cook's shelf.

Moving past Cookie, Half Breed shakes his head. "Flu's goin' 'round, kinda," he says.

Though his teeth are clenched, Odell speaks in a low tone. "Old drunk's all's goin' 'round. Chili, want to go see if you don't cure 'is kinda flu with couple cans of beer in 'at sack back at pickup. Get it cured up 'fore bunch others get it."

Virgil seems amused. "Never heard hardly no flu up 'is high country."

To a man, everyone else seems anxious to start working. Some already are restless. Frosty smiles mischievously, conveying an inner amusement, as he watches Cookie pitch eggshells into the fire. "Maybe I'd better volunteer to run into town tonight and get you some more eggs, huh?" he says, winking. "Get myself little somethin' too."

Walking into the air outside the tent, alive with the chirping of small birds, Woody squats in the dirt between some cat's-claw and a cactus that seems dead. As he faces a distant mesa to the east, its rim turning into a faint pink, he does not see why his presence excites a gray bird. Beside him, a pale green lizard, which a bird either shook or pummeled unconscious, is stuck on a thorn.

"Doing all right?" Pancho asks.

"Aw, wish old Rio'd hurry up and get his butt here with the horses," Woody replies, half smiling. "I get 'at little black bugger — Squirt — saddled up. His butt is gonna ride good today — let me tell you."

6. Driving and
Branding / Dust and Blood

GALLOPING ACROSS the chilled bottom between the mountains, about all that the men can see, at first, is the shadowy figure of a cow; then, a few seconds later, comes the outline of a calf rushing toward her. But, knowing that the cattle always see or hear them, the cowboys continue across the brushless holding pasture until now, in twilight, the irritating bawls remind them that they have gathered more than 850 cows and calves against the barbed wire.

Yesterday afternoon the men drove the cattle down from the piny mountains to reach the pasture. This morning they start them on the longest drive of the roundup. They must push the cattle fourteen miles at a calm, sustained pace that will keep them from losing much weight but still reach the far corner of the Double Diamond Ranch's Flying A Flat, the nearest place where they can be loaded onto trucks, well before night falls. The early deadline, as Odell explains during breakfast, is a choice born from the chaos of chasing runaway cattle in the evening. "There's only one way to get there good before dark," he says, "so we ain't looking for a bunch old crazies in the dark someplace — and 'at's to get the cattle goin' out before it's light."

Six of the ablest men position themselves outside the west end of the pasture. It is not easy for them to remain there. On the coldest morning of the roundup, each breath leaving light vapor around the mouths of men and horses alike, the cowboys continually tug at their reins to force the frisky animals to stand still for about twenty minutes.

Crowded and cajoled by other men, the cattle move suspiciously toward the gate and then, suddenly, four or five of them at a time lope through the opening. Heads swinging toward the cowboys, poised on each of their flanks, the cattle move straight ahead but always stay behind Odell. As the point man, Odell moves at a leisured gait, which, as he planned, "has the cattle half thinkin' they're takin' us someplace."

The more they stream out the gate, the more the older cows trot and jostle to get ahead of the younger ones. Soon the scuffling increases. After most of the cows pass another trap, 273 steers, also gathered earlier, are added to the end of the column. Instantly, aggressive steers begin to force their way toward the front of the line but, without horns, seldom prove serious opponents for the horned, heavier, and sometimes excited mother cows. Several steers trot ahead of cows intent upon protecting their calves. Yet, for all the semblance of social order arising from the commotion, the cattle must travel for a considerably longer distance before the role of a boss cow, or lead steer, is as pronounced as those during the era when longhorns were driven eight or nine hundred miles. Even then, the lead steer, which often had a bell tied to his neck, needed uncanny instincts to approach the reputation following Old Blue. Never forgetting a trail or that he was the leader, Old Blue gained a legendary status during the eight years that he helped the men riding with Charlie Goodnight, the pioneer cattleman–trail driver, move herds from the Staked Plains of Texas to Dodge City, Kansas, or into a developing cattle region. Fed and watered with the horses, Old Blue always returned to Texas with Goodnight's crew to await another drive northward.

But positions gradually develop for both the 1100 head of cattle and men. Leaving the high hills, which have long blocked the rising sun, the sudden brightness uncovers an immense line of cattle swaying between sagebrush and rocks. More than half the cows in single file with their calves, most of the others two or three abreast, the cattle form a line so long that, even when viewed from an adjacent ridge, it is difficult to see from one end to the other.

Remaining ahead of all cattle and men, a position of stature and responsibility that few foremen or wagon bosses see fit to relinquish, Odell sets a pace seeming as slow as someone strolling through a garden. He remains erect, seldom looking back; when he does twist toward the cattle, he ignores the sight of a straying calf. Eyes surveying the land ahead, he continues to pick the shortest path to the Flying A Flat but one that still avoids the buttes or deep parts of dry creeks which provide nervous cattle a place to sprint.

Spaced out behind him, on each side of the herd, many of the experienced cowboys appear relaxed for hour after hour. Tucking windbreakers behind their saddles, as the sun burns off the chill, the men seldom take their eyes from cattle, which for the most part appear thirsty but calm. To keep them passive, the men quietly close each widening gap. Or, almost continually, somewhere along the column, a cowboy decides if a calf moving away from the herd merely seeks to rejoin its mother. If not, he must react before the calf — or steer — draws many skittish cattle behind him. Pursuing each runaway as fast as he can ride, the cowboy sometimes disappears behind the brush or rock, but, inevitably, he reappears behind the runaway, which, if a calf, is directed toward an impatient cow likely to be its mother.

Even with their experience, the men cannot always predict what excites cattle. For example, the full-time cowboys are particularly alert for frightened cattle in the foothills, which turn into bumps and then flatten into an immense, empty valley fringed by distant slopes that will seem strange to calves raised in stony or piny mountains. Eyes search for restless cattle given to sprinting. Suddenly, in a clearing to the left, seven pronghorn antelopes — heads cocked toward the herd — spring off their delicate hind legs as if to taunt the cattle into a race. Except for a heifer calf breaking in the opposite direction, the herd shows no reaction. Then, coming upon an arroyo, several roadrunners unexpectedly skip out from behind the brush and, momentarily, run toward the herd at seemingly maximum speed. But only one steer swerves from the column and, then, he soon stops to look for a place to return. Not long afterward, toward the middle of the herd, a single, familiar jack rabbit bounds beside the herd — causing three calves to panic. Instantly, fourteen other head of cattle follow them. Swinging out, aware that similar reactions have precipitated stampedes, Chili and J.J. are hunched over their horses. Now about twenty-five other head of cattle veer behind Chili and J.J. Three other men rush ahead of them. But, as the herd continues westward, the five men intercept all the runaways before any others can follow them.

The challenges occur far more frequently near the end

of the column. Riding in the "tail" or "drag" positions, the young Anglo and older Mexican men — all with less experience and standing — continue to find that their job does not entail, as suggested, "sitting there like scarecrows" to discourage any cattle at the end of the herd from turning back. Whatever these men do, as they persevere through the day, involves far greater effort than for the men riding well ahead of them. In what is typical work for a "drag" rider, Sheep repeatedly needs to swerve, slap, or yell to prod on a disproportionate share of the stubborn, skittish, lazy, or, perhaps, ill cattle. Then, instead of a seasoned horse whirling toward a fleeing calf, he needs to tug or spur a young chestnut gelding that Odell felt needed the experience of making a "straight drive."

At the same time, though the dust spirals higher and higher above the herd, enough of it carries past the tail riders for Sheep's view of the cattle, at times, to resemble a hazy movie photographed through a filter. When the wind dips, it sprays him with sandy dust that dries the mouth and stings the face much like a windburn. Even the welcome breeze blowing across the herd sometimes turns out to annoy rather than cool. Routinely, Sheep races after a steer breaking between some thick sagebrush. Drawing closer, he notices an elderly Mexican cowhand galloping from another direction in time to turn back the steer. The man's head dips as he spits out a stream of tobacco juice. Within seconds, Sheep feels moisture splatter his face. Rubbing a hand across his cheek, he finds that the tobacco juice carries about as fast as dust. Pretending to examine a loose horseshoe, Sheep stops to rub both his groin and spine.

Few other chances exist for anyone to leave his horse for more than a few minutes. Aside from the times that cattle snatch at sprigs of grass, the men push them so steadily that they find little time to stop and spread. Around 12:30 A.M., the earliest that the terrain permits Cookie to reach the men, a green pickup truck appears about a quarter of a mile to the right. Staying wide of the herd, he is careful to avoid spooking any of the calves and steers that are seeing a truck or an automobile for the first time. As the herd plods on, six men gallop toward the truck and eat dinner in less than fifteen minutes. By the time they return to their positions, Cookie has moved ahead of the column to await another group.

Reaching the truck, the young men assigned to the rear of the herd swallow a full cup of water and then, as someone else dips a cup into the can, wait to refill their cups.

His thoughts undisciplined as ever, Frosty turns toward two men wiping their sleeves across their brows. "Hell, 'em old days," he says, "had same dust as 'is comin' at ya one way and Indians 'nother way, you know. Steal your water cooler 'sides."

One, shaking his head, smiles slightly. "Little more this and I'd gone off with 'em."

Turning away from the sun Frosty looks around. "Where's old Cecil? " he asks. "Wonder he ever screwed a Indian girl when he worked up'n Arizona, New Mexico? I don't blame some 'em fellows marrying Indian women. Some of 'em today still damn sharp-lookin', ain't 'ey?"

Their mouths full, two Mexican men nod.

"Ones pretty as all hell and gone," says Woody. "You think they'd be dying to put up with you."

Frosty seems mildly embarrassed. "Naw, ever'thing don't always turn out way you hope, you know," he continues. His voice rises again. "You ever get you one 'em good-lookin' women from San Antone, you got somethin'. Buddy, 'at's best class stuff the world, let me tell you. What I wouldn't . . ."

Woody remains skeptical. "When'n hell you been all

way to San Antone 'out 'at fat old woman yours and your
kids?"

"Let's me and you go sometime, want to?"

There is no more time to talk. Back in their positions,
the cowboys continue to drive the herd westward. Some
young men feel as though they have ridden all day. It is
barely 2:00 P.M. But, as long as the drive seems, it is relatively short to cowboys working in still higher country.
During a spring roundup he worked in New Mexico,
Odell rode with a crew for two days to drive a herd from
the prairies, where the summer heat grows oppressive, to
the grassier sections of the mountains. And if a cowboy
works in northern Nevada or Wyoming today, for example, he often drives a herd for seven to ten consecutive
days across open range — and, where impassable, detours
along a country road — to reach the summer pastures in
mountains sixty to eighty miles away. Once again, in
early autumn, before a premature snow can block or kill
the cattle, the men drive them back to the plains to be
sold or turned into their winter pastures. Still, as the
cattle plod across the Double Diamond, keeping to a pace
taking them little more than one mile per hour, each step
evokes the style of the historic cattle drives a century ago.
Starting from Texas in early March, a trail crew pushed a
herd up to twenty or twenty-five miles in each of the first
two days in order to leave them so tired that they preferred to sleep instead of stir at night and, failing this,
would be beyond any familiar range that might tempt
them to turn back. Then, much like today, most of the
cattle fell into a routine. Grazing as it moved, the herd
advanced an average of ten to twelve miles a day for each
of the seventy to one-hundred days needed to reach the
railroad sidings in Dodge City or Abilene, Kansas.

The sun sinks behind the hazy peaks ahead of the men.
Finally, at the front of the herd, the tall, skeletal frame of

a metal windmill comes into view. A half-hour later the men approach the holding pasture. Dragging back two rust-colored gates, Odell leads only a few dozen cattle through the entrance before enough of the others, bawling from thirst, stop and block it. Though within sight of the water, the cattle are so confused that they move toward it only after Odell slaps his rope at them. But, more and more, he is engulfed by cattle pushed forward by tail riders, their view obscured by the distance and dust, not yet aware that the other men have reached the pasture. Handling his reins to the nearest man, Pancho squeezes between the barbed wire and, flailing at any head or rump within reach, forces some of the cattle away from the gate. At the same time, three other men wedge their horses behind the cattle approaching the gate, somewhat like football linemen creating space for a running back, and help scatter the cows inside the pasture.

Later, the men chase away the few cattle that have found the concrete water tank; then, as some of their horses drink beside them, the men brush back the top of the water and slurp it. Back on their horses, the men drive about 150 head of cattle onto the edge of a long earthen dam that has been built to trap the rainwater which rushes down these hard, sunbaked draws and slopes — instead of soaking into the ground — with such awesome force that it often drowns anyone in its path. Recognizing the land, the men realize that the pasture lies only a mile or so from the chutes where the cattle will be loaded onto trucks. "Gonna let 'em take fill tonight," one asks, "and ship out 'morrow?"

Odell's voice rises. "Naw, suh," he says, "they gonna stay here tonight, and all day 'morrow and all 'morrow night — then we'll weigh 'em up."

On the other side of the fence, the men with J.J. finish diverting the steers at the end of the column into an adjacent pasture in order to simplify loading them onto separate trucks. Several men then turn to watch a tan pickup truck pull the long stock trailer through the gate to the west. The instant that Rio stops the truck, all of the men reach hurriedly into it for the cups and water can.

Riding up to the men, Odell gazes at Carlos, the dark-complexioned wetback. But, beginning to appreciate his skill, Odell has second thoughts about assigning him another unwelcome job. Instead, he climbs down from his horse to wait until Dairy and Half Breed gulp down some water. "You fellows, you all want to throw a saddle on couple fresh horses Rio's got in 'at trailer," he says, "and help him drive horses back to Two Mile Mesa."

An expression of surprise covers Dairy's fatigued, dusty face. Still scratching his thighs, he turns toward the nearest men. "Be dark practically 'fore get all way back, won't it?"

Chili directs a stream of tobacco juice against a post. "Naw, go pretty fast fresh horses. Rio cut over hills you couldn't bring calves over. Be quick."

The men begin to remove their saddles and drop them into the trailer. Several put on their jackets. Climbing into the pickup, someone comments, "Gettin' chillier too."

"Ought to you old son-bitch," Woody snaps. "Don't you know it half frosted last night, huh?"

With the wind lashing them, it seems much colder as the men huddle in either the open truck or trailer jolting over nearly twenty-five miles of trails leading them back to their camp.

"Hey, Odell, frost good 'gin tonight," somebody says. "Kill off all 'em screwworms good, won't it?"

Cecil seems anxious to speak. "I 'spect it'll frost good. Killer rattler — old diamondback with eleven rattles next to my old shed twenty-second of March. 'at early, 'at's

good sign you'll get moisture.   Or little bit early winter.
Hot one day and big snow blow in day-two later."

"Kill'm with rock or stick? " somebody asks.

Cecil's face wrinkles into a smile.   "Both.   Waited he
got all straight and not curled up where he could jump at
you.   Hit'm with rock and had old piece of two-by-four in
other hand case didn't stun'm first lick.   Ain't gonna lie
'bout it.   Long I seen'm, I'm still afraid rattler."

"You ain't pissing through a rock," somebody answers.
"Ain't nothing be shamed of."

"Damn, I hope you're right 'bout frosting again," Odell
says enthusiastically.   Propped against the cabin of the
truck, pondering the schedule for tomorrow, Odell realizes that much depends on the temperature plunging
enough to kill the screwworms.   If so, the weather would
enable him to finish what it forced him to stop last May.
Just as the fall roundup is for sorting, selling, weaning,
and moving cattle, the spring roundup is intended to
brand, earmark, dehorn, castrate, and vaccinate them.
But a staggering drought, once again recurring on the sev-
enth year, had been followed by another dreaded pattern
during the previous spring.   The vital spring rain came so
late that, until virtually the eve of the roundup, Warren
and Odell agonized over canceling it.   When the rain finally fell on the Double Diamond, Odell discovered that
some divisions had been drenched while adjacent valleys
or mesas, almost as if they were cursed, had not received
the barest sprinkle.   A lifetime of hearing the pattern that
has ruined some small cowmen reminded Odell of what
would follow.   "Your pasture gets missed once when it
rains," he recalls, "then it's gonna get missed again."
Reaching the withered pastures, after branding all of the
other calves, he saw that these calves were in such poor
condition — and the grass so thin — that it would be ex-
tremely difficult for them to recuperate from what he

called "getting worked over from one end to the other."
Even with sufficient grass, bull calves are often left so
stunned from castration and dehorning that they lose
about twenty pounds in the two or three weeks before
they begin to graze normally again. "Boys, you can go get
you a bottle," Odell said. "The roundup's over."

When sold in the fall, any unbranded, horned bull calf
brings from two to three cents a pound less than the
price paid for steer calves. The discount is standard. If
allowed to keep their testicles and horns, cattle feeders
insist, growing bull calves "bruise the meat," become "all
rambunctious looking for hot cows," and, most of all, tend
to accumulate more of their weight in the forequarters
than in the hindquarters, which provide the choice cuts of
beef. Now, with adequate grass on the Double Diamond,
Warren and Odell have agreed, after freezing weather
kills the screwworms, to "work" all the bull calves that
they will keep until they are yearling steers. At the same
time, the men can also brand and vaccinate heifer calves
against the fatal blackleg. Odell had not expected freezing temperatures until the roundup ended. But when the
weather changes in these mountains, it usually changes
rapidly. If it frosts again during the evening, Odell decides, he can mark and brand the calves that are already
gathered in a holding pasture.

As the air grows chillier below Two Mile Mesa, the
fourth place that the men have camped during the
roundup, Odell is convinced that it will frost. Leafing
through his notebook, he stops at a frayed page of an al-
manac that is held in place by a rubber band. He studies
the pictures of a human head, heart, arms, and feet that
are part of the twelve signs of the zodiac always appearing
for at least two days every month. Like many foremen
and farmers, he maintains a high faith in signs indicating
either a favorable or ominous period for marking livestock

or planting certain crops. "Yeah, timing couldn't be no better," he says, looking pleased. "Signs in the knees for 'nother day and then be in the feet next two."

"Right for cuttin' and markin'," replies Virgil. "It'll go right down their feet and get it out their system."

At dawn, as soon as he fits on his boots and jacket, Odell pulls at the cold, brittle grass. He drops it and, approaching the cook's fire, takes another handful of grass. "Good 'nough frost to get rid worms, huh?"

Some older men snap their heads in agreement.

"Thing wanta make awful sure of," Odell replies, glancing at the experienced men, "is we still doctor any calf 'at's done got worms just to be sure. Freeze kill off ones 'round here sure. But them 'at's done in calf, some liable to go down deeper to get 'way from the freeze."

Soon the heavily aged corrals, rising much like petrified ruins on the floor of the valley, become a sea of swinging sticks, tossing horns, and swirling dust. Cursing and hollering, several men press the cows and their calves into the corral. Inside, as their sticks pummel rumps and heads, the other men begin to force the calves into separate compartments.

In the commotion, Luke fails to see a mother cow charging toward his right hip.

"Look out! " somebody hollers in Tex-Mex.

Reacting slowly, as if the remark were meant for someone else, Luke spins around to find the cow only inches from him. Stumbling, he falls away from the cow. A horn catches only his left hand and, at that, does not penetrate the glove.

J.J. strikes the cow across the brow; then he turns to see the young man shake his hand. " 'ese old bitches go wild in pens," he says. "Come over on ya hookin' if ya ain't lookin' out."

Outside the corral, Billy Bob settles against the pile of fence posts and skinny oak and pine branches. With a crutch he pushes a pine stump farther into the fire. "Least I do, keep fire up," he says. "Huh? Hey, you like wood fire better'n 'em gas heaters I seen picture of?"

Nodding, Odell removes the oily burlap bag that has been wrapped around the three branding irons to keep them from rusting. "Not so hard on your irons or cattle both."

Cecil rubs a thumb over the two connected diamond-shaped characters, together four inches high, that have been forged onto the end of a long handle. " 'ey been took good care of," he says. "Betcha 'ey's old as half 'ese boys here."

Odell nods. "Yeah, 'ey'll get you brand 'at's good'n clean and clear pretty easy."

A design considered clear and attractive, as well as difficult to alter, is the reason for choosing the pair of diamonds as the brand and, in turn, the name of the ranch. Much the same practicality lies behind the vast majority of the combination of characters, letters, and numbers used to form the 125,000 cattle brands and supplementary earmarks registered by their owners at county clerks' offices across Texas alone. Several brands do, as cowmen say, "stand for something." Aside from cattlemen using their initials as brands, that motive has been established by the likes of M. A. Heart in choosing a heart-shaped imprint, and F. R. Lewis the letters COW. But, most often, the romantic symbols prove to be apocryphal even on the historic ranches. For example, the wavy, stretched-out "W" that is instantly recognized in much of Texas as the King Ranch's "Running W" brand evidently owes its origin less to a cryptic snakelike message to would-be rustlers than to the fact that cowboys originally had to etch the "W" on a wiggling cow with the Argentine gaucho's poker-shaped running iron. "Yessir, you draw son-bitching brand on even old Jersey cow way 'ey be all squirming," Odell says, "and you gotta be a good hand just to get brand on with little curls and bumps — one you can read anyhow."

Little more romanticism resulted after blacksmiths forged stamping irons to merely press on any brand chosen by a cowman. The genesis is much the same no matter if a brand is a simple X, a framed X, long X, or the pioneer XIT, which has long been said to symbolize the ten counties in the Panhandle of Texas ("Ten In Texas") that the XIT ranch stretched across — despite the fact, according to Ab Blocker, who designed the brand solely for clearness, that the deed shows that the ranch never extended into more than nine counties. Nor can any historic connotations be established for a brand whether it is that -J6, 06, or even the famous 6666 ("Four Sixes") that is said to have originated from the memorable poker hand that Samuel Burk Burnett, founder of the 6666 Ranch, won with four sixes. Typically, when asked the origin of his brand, H. L. Kokernot, Jr., owner of the largest 06 Ranch, shook his head and continued to gaze at hundreds of his calves being herded into a trap. "It'd be nice to say my great granddaddy wanted the O six brand to mean something special when he started it in Texas before the Civil War," he reminisced. "But he didn't. It just looks good and doesn't have a lot of little parts and points and corners in it that could blotch and close up the brand."

To then prevent someone from adding characters to a brand, instead of depicting the shape of their ranch, many cowmen framed the brand with either a triangle, circle, box, square, diamond, bucket, or horseshoe. Or they underlined their letters with a quarter circle known as the rocker ("The Rocker B") or preceded it with one or more of the popular hyphens known as the "Bar" (hence, the -BQ that is called "The Bar BQ" or the --J interpreted as the "Double Bar J"). Even then, few cowmen have been comfortable with just the only brand of its type in a county of Texas or anywhere in another state. As a safeguard against a brand being changed or duplicated — as well as to help identify distant cattle from the front or rear — cowboys have found dozens of recognizable ways to cut out a section of their ears.

Making certain that he stamps on an indelible brand, a cowboy knows, requires craftsmanship. Now that the calves are dry, and their hides less likely to scald from a brand, Odell examines the irons. He picks up an iron that has turned pink, an indication that it is too hot, and wipes it across the ground to cool it. "Guess we can flank some 'em little late calves 'at gonna stay with their mommas," he says, laying down the iron.

Seeing a small heifer calf being pulled toward him, J.J. holds his left hand in front of a branding iron, as gray as the ashes, to gauge its heat. Looking satisfied, he shakes the iron to rid it of any small coals.

Woody grabs the calf's ears and front ankles. At the same time, another cowboy clasps her tail and a rear leg, flipping her onto her right side. Working as the "front-end man," Woody presses a knee into the calf's neck as he pushes on her bottom foreleg and draws back the top leg. As the "hind-end man," the other cowboy sits on the ground behind the calf, and, while pulling back the top rear leg as hard as he can, hooks the arch of his boot around the bottom leg and pushes just as forcibly in the other direction. Quickly, immobilized, barely able to squirm, the calf strains her eyes in fear. She bellows softly.

J.J. bends over the calf's left hip, the standard

place for a brand in Texas. In the two or so seconds that it takes to burn through a calf's hair, as well as outside layer of skin, he presses the iron with the firm touch needed to leave an imprint that will be clear but not deep enough for it to scab and peel. Flinching, the calf emits a drawn-out bawl that continues as long as the iron touches her. J.J.'s hand remains so steady that there is no chance, as sometimes happens, for the calf to jar the iron.

When the calf scrambles to her feet, Cecil looks admiringly at the dark red imprint. "Boy, 'at's straight 'cross you can get."

"Yeah, better be."

As he well knows, the angle of the brand needs to be as precise as it is clear to satisfy Odell, Warren, and, many times, legal requirements when cattle are moved to another state. Except when earmarks differ, about the only distinction between some brands is the angle. If an "11" is vertical, for example, it signifies the Standing Eleven brand. But if the same "11" leans to the left, much like a hand pointing to eleven o'clock, it would be immediately interpreted as the Callaghan Ranch's "Lazy Eleven" — providing that the brand touches the calf's left backbone. Similarly, any A-shaped brand, known as the Straight A if perfectly erect, legally becomes the Tumbling A if it lists to the right. Or a letter, such as an A or K that is inverted or backward, becomes the "Crazy A" or "Crazy K."

"Some you seen sure ain't 'at good, huh?" Virgil says, smiling slightly.

"Way some old boys jiggle irons 'round they get it half wrong," Odell replies, as he moves toward another calf. "You'd think 'ey had erasers on their irons. Get brand all blurred up, peeling. Some buyers 'bout half don't want to take'm off you. 'Course, it's Warren's cattle. But you know how he likes ever'thing all alike. I swear, he 'bout as soon see lightning hit half-dozen head as see a brand half smeared or little crooked."

"Sure hurts'm more when get it all sored up."

"You bet it does," he snaps. "No sense hurtin' more'n have to."

Though it hurts any calf to be "worked," a bull calf now being thrown bears out the fact that the pain and trauma is far greater for the male.

As the knife man, a job entrusted to only the most skilled, Odell bends over the calf's hindquarters. He pulls down on the calf's sac until the skin is taut and, using a pocket knife, slits the end of it. He pulls out the testicles, one at a time, and severs them from the cord. Raising up, eyes already searching toward another bull calf, he lobs the two testicles into the fire.

J.J. walks up to brand the calf.

Then, before J.J. moves on, Virgil drops to one knee and grasps the calf's left ear. Using the ranch's registered underbit cut, one of a dozen recognized types of earmarks, he folds the ear crosswise and begins to slice out about one and one-quarter inch of the bottom section of the crease. He frowns as he finishes cutting through the thick cartilage — leaving a triangular indentation in the bottom of the ear.

He walks away rasping his blade on a small, deeply grooved whetstone. "Damn 'at old ear muscle ain't tougher'n I thought or my knife needs sharpening some."

The next man to work on the same calf, Chili demonstrates why the job of dehorning is never left to a novice or squeamish cowhand. His right knee sinking into the dirt, he fits over one horn a long instrument that is grooved on the inside, much the way that the outside of a pipe is threaded. Twisting and pressing the tool, digging well below the calf's white hair, he cuts out both the horn and enough of the cells under it to prevent any eventual regrowth. He flicks the horn onto the ground and quickly pushes the tool over the other one. The calf winces and slobbers.

Snapping his head, Woody looks at the bloodied cavity which, seconds ago, held a horn. " 'at even hurt me. Hell, I see his brain in 'at hole 'ere, don't you?"

"Bleeding stop better if you get all old artery out," Chili says, twisting the tool. "Like getting tooth pulled. Don't hurt long." Flipping the other horn onto the ground, Chili turns toward a larger calf being thrown. "Where the big squeezers for big old calf's horns?" he asks.

"Hey, keep rope on 'at old calf," Woody hollers.

One man sprinkles a medicated powder to clot the oozing wounds. Another pushes a hypodermic needle into the neck to vaccinate the calf against the blackleg disease, which a few generations ago sometimes struck half of a herd so swiftly that many cattle seldom even squirmed before they died.

Woody and Sammie release the calf. Scrambling to his feet, he slings his head twice, as if trying to shake away the pain. He sprays a few drops of blood on the nearest men. Wobbly, he stands looking around.

Odell, routinely flicking the blood from his blade, wants more space to work on the next calf being thrown beside him. "Yeoooo! Get outta here!" he hollers, throwing out both arms.

Confused, the calf runs about 50 feet before he spins toward a heifer calf that has just been branded and marked. Both are quickly joined by other calves searching nervously for their mothers.

With little visible difference in their appearances, the calves are met by two older cows sniffing angrily for the scent that identified their own calves. The two cows jostle to smell under the chins and bellies of the calves scrambling back to them. But, finding that these belong to neither of them, the cows knock them aside in their anxiety to locate their own calves.

The bull calf, separating himself from the others, continues to sniff around the udder of any cow he can reach. Suddenly, looking momentarily stunned, he stands motionless for little more than a minute. He seems oblivious to the cows sniffing him. Then he and an older mother cow whirl almost simultaneously as they recognize each other's scent. Moving along the calf with increasing affection, the cow licks his chin and side until she notices the deflated sac that had always bulged with testicles. She sniffs above the sac, and then, as if conveying her sympathy, hurries in front of the calf. Now she discovers the blood trickling from either the marked ear or the wounds where horns had protruded. Turning toward the cowboys, she emits a short, deep bawl. The glare in her eyes seems to transmit a protest that, perhaps tempered by the joy of being reunited with the calf, seems to fall just short of avenging his wounds.

The cow has absolutely no doubt, as any cowboy knows, that she has found her calf. These cows are never mistaken. Even during a spring roundup, when 400 or more cows in a pasture are separated from younger calves, all seemingly identical in size and appearance, their inherent ability to find their calves is legend. A cow's method of identification is considered so infallible that a sheriff or impartial jury in the cattle region would, as always, consider it far more positive evidence than any submitted by a federal investigator or laboratory technician. Not long ago, for example, J. R. Branch, the tall, relaxed sheriff of Wise County, Texas, reaffirmed the continuing faith in a cow when the only clue to the theft of a calf found on a small, dusty ranch was a lonesome, white-faced calf matching the age of one that had been stolen.

Branch left quietly after both the rancher and suspected rustler claimed the calf. When Branch returned to the small ranch, he was leading the mother of the calf thought to have been stolen. In the meantime, the cow had reluctantly adopted an orphan calf that the rancher had bought for her at a sale. But as the cow began to sniff each calf in the man's pasture, she quickly found her calf and, in turn, was easily recognized by the calf. The rustler knew that he had no defense as he watched the cow angrily kick away the adopted calf, trying to kill it, and happily allowing her own calf to nurse. Branch turned toward the embarrassed rustler. "You'll have to go to town now," he said. "This is better than fingerprints."

By the time a newly branded calf finds his mother, the crew has already "worked" two or three others. With all the efficiency of an assembly line, the cowboys keep to a deliberate, imperturbable pace in spite of conditions that might overwhelm men unfamiliar with their job. Moving around, trying to avoid the dust or smoke blowing into their faces, the men scarcely notice that patches of tan grass are splattered with blood or wallowed down to bare dirt, or that the earth around them is littered with horns, pieces of white ears, and fresh manure. Every minute or so — or an average of forty times each hour — they release another calf.

Awaiting his next calf, nobody complains that the moistureless air is heavy with the scent of manure and burning hair or the unending sound of bawls. They rotate the conversation from cattle to women; reach for more tobacco, snuff, or an occasional cigarette; and, if assigned a lesser job, finds ways to busy themselves.

Seeing several testicles plop in the dirt, missing the fire by more than a yard, Carlos sets a bucket behind Odell. Every few minutes, someone picks up the bucket and spreads the testicles over the red, crackling coals.

Like many of the men returning to the fire throughout
the day, Chili opens the long blade on his pocketknife
and studies the roasting testicles — a regional delicacy
that cowboys often call "desert trout" and restaurateurs
sell as "mountain oysters." He spears a browned, sizzling testicle with his knife but, after biting into it, tosses
it aside and looks for another one.

"Ones 'at's done popped open good," Cecil says,
"they's best eatin'."

Tightening his grip, another cowboy sees Odell grab for
the sac after the calf squirms away. "Hear 'bout 'at new
pincher thing 'at some little old ranches using up in the
Panhandle on the nuts?"

A cowboy on the front of the calf looks puzzled. "How's
'at get 'em out?"

"Kinda like big long pliers," Woody answers. "You
pinch the cord up top the bag and the nuts supposed to
dry up pretty soon."

Odell frowns. "Don't catch none 'em things 'round
here," he says, patting his knife against a palm. "Just get
hold nuts good and whack 'em off — only way to do it
right."

Waiting, with thumbs resting on the edges of his worn
pockets, Odell also has mocking skepticism for about the
only other innovation that has come to branding and
marking anywhere in the cattle country. Instead of hiring
more cowhands or to make the ordeal slightly easier for
the calves and men alike, some ranchers now drive the
calves into a metal chute and squeeze one side of it. Immobilized, the calf is then branded, dehorned, castrated,
and vaccinated as he stands. Since the chute is impractical on many huge, rugged ranches, Odell doesn't even entertain the thought of hauling one across the Double Diamond. "Ones fooling 'round 'em old pincher things," he
says, "same kind 'at's got somethin' 'gainst a rope and use

'em old chutes and taking twice long to work a calf. I don't like chutes a-tall."

Frosty looks around. "Hell, you got chute back at headquarters, ain't you?"

Odell's head turns quickly. "Yeah, it's all right when just you and 'nother boy got to doctor a bull or something. 'at's like tryin' hold on a train. But out'n the pasture, uh-uh. They try'n dump one 'em things in pasture and 'ey wouldn't get through 'at number four gate 'thout a fight on their hands."

None of these men see any reason to improve upon the way that they throw calves onto the ground. By 5:30 P.M. they have branded all 371 calves Odell had selected — an output comparing favorably with the highest number that any spring crew branded in any day on the ranch.

Returning to the camp, even the dust coating Odell and J.J. does not obscure the satisfaction sweeping across their faces. Wiping his boots in the grass, awaiting his turn at the washpan, Odell comments that just the opportunity to brand while he has these men together points up how smoothly the roundup has progressed. As he recalls, there have been no costly stampedes of cattle; with the exception of Billy Bob's accident, no injury has been any more serious than the usual shoulders and hips stiffened or scraped from collisions with cattle or horses. Only one man, hinting to quit anyway, has needed to be told, after his second fight, "Well, much obliged for your help — we'll be able to handle ever'thing from here on out." Then he was driven into the business manager's office for his check.

But the wear of the entire roundup, now in the middle of the fourth week, is increasingly noticeable. Ridden almost every day, many of the favorite horses have each lost 100 pounds or more. Conversely, the two to three pounds apiece that many of the men have gained from the hearty meals form, or enlarge, slight paunches above the wide belt buckles and tight pants.

Most of all, after a particularly grinding day, it is now easier for the most agreeable men to start a fight. By habit, as he coils his rope, Woody looks around for the closest target and pitches the loop around Frosty's right ankle. Surprised, struggling for his balance, Frosty flings a rock at Woody's boots. "Son-bitch, you."

Odell's wide smile ends the tension. "Yeah, think your temper get to you 'bout now — wait your butt's all galled with 'at old dust in 'em pens."

Looking moderately apologetic, Frosty regains his balance and composure. "Yeah, your temper keeps gettin' shorter," he says. "And your dick gets longer."

"Not be much longer," Chili interjects, "and then women chase you."

Chili can, no doubt, look upon the prospect of women and whiskey much more dispassionately than the other men. A few nights ago, as a reward for Chili's dependable work, as well as the suspicion that he would find a reason to slip off anyway, Odell allowed him to put a fresh horse in the small trailer behind a pickup truck and leave to "see about the two heifer calves I forgot to untie when I chased." As usual, after driving for nearly two and a half hours to reach a girl friend, he stayed at her house somewhat longer than he planned. Speeding back toward the camp, occasionally reaching for a bottle, he went around a corner so fast that the hitch on his truck snapped, sending the trailer into a ditch. Chili knew that he could not wait for morning or until a motorist could ask the nearest service station to send a wrecker. To lighten the trailer, he unloaded the horse and tied him to the frame; then, after chaining the trailer to his truck, he pressed the throttle until he pulled it from the ditch. He arrived back in camp just after Cookie prepared the coffee for breakfast. "Hell, didn't you do no good?" Odell said quietly. " 'at horse looks tireder than you do."

Now, Odell notices, J.J. is impatient in his search for a chance to spend part of the night with his girl, a young and attractive Mexican-American divorcée who, J.J. has previously demonstrated when necessary, "is damn worth fighting over." J.J. stops briefly to watch Willie replacing a front shoe on a black horse and saunters near Odell. "Practically more'n half out double ought shoes," he says, snapping his head. "Popular size as this is — 'at's liable to mess somebody up."

"Pretty good time to go get more," Odell says. "Light work day comin' up — just scouting and cleaning up. Then shipping. Old pissant's trucks, they don't never get here till after eight o'clock nohow."

"Yeah, I want to get my other pair pants and shirt."

Odell's brow wrinkles. "Oh, hell, you'll get 'ese boys down dumps good 'ey see you changin' to go get a piece."

"Naw, I'll change out by the road."

"Pick me up 'nother fifth in case of emergency," Odell says, turning around to reach into his wallet. "Yeah, get 'ese boys some beer too and keep their spirit up some night. Four cases Coors and three of Lone Star. Tell 'at old boy you get the beer off of to put it on the Double Diamond's grocery bill. 'at's his mother, you know, 'at owns 'at grocery store."

J.J. turns around. "Old Rio looks like he could use couple cans right now. He's done run out."

"Get'm two biggest damn bottles vanilla extract you can buy," Odell replies. " 'at's got more alcohol in it'n half wine he'd buy. Let'm see you put one bottle up by spices, then put other away where he don't know where's at."

Woody notices J.J. carrying a rope, halter, and canister of P.E. 335, a pinkeye medication, down to a pickup truck

and disappearing between two slopes. "Where's old J.J.
goin' 'is time night?"

Cecil spits forcibly into the fire. "I don't know. Doctor
calf, he said."

7. On the Road /
The Rustlers Ride Faster

THE BORDERS of the Double Diamond Ranch are well behind him. Yet mile after mile, J.J. keeps his pickup truck in the middle of the asphalt road with little thought of meeting another vehicle. Suddenly, surprised to see a red pickup parked on a distant hill, J.J.'s face stiffens. A boot already shifts toward the brake.

He anticipates a problem even before he notices that the truck is empty. With no gates or cattle guards along this fence, J.J. knows, any cattle in the pasture are usually driven toward a pass that leads to the ranch's main pens located in the opposite direction. Before opening his truck, J.J. removes the .22 caliber automatic rifle from the rack, unfastens the safety, and lays it on his seat.

Spinning, his eyes follow someone moving between the rock outcroppings about seventy-five yards away. He suspects that he has caught one of the growing number of rustlers who shoot a cow with a high-powered rifle, then haul away the choice hindquarters and rib section.

But, as J.J. drives slowly along the road, the man

emerges from the rocks with a friendly smile. He recognizes him, even beneath a tall Silver Belly hat, as well as he does the land: Beans, a middle-aged cowboy whose full life as a hand on a dozen ranches, a steer-wrestling champion, and minor cow-trader has not shed the youthful nickname gained when he sold twenty-five-pound bags of dried beans swiped from a source never revealed.

Beans, his eyes glancing at the Double Diamond insignia on the truck, is anxious for some information. "Didn't see no truck headin' back up through your way with eight, ten steers, did you?"

"Naw. What's the matter? You leasing grass back up through there?"

Beans shakes his head. "Runnin' some for a fella who leases 'is and looks like 'ey stole eight, nine head off'm."

"Done shook out all the bushes up 'ere?"

"I got a Mexican boy poking 'round again just to make sure." Beans's right arm sweeps toward the notch between two steep hills. "But 'ey ain't liable to be 'ere. Wasn't enough grass in 'is pasture and we been putting out little feed for 'em once a week. Them cows get used to following a truck for 'at feed and get a little tamer. They all showed up when I counted 'em last week."

J.J. throws down his toothpick. "Yeah, 'at don't look good, when 'ey 'at tame. Week don't leave time enough for 'em to get down with something like worms. Found any fence cut?"

"Some tracks and fence posts all rotted and broke off over where I was at 'ere," Beans answers. "Looks like 'ey laid the posts down and put a couple planks over the barb wire and backed right over it. Way the posts are stuck back up you wouldn't notice they'd been broke until you noticed all the tracks and knowed the steers were gone and was looking for 'em. Big outfit like you're workin' for wouldn't never miss no eight or nine head.

But 'at fellow I'm tied up with is gonna get awful mad 'bout somebody taking eight three-hundred-dollar bills outta his pocket like 'is."

Other than the occasional times they kill a cow on the perimeter of the Double Diamond Ranch, rustlers know that the cattle and land are too wild for them to venture inside. Much like the days of the Old West, moreover, a prudent cow thief still finds that there are several other places where he had best keep riding. For example, rustlers show no inclination to challenge either the mystique or the fence riders who patrol the boundaries of the 950,000 acres of partial wilderness that encompasses the King Ranch in Southeast Texas. A cattle inspector summarized the hazards succinctly: "A cow thief ain't much smarter than a cow if he doesn't know why they don't mess with King Ranch. Get shot hell — they's been people who tried to go in on 'em boys and never been heard from again. I ain't saying 'em boys shot 'em. But they didn't come back."

In another still larger zone, Sheriff Jess Harris continues to make the vast mountainous range in Elko County, Nevada, far less profitable for cow thieves than many other parts of the state. Though a quiet, soft-spoken fellow, Harris honed his techniques against rustlers in the twenty-eight years that he watched his late father as sheriff of Elko County and subsequently since he became sheriff in 1951. The other morning, Harris exemplified the priority that he gives to rustlers when a cowman recently telephoned him that a young man "in a blue pickup looks like he's up to no good." Knowing that it would take six hours to drive to the range in question, Harris hustled out to a Debonair plane, which he rents for such occasions. After he found fresh tire tracks twisting across a range, Harris climbed back toward the clouds and remained above a blue truck carrying two calves until a cattle inspector, whom he radioed, reached the area. With Harris' directions, the inspector was able to stay one canyon behind the suspected rustler, regain his trail when it wound through cedar thickets, and then wait beside a cliff when the man stopped atop a ridge to see if he was followed. That precaution convinced Harris that he was a thief. He radioed: "Go get him." Suddenly, the man saw a jeep speeding toward him and canyons sealing his path in two other directions. Just as the man turned toward the remaining route, he saw Harris landing beside him.

The rustler, his eyes rotating between the jeep and plane, finally shrugged his shoulders: "All this for two old calves?"

"Fellow," Harris said, "we don't even like to hear *talk* about cow stealing in 'ese parts."

But with increasing frequency, rustlers are stealing from ranches of other sizes when they find a situation to their liking: Cattle in small pastures that are isolated from headquarters but still accessible by truck, unbranded calves not likely to be missed by either the owner or nearest cowboy, or any cattle gathered in a corral to be fed, sorted, or shipped or, many times, already on a truck.

In taking these cattle, a few rustlers show sufficient boldness to arouse even men as removed from them as J.J. and Beans. "Now I tell you one thing sure," Beans says "I wouldn't haul a load out nowhere at night 'out my thirty-eight 'side me — not after what happened 'em young fellows up the Panhandle 'is summer."

"I heard little something 'bout 'at," J.J. replies. "But fellow tellin' it 'bout half didn't get it straight."

"Yeah, these boys had over ninety calves on a trailer and heading back over toward Clovis," Beans continues. "And 'is cow thief must been followin'm ever since 'ey loaded up and waiting for a place to jump 'em. They stopped to see what's wrong with their lights, you know,

and 'is son-bitch with a mask on pulls up with a gun and
ties 'em to a post and blindfolds 'em. He must've kept 'at
truck too long 'cause the law supposed found the calves
halfway 'cross the state. 'Course he got away."

Only the way that cattle thieves get away has changed.
The present state of rustling is apparent when, gaining a
respite from the sweltering heat of 102° F. in Fort Worth,
you enter the air-conditioned headquarters of the Texas
and Southwestern Cattle Raisers Association. A suggestion that city folks might consider cattle rustling an an-
achronism brings an expression of surprise to the face of
Don King, the spunky general manager of this federation
of 12,225 ranchers in Texas and Oklahoma. Clearing his
throat, he straightens to an upright position in his swivel
chair. "Lord, what people don't know," he says. "We'd
better start from scratch. This association got started back
in eighteen and seventy-seven when forty-four ranchers
banded together in Graham, Texas, to stop all the outlaws
and renegades from rustlin' their cattle. Since then, our
people's caught 'em. The Texas Rangers, county sheriffs,
constables — they've caught 'em. But there's still more
cow thieves around than you can shake a stick at."

For documentation, King opens a copy of the association's weekly *Missing-Stolen Livestock Bulletin*. It lists
twenty-eight new cases that extend in size from "21
white-face steer calves and an unknown number of cows
branded CL" that are missing from a ranch in Hudspeth
County to the "1 red white-face bull, 3 years old, nub
horns, -C brand on right hip" that disappeared overnight
from a pasture in Ochiltree County. Typifying their
adaptability, rustlers are also accused in the bulletin of
stealing 109 longhorn and Mexican-made saddles, or,
while free on bail for theft in one county, they now are
sought for buying cattle in other counties with worthless
checks.

Across the hall, six women, any of them proud to volunteer that "I used to rope calves and give 'em shots myself," work full-time transferring information from a stack of forms onto a microfilm record. These forms, mailed in each workday by ninety one-time ranch hands, now employed by the association as brand inspectors, show the age, sex, breed, color, brand, and horn size of any cattle, along with the seller, arriving at the 195 livestock auctions in Texas. Once the microfilmed information is inserted into the machine, it can be used to show exactly where someone sold cattle that are similar in number, breed, and age to those reported missing. Since most of the stolen cattle are either unbranded or sold in another state, the microfilm cannot be used to detect all suspicious sales. But, when it does, the information often enables the association's twenty-seven field inspectors — all experienced cowboys commissioned as either special Texas or Oklahoma Rangers — to invite a sheriff to join them in arresting someone or to ask some specific questions: "You heard about any old boys being big spenders around a beer joint?" or "got a license plate from 'nother county?" Or, since almost everyone's status is known in the small towns, have "you seen any manure?" in a pickup truck of someone who doesn't own any cattle. Many people have these answers. By knocking on just two front doors, a TSCRA inspector once followed the devious trail of rustlers hauling eighty steers over three different roads through the Panhandle. When nobody saw three trucks pass a crossroads, the inspector was so certain that the cattle were aboard railroad cars that he drove along the tracks until he found one of the stolen steers wandering in a pen. "Fellows packed cattle in 'em cars so tight," an old man grinned, " 'at they couldn't even get one more in." The inspector was waiting when the steers arrived at a terminal.

In searching for clues, the inspectors know never to waste time poring over police files. A rustler, unless he seeks young calves or cattle already in a pen, can only have been a one-time cowboy skilled at maneuvering cattle. Seldom having seen a truck or loading chute, many wild cattle fight rustlers so desperately at night, even when roped, that they dehydrate themselves. And not even experienced rustlers attempt to steal many of the huge, humped Brahman, a breed that remains gentle in the streets of its native India but has become so fierce through crossbreeding and growing up on ranges that, inspectors say, a crew is fortunate to load them without being attacked — let alone steal them at night. "How good does a cow thief have to know cattle to get by?" muses Don King. "You let a busload of the toughest thieves in New York sneak around these pastures. They couldn't take one cow alive — unless she's awful sick."

It takes, in turn, a cowboy with even greater skills to find most rustlers. "I don't care if the greatest investigator in the world walks through those doors," King adds, a hand slapping his desk for emphasis. "No, sir, he can't get a job here as a field inspector. Anybody who goes out with the men here will see why we can't hire him unless he's a *good* cowboy above anything else — and these men are as good a cowboy as you'll find."

Stepping into the hallway, King sees one such inspector, Charlie Hodges, walking through the parking lot. A friendly, big-boned cowboy, with a .38 caliber Combat Masterpiece slung low on his right hip, Hodges smiles just enough for the sun to shine on a gold-trimmed front tooth. During his twenty-eight years as a field inspector, Hodges' skills have enabled him to emerge from a hiding spot precisely as one group of rustlers unloaded the cattle and another put the money that they received for some cows in their wallets. But, now recalling what happened at a ranch in North Texas, Hodges explained that he had not been deceived in the slightest when a cowboy found tracks where rustlers drove off twenty-six Hereford cows between some scrub oak. He borrowed a fresh horse, strapped on enough food, water, and cartridges to last a day or so, then galloped in the opposite direction. As he sensed, two rustlers had taken an evasive route toward the Red River separating Texas from Oklahoma. After fording the river, which only reached his horse's belly, Hodges followed the faint tracks through Oklahoma until he found two of the stolen cows straying aimlessly. He continued to search until nightfall, but, by then, the tracks disappeared on a dirt road baked as hard as pavement. Once again, the rustlers escaped.

It is equally challenging, in the rugged areas, to predict just how contemporary rustlers will ride away. About this time, another veteran inspector, Cullen Robinson, ambles into the Texas and Southwestern Cattle Raisers Association headquarters to finish his report on a rustler he found had stolen seventy-nine heifer calves over a period of several months. A lean and lanky man, who tilts his straw Stetson over his forehead, Robinson buries his thumbs behind the wide belt buckle that is a trophy for winning a team calf-roping contest years earlier. "Sure, I practically wore out a good horse chasing after 'is rustler sneaking cattle out of the rough country," he drawls. "But, in some of these ranches not too awful far from town or a road, I'll tell you, you need more'n just a horse now'days. You'd better be ready for somebody in a U-Haul moving truck. We caught one bunch goin' one way with a big gooseneck trailer full of steers. 'fore I practically turn around, here's another old boy heading the other way with a big bull calf crammed in a little old Volkswagen."

Rustlers are heading up roads throughout the remainder of the cattle country. Though the seventeen other cattlemen's associations maintain that many large rustling gangs escape, they each still catch, or help arrest, anywhere from thirty to eighty thieves a year in each of their states — or a total of 1500 every year in the region. From its investigations, many of them conducted with a Texas Ranger or county sheriff, the Texas and Southwestern Cattle Raisers Association alone saw 120 men convicted of stealing cattle within the past year. But the convictions, though far exceeding those of any other association, only remind some men of the irritating technicalities that have crept into the judicial system since the days when it was considered an honor to be in the group of ranchers like those who promptly hanged three careless rustlers from the lone tree along Goose Pond, in Grayson County, Texas. "There should've been practically five times that many rustlers prosecuted right here in Texas alone," says Don King, fanning himself with his wide-brim hat. "Even half the ones you catch don't even get brought to trial. Listen, after you finally run down a cow thief nowadays, the law says you have to warn him about five times that he's not supposed to tell you anything he did. If he finally asks for a drink of water, you have to warn him all over again to keep quiet."

Few cowmen or cowboys attribute rustling to the rising price of beef. One reason, readily mentioned by them, is transportation. Even if a theft is discovered early the next day, the rustlers are not limited to the twelve miles that they could have driven the cattle during the night. By then, the rustlers have traveled much of the evening on a highway that is frequently crowded with trucks hauling cattle while it is cool and are no longer bound for just the few large terminal stockyards such as those in San Antonio, Fort Worth, Oklahoma City, or Kansas City. With the proliferation of decentralized livestock auctions, a rustler can take unbranded cattle to any of 135 such weekly sales in the county seats of his own state. Even when a rustler steals branded cattle, he still has time to reach an auction in a state where brands are seldom recognized or inspected. Since many cattlemen routinely cash their checks at the auction office, the rustlers also drive away with the money. Moreover, unlike most stolen property, cattle are never a secondhand item that must be sold cheaply and quietly to fences. Before the cattle are even unloaded into auction pens, rustlers are often approached by traders or small cowmen wanting to restock their herds. And in some instances, rustlers also sell to small packing houses, which pay a little less than the average auction price of $425 for a steer but routinely butcher it (and dispose of the hide) before the brand can be traced. "I've looked a fellow in the eye and knowed he had a hot cow," volunteers Juddie Cannon, a brand inspector at the Fort Worth Stock Yards. "But you tell me how you prove a steak was rustled?"

A far deeper reason fosters the enduring practice of rustling cattle when, by contrast, relatively few horses or hogs are stolen in the regions where they are predominant. Rustling was ingrained into the western culture so early that it popularized the phrase "cowboys." After taking the grasslands of Central and West Texas, the hard, calculating men realized that in their lifetime the few, if any, cows that they purchased would never reproduce into the size of herd that they coveted. Starting with the first "cattle king," most such pioneer cowmen stocked ranches, now the property of a Texas oligarchy, with longhorn cattle driven from the Mexican ranchos under the pretense of advancing the state's independence from Mexico. When bands of Mexicans rode north to recover their cattle, by then often carrying the Anglo brands, the cowmen attached an aura of righteousness to their practice: "We've got to steal our own cattle back." As hatred intensified between the two protagonists, any thief found a willing customer for cattle that he stole from either Anglo or Mexican ranchers. For at least fifty years, large Mexican rancheros extended a standing offer to buy any "grandma's cattle" driven from Anglo ranches in Texas. At the same time, Texas ranchers built huge pens in the mission town of Goliad, Texas, to hold stolen Mexican cattle until they could be sold or distributed. The theft of cattle gained such widespread acceptance, even before "cowboy" was ever heard in the East, that in an official report to the adjutant general, Army of Texas, a Lieutenant John Brown emphasized: Between 300 and 400 "hard-riding bands of 10 to 15 horsemen are in the cow-stealing business . . . predominantly young veterans of the Army, now calling themselves 'cow boys,' these men pretend to steal only from the enemy [Mexicans] but steal from Texans as well."

As both cowmen and cows multiplied in Texas, more and more cowboys heard how a fortune awaited them. Instead of working for a dollar a day, a cowhand usually averaged about seven dollars if he could "hustle up" six or seven head of cattle a day — an expression later colloquialized to "rustling." In the more sophisticated method that followed, bold cowmen advanced the practice of "mavericking" by claiming any unbranded cattle that they could catch. Such a method owes, at least, its name to the time in 1861 that Samuel A. Maverick, a lawyer, land speculator, and signer of the Texas Declaration of Independence, sold about 400 head of cattle, "as they ran," which he had taken for a debt of $1200. Far wiser in the subtleties of ranching, the new owner, Toutant de Beauregard, insisted that for years a sluggish Negro cowboy failed to brand most of the calves borne by Maverick's herd and, therefore, any unbranded cow that his armed cowboys found had to be a "Maverick." Hearing how quickly it created or enlarged a herd, "mavericking" was adopted as the way for cowboys to become cowmen and cowmen to become cattle kings. And with the use of the running iron, a rod with a curved tip that is used to alter brands, rustling became a way of life for entrenched cowmen wanting to restock a herd lost in a drought or blizzard or to fill a profitable order. Typically, the famous Lincoln County War, which was fought in New Mexico's Ruidiso Valley throughout much of 1877–78, matched two ranching factions so determined to gain the federal contract to supply beef for forts and Indian reservations that they hired the toughest gunmen and cowboys to rustle from each other. Finally, the rival Murphy and Tunstall-McSween blocs fought for three days from the adjacent stone buildings in Lincoln, New Mexico, a town that still looks much the same, before enough of the men (at least six) died to end the war.

Amid this atmosphere, many a cowboy saw little distinction between "mavericking" for a cowman than for either himself or the cowhands who formed rustling groups during long periods of unemployment. Since they often drifted into rustling from honest ranch labor instead of another crime, many members of the notorious gangs have reputations advanced by fathers and grandfathers of some cowhands as "good old hard-working boys" or "never did nothin' wrong 'at I heard of until he got shot." Still, both ranchers, forgetting their own beginnings, as well as scrupulous ones victimized by indiscriminate rustlers, eventually found that posses, hangings, cattlemen's associations, and the Texas Rangers eventually reduced the rustling gangs — who later were swelled by the renegades immigrating to the cattle country after the Civil War or the extinction of the buffalo. But the cattlemen only eliminated the openness of rustling.

What many cowmen found as ineradicable as worms or

mesquite is the system that they pioneered. Today, cognizant of how many families stocked ranches, some cowboys drifting through the cattle country for roundups or seasonal jobs still see that they can leave with enough cows of their own to tide them through the winter. As always, when the time comes to drift on, such men are so familiar with the cattle on either their employer's ranch or surrounding ranches that they can be selective in what they take. Apart from any surveillance patterns, they know what and how certain brands must be altered, where and when unbranded calves are in accessible traps for a few days before they are transferred or sold, and the location of expensive young bulls purposely left unbranded in order to preserve both their appearance and chances for sale to another rancher. When the rustlers slip back onto a ranch today, they seldom need to guess the slightest details about the cattle. In the Oklahoma Panhandle, two rustlers recently drove onto a dusty ranch in a Ford truck equipped with the same type of Chevrolet horn that the cattle had learned to recognize as the signal for feeding time. Another pair enticed eleven Angus cattle toward loading pens with the identical brand of "cow cake," the molasses-sweetened cubes of grain, which the hands used to move them through gates.

In a more systematic practice, an ambitious foreman has long known that the fastest way to become a cowman himself is to periodically hide unbranded calves in an isolated pasture until they are grown beyond recognition — then transfer them to his own or a married daughter's small ranch. Once, many cowmen refused to hire any cowboy who owned land, cattle, or a registered brand. Starting with members of the Texas and Southwestern Cattle Raisers Association, other ranchers kept a blacklist of seasonal cowboys suspected of stealing "maverick" calves. But today, as did their ancestors, some such cowboys disguise their rustling — if the cattle are ever missed — by reporting that thieves cut a fence or coyotes killed several calves to feed their pups. When he doesn't own any grazable land, an "inside" rustler usually works with a small group or a heavily indebted cowman whose herds continue to expand fast enough for each of his cows to bear a dozen calves a year. (While they lack incriminating evidence, employees of at least two cattlemen's associations feel certain that not one original cow in some current herds of 2000 to 3000 head of cattle was purchased legitimately.)

When caught rustling, a cowhand tends to view himself as the Robin Hood of the range — a man scrupulously avoiding any ranch unable to afford the loss of even a single cow. Typically, just before his fourth conviction for cattle theft since 1960, Ted Charles Thompson, a stockily built man from Nowata, Oklahoma, seemed nearly as concerned about clarifying his record as he was about spending another one or two years in a state penitentiary, this time for selling fourteen Hereford heifers stolen from the Harrington Ranch in Rogers County, Oklahoma. Sitting beside a tape recorder in the county sheriff's office, he offered to Sheriff Amos Ward and cattle inspectors his theories on how ranchers could avoid losing cattle to other rustlers. Then, after maintaining that he began to rustle only when someone refused to pay a debt of forty dollars, Thompson emphasized: "I guess you could say I was a sneak thief. [But] I never did steal in my own county . . . I have never stole from anybody who I claimed to be their friend or from anybody I really knew. And another thing, if I knew a man was a poor man, I wouldn't steal from him. It was people who were not really making their living on the farm such as doctors and lawyers. If a fellow would hire me and trust me, and not bird dog me all the time, I wouldn't steal a bale of hay from him."

With rustling rooted in their culture, some boys who grow up on ranches without seeing them stocked in any manner but "mavericking" repeat the cycle at such an early age that an inspector has caught one needing to sit on two pillows to see out the window of an uncle's truck that he used to steal calves. In a recurring, and more typical case, Charlie Hodges, the veteran inspector, was intrigued by the information that an ill, elderly rancher telephoned to the Texas and Southwestern Cattle Raisers Association: "Over a thousand head cattle have been stole off my place in the last year or so. And when I lay out and watch for 'em they always steal som'er's else." Immediately, Hodges knew that any rustler would need to be particularly astute to continue eluding this wily old cowman. In that area of West Texas, Hodges remembered, it is common knowledge among cowboys that the cowman stocked his own pastures by systematically stealing cattle from a larger ranch while he managed it. Arriving at the cowman's ranch, Hodges found the owner's two sons had slung .45 caliber automatic pistols on their hips and 12-gauge, double-barreled shotguns in the racks above the seats of pickup trucks. "If I catch 'em Mexicans," the youngest son said, slapping his holster menacingly, "they gonna be ready for burying."

No rustler was in danger of being shot by either son. After telling both the cowman and his sons that he would hide near a remote pasture, Hodges instead waited in a clump of scrub cedar bordering another pasture where calves were already penned. In time, he found that the sons were rustling the cattle because each suspected the other would steal enough to deprive him of inheriting his rightful share by the time their father died.

Enough other men, even if in less inviting circumstances, perpetuate the family tradition of rustling anyone's cattle to occupy many an inspector or sheriff. "Yes, sir, there're whole families who rustle for a living," points out Lee Garner, executive director of the New Mexico Livestock Board. He needed to leaf through only two reports on his desk for a case in point: A cowhand and his wife from Alamo, an Indian community near Albuquerque, New Mexico, walked uneasily into a state police station and laid three steer hides in front of an inspector. A small cowman always paid him with beef and hides for helping butcher cattle, the Indian cowboy explained, but those three hides, from about thirty steers that had just been killed, bore a total of four different brands and another that had been obliterated. In questioning other men who worked on that ranch, police and state cattle inspectors heard that about 200 cattle had been rebranded or butchered there. Two inspectors, while tracing the brands on several hides discovered in an odorous sinkhole, found more than 250 stolen steers the rustling cowman, or relatives and associates, had rebranded and sold in Texas, Arizona, California, and Kansas. There was little possibility that anyone at the ranch needed to learn the techniques of rustling from strangers. "This bunch of rustlers," Garner adds, glancing at an inspector's report, "involved a daddy, two sons, a grandson, a nephew and, let's see, who else . . . ?"

With little exposure to any other vocation, most lifelong rustlers believe the only thing immoral with their livelihood is sloppiness. Even if imprisoned seven or eight times, many such professionals rustle until they grow too old to outmaneuver a cow and, even then, sometimes try to prolong their life-style by using a battery-powered cattle prod. Showing the diligence of a skilled bank robber, the seasoned rustler scouts a herd so efficiently that he rarely needs to draw his pistol or steal more than forty head of cattle at a time. Most operate with the finesse of a one-time cowhand and bareback bronc rider known to cattle inspectors throughout Texas as "Rattlesnake Red." A gaunt, windbitten, and red-haired man, who owes his name to a resistance to razors and combs, Rattlesnake Red has meandered for years through the ranch country with a pickup truck and two cutting horses in a small trailer. Seldom pressured into unwise thefts, he has seemed content to sleep in his truck, or vacant line camps, until meeting another drifting rustler or cowboy with either a large trailer or the nerve to steal one.

One spring, he met a man called Boots, far more bow-legged than most old cowhands. Then, in a typical night's work, Rattlesnake Red quietly pulled the small trailer, followed by his new partner with the gooseneck trailer, into a moonlit pasture secluded about six miles from the nearest house. After cutting the barbed wire, the men eased toward several cows, nursing newborn calves, near a water tank. With their maternal instinct, such cows fiercely resist being separated from calves barely able to romp. But Rattlesnake Red's two cutting horses were so trained, men say, that lightning couldn't force them from a pasture until they had driven the cows through the pens that narrowed into a loading ramp. After squeezing thirty cows into the large trailer, plus another three into the pickup truck, Rattlesnake Red and Boots reloaded the horses in the small trailer and drove to Woodward, Oklahoma, in time for a leisurely breakfast of ham, biscuits, and milk gravy before the start of the weekly livestock auction. Since no ranch in that county used the brand appearing on these cows' left hips, the two rustlers soon found a small cowman-trader, known around the auction as a fairly good old boy, to sell the cows for a commission.

Rattlesnake Red and Boots, with fifty-four white-faced heifers already in their trailers, could have rustled a lot longer this time around if a barrel-shaped old cowboy's conversation hadn't found its way to a deputy sheriff and cattle inspector relaxing on the opposite side of the sales arena.

"Somebody's sold a load of old cows bawling their head off," he said. "Boy, their old bag so full that they've got babies som'er's. A fellow'll sell one or two cows like 'is after their calf died. But I ain't never heard of nobody selling off a whole big bunch like 'is till their bags dried up a little and their calves were weaned."

After hearing that a similar number of cows had just been stolen in Texas, a deputy sheriff and an inspector told the trader who sold the cows how many decades he might be imprisoned, with a jury composed entirely of cattlemen. They soon had the identity and destination of Boots; a few days later, following an equally intense conversation with Boots, the men also had Rattlesnake Red sitting in the plastic-covered chair normally reserved for the sheriff of Potter County, Texas. Looking unperturbed, Red cut off a chunk from his twist of tobacco and watched the space around him fill up with more cattle inspectors, a couple of Texas Rangers, and deputy sheriffs from six counties. "Ever'body better get good'n comfortable," a deputy said with a smile, " 'cause this is gonna take lotta time."

As boots piled atop desks, Rattlesnake Red was accused of rustling hundreds of cattle from ranches stretching all the way from Abilene to Amarillo. The evidence, Red heard repeatedly, was indisputable. One inspector claimed to have the prints of Red's truck tracks in a pile of cow manure that he had picked up in a pasture where some cattle were stolen. "It's dried up like a plaster cast detectives use," he added, as he walked toward a door.

"Maybe I ought to go get it and show you what I got to pitch down in front of the judge."

Rattlesnake Red waved a hand, enough to imply that it would not be necessary, at this time, to bring in the manure. Still considering his own reputation, Red only mildly offered both of a rustler's standard alibis: "I traded for 'ese cows off an old boy who didn't tell me his name."

Since the remark was a common ploy, it fell on rather deaf ears.

Red did not put much enthusiasm into his next effort. "What I mean is this old boy hired me to load 'em cattle for'm," he said. "But he didn't tell me he done nothin' agin the law."

Nobody seemed to hear that remark either.

Red barely suppressed a smile. "Well, like I always say, boys. I may steal a few cattle, but I don't tell no lies. How many head [of cattle] is 'at warden gonna have at his place 'is time?"

As experienced as the professional rustler may be, his volume is now rivaled — if not surpassed — in more populated areas by a growing breed whom inspectors call "dudes" or "town boys who want to be cowboys without working." Their attitudes differing little from many Old West rustling gangs, the dudes are predominantly young men with a similar fondness for all the trappings of the good life. They are partial to cream-colored automobiles ornamented with statues of bulls on the hood and heavily embossed saddles trimmed with silver. Though wearing the customary denim pants, they are seldom without high, smartly creased hats tilted over their foreheads; two-tone lizard-skin boots, with wing tips, costing up to $150; and rings with small diamonds mounted in the shape of a horseshoe. With this ensemble, dudes often have no difficulty in befriending — then spending their profits to amuse — the feisty women with towering beehive hairdos and breasts pressing through nylon sweaters with sufficient force for other men to shake their heads appreciatively. And when a dude takes the woman into one of the raucous saloons, better known in Texas as beer joints, she just may command enough attention to provide him the chance to defend her honor. "Seems like more cattle some old boys steal," said one inspector, "the bigger their old girls' tits are."

Much like some Old West rustlers, moreover, the dudes know that if they loaf in town for an opportune moment they seldom need to thrash through the mesquite and prickly pear. By observing the patterns of guards, these rustlers are able to repeatedly steal cows already on a truck or near the loading ramp in a feedlot — while one of them simply opens enough gates to create a noisy stampede. Their tendency to "hit 'em at the pass," as one dude boasted, has not gained them much respect among old-time rustlers. One spirited gang of dudes, operating from Seagoville, Texas, even gave a lifelong rustler, waiting to sell fourteen heifer calves, reason to contend: "These young fellows comin' up now'days don't have a ounce of honor." Though the younger men had already stolen more than 200 head of cattle, two of them engaged the old rustler in a crap game while the third stole his heifers.

When a dude does slip onto a small ranch, he seldom needs to search a pasture or stomp around feed troughs emitting the common cattle call of "suc . . . suc . . . suc." Many arrive as well prepared as Dog, a tall, slope-shouldered young man who "mavericked" unbranded calves throughout Central Texas. Once he cut a fence and aligned a portable ramp to his pickup truck, all he needed to do was rub the chins of his well-trained border collie and German shepherd as the signal to drive the calves up into the truck. Within a few weeks, fifteen deputy sheriffs and cattle inspectors, far more men than found on many a posse, hid all night in accessible pastures in the hope of trapping what they envisioned as "a big mavericking gang." Yet Dog and his cowdogs went on to steal more than 125 fat calves from thirty different ranches without being seen or heard. Though admittedly nervous, he demonstrated just how well he eluded his pursuers when, early one bright morning, he noticed that he had also stolen a handsomely proportioned bull calf. Suspecting that it was a prize calf, perhaps one a child had groomed for a cattle show, Dog did not want to ruin the youngster's goal. Scrupulously, he sneaked back alongside the pasture around 10:00 A.M. and returned the calf.

Dog might still be stealing into pastures if Cullen Robinson, the tall field inspector for the Texas and Southwestern Cattle Raisers Association, had not found, in investigating one theft, a narrow slab from the walnut-colored rack on a truck that splintered when pressed against a post. One afternoon outside Waco, Texas, Robinson instinctively slowed down while passing one of the beer joints that, as in the Old West days, remain the places where rustlers most often leave clues about their thefts. He found that the piece of wood he had been carrying for many months fit perfectly in a crack on the cattle rack of a pickup truck parked there. Waiting until the blare of "Galveston" faded from the juke box, Robinson suddenly poked his head through the door of the beer joint. "Somebody hit the side of 'is green pickup out here," he yelled, pointing, "and they 'bout to get away!"

When Dog ran toward the truck, Robinson showed him a badge. After considerable cussing, Dog not only admitted that he "mavericked" but also accepted the suggestion that he point out every pasture where he had stolen calves in order to "clear your record good," thereby removing the threat of arrest for undetected thefts after finishing his prison term. Underscoring his elusiveness, Dog led deputy sheriffs and inspectors to ranches where the owners or hands had not yet realized that any calves had been stolen.

When told of this type of case, J.J. always dismisses it, philosophically, as "one of 'ose boys who don't think good or thinks he's too smart." Shrugging, he has added: "Old fellows'll tell you if practically ever'body got caught mavericking then 'ey wouldn't have as many little old ranches as 'ey do now."

But on this morning, about twelve hours after he has left camp, neither rustlers nor calves occupy J.J.'s thoughts. Speeding through the darkness toward Two Mile Mesa, he continues to bounce the pickup truck across the dipping land. He slows down only when approaching the camp. Carrying his rope and his pinkeye powder, he strolls toward the men lingering over their third cups of coffee.

Billy Bob snaps his head. "Damn, if I heard you go down 'em old pens 'is morning," he says. "I 'bout first one up too."

Offering a weak nod, J.J. saunters past the fire.

Odell seems relieved. "Don't look like you had to whip nothing to get it," he says. "No bad luck to slow you down, huh?"

J.J. swabs a pancake in his plate of syrup. "Naw, only thing is 'bout half-hour last night 'is Beans; know 'at old boy, don't you?"

"Know him!" Odell says, eyes narrowing. "He have on 'em old pig-toe boots and old belt bucket big as frying pan — one he supposed to got wrestling steers?"

"Yeah," J.J. replies. "But he was havin' some trouble. Little place he's takin' care of — somebody took eight head off him. Steer calves they's feedin' out."

"Just lasso 'em and cut the fence and made off dark the moon again."

J.J. nods. "Yeah, but I didn't have time to help him none."

Odell grimaces good-naturedly. "I could help 'at son-bitch real quick," he answers, still smiling. "First thing I'd do is tell him a real good place to look: some old place he's got som'er's."

J.J.'s expression turns quizzical. "Know him pretty good, huh?"

"Know him better'n people who hire him." Odell shakes his head. "Always eight head. 'bout ever'where he goes for any time a-tall, somebody always takes eight head. Never ten. It's always eight."

8. Shipping / Watering, Weighing, and Whiskey

STARING ABSTRACTEDLY into the twilight, Odell stirs another cup of coffee with the handle of a spoon. Then, pitching the spoon into a tub filled with metal dishes, he backs against the fire, seemingly scorching his pants, and ponders the logistics of the thirtieth — and last — day of the roundup.

On the previous day, as the other men searched for stray calves, Odell drove to the Double Diamond Ranch's Little Hills Division to confirm details such as when the trucks should arrive and the number of days that each man has worked. Now, he studies the numbers and marks in his notebook, all smudged by perspiration, that summarize the results of the roundup: 5725 calves and steers delivered to buyers, 644 ill or older cattle sent to stockyards in San Angelo, 828 heifer calves weaned and kept to replace older cows, 653 steer calves, including those he branded and marked, moved to the valley below Panther Hill, and all the healthy bulls and mother cows driven to winter pastures. Today, the notes show, he needs only to move from the holding pasture the remaining 185 yearling steers and wean about 215 calves to fulfill the ranch's contract with two brothers from Amarillo, Texas. But in a low, firm voice he first reminds J.J. of the sequence in which the cattle must be moved in order to have available some men to drive the horses and mother cows back to their pastures and still allow all of the men to return to Little Hills by late afternoon. Next, frowning as he speaks, Odell cautions J.J. about the attitude of the men. "Last day like 'is, you have to watch some hands worse than the cattle."

Clearly, most of the men show that they are tired, irritable, and anxious to leave the ranch. Instead of drinking more coffee, a dozen of the men walk to the frosted grass to roll and bind their mattresses or toss cots and satchels onto the supply truck. Three others, each squeezing a mirror with their knees, shave the stubble that has coated their chins for four or five days at a time. After a short argument, Luke and Half Breed each glare at the other, waiting for a remark that will justify hitting him.

Odell's head turns away from the men. "Yeah, wait till sun gets out good later and dust and manure's a good six inches deep 'em pens. Sweat be pouring down cracks of their old butts where it's all galled. Them hot-tempered ones'll be swingin' and starting your biggest fights today for sure."

"I'll put some of 'em old hot-tempered ones driving the cows back later," J.J. says, nodding slightly. "Let 'em fight little dust 'stead of each other."

Several of the men laugh when Chili grabs his groin and pretends to run toward a pickup truck.

"You gonna have to drive like a Mexican to beat me to town tonight," Frosty says. "Damn, I swear if I didn't wake up feeling like I was sleeping in a tent again. 'at's true."

Moving beside Odell and J.J., Virgil shakes his tattered chaps against the fire. "Going 'is long without a woman," he says, glancing sideways, "lotta old necks sure get all swelled up, don't 'ey?"

Odell, just as he starts to speak, hears Woody taunt someone: "Hey, you acting like you got a piece of tail on your mind." Pressing his teeth together, Odell continues: " 'at right 'ere's exactly why somebody always spills some cattle or gets hurt the last day a roundup. Here his old arms be shooing some wild cow and his old mind be thinkin' 'bout the women and whiskey he's going after tonight."

Virgil's bushy eyebrows jiggle. " 'at's on lot a cowboys' minds for sure end of a roundup. One time, I gathered cattle with old boy from Arizona who'd be worried at goin' without a woman too long would put more strain on his gall bladder and get him in poorer shape."

Squatting over the coffee pot, Frosty reacts quickly to the comment. "Naw, naw, 'at couldn't be right," he says loudly, pausing until several men look toward him. "If goin' a long time without a woman is hard on your health — then Chili'd done be dead long time ago."

Raising up, stretching his arms as he walks, Odell glances cheerfully at the men. "Better throw anything you don't want to leave for the coyotes on the truck, fellows. Cookie'll be bringin' dinner over to the pens later so you all won't have to come back here."

At the corral, the full-time cowboys load the twelve stray calves that they found into a stock trailer. Everyone tosses his saddle and bridle into the pickup trucks. Slumped into the back of the trucks, trying to avoid the cold wind as they ride, the men seldom speak until they reach the dilapidated wood corral between the two holding pastures.

The first to saddle his horse, J.J. rides in a small circle

outside the corral. He seems impressed with Odell's method to temporarily increase the weight of cattle. Any time cattle are sold, he knows, the buyer customarily deducts 3 percent of their total weight for the normal body fluid that is considered to be "shrinkage." But these cattle should contain much more than the usual amount of fluid. Looking at the long pond in each pasture, he is confident that these cattle have drunk enough water to regain all — if not more — of the water and weight that they lost during the stress of being rounded up and driven from the mountains. "It sure pays to rest the cattle couple days to get 'em used to place like 'is, don't it?" he says. "They get a windmill and pond both and ain't nervous no more — I swear 'ey'll take more fill than 'ey usually do."

Odell smiles. "You bet 'ey will. You don't never cut calves off from their mommas till the last minute so 'ey don't get all nervous. But with 'em Panhandle boys buying 'ese cattle, I want ever' head watered up good."

"They ain't those Oklahoma boys, are 'ey?" J.J. asks. "Ones 'at always wanting us to give 'em a good horse."

Virgil spits a stream of tobacco juice that the wind carries against the backs of Pancho and Woody. "Naw, it's 'em foreign-lookin' brothers 'at was here last fall when it rained so much. Ones 'at didn't look American to me."

"Way 'ey'll skin you," Odell says, "I hate to admit it, but 'ey born and raised right in Texas."

J.J.'s voice grows enthusiastic. "Look at 'em sonbitching calves drink, would you?"

Odell's smile widens. " 'at's why it even pays to have your hands just cleaning up a pasture while you leave cattle here taking fill another day. Cattle get a pond like 'is 'at 'ey can walk around in and piss in. 'at old cow 'ere'll drink twenty-five gallons a day just to have something to do. Steers we shipping — they'll drink twelve.

'at little old heifer calf right 'ere she'll drink six, seven gallons, I betcha."

"Least 'at with the full moon 'at's been out," Virgil says. "When 'ey can see better 'ey'll drink lot more than when it's the dark the moon."

J.J. pushes back his hat. "Wonder how much extra weight you get out of four hundred head time you get a whole bunch watered up 'is way?"

"I ain't smart enough to figure out all the pounds," Odell says. "But I'll tell you one thing: 'em Panhandle boys might have sharp pencils. But 'ey still gonna buy lot of cowshit and water."

"We supposed to get first bunch cattle to 'em 'round eight, ain't we?" J.J. asks.

Odell steps on a cigarette. "You can't go by what 'ey say. Their old trucks'll be late or 'ey'll have something else up their sleeve to have the cattle stand around. See, they're buying cattle ever'day and way 'ey figure it, if 'ey can just slow us up enough for ever' head a cattle to get nervous in the pens and take just one good leak apiece 'fore we weigh 'em — 'at'll save 'em least six hundred dollars a day. Then sun gets out good and 'ey get to sweatin' and pissin' again — 'at's about another six or seven hundred dollars to 'em."

J.J.'s eyes turn toward a pond. "Hell, I'll keep 'em 'round the water till last minute 'stead the pens."

"Yeah, we'll just take the cows and calves up to the pens now," Odell answers. "We get 'em half cut out, then you can take a bunch to go get the steers. Drive 'em son-bitches right through the water again."

As the cows and calves are quickly gathered, then strung out in an irregular line behind him, Odell rides along, doubting his arithmetic. Approaching a fence, which the men use to cluster and separate the heifer calves from the cows, Odell gallops alongside J.J. "I figured out we're least eighty head over the order," he says. "So cut out the prime heifers and keep 'em in a bunch way off to sides and get another bunch not quite so good case 'ey got room to buy more of 'em."

Shaking his bridle, Odell turns toward the rambling collection of chutes, covered scale, and pens — the occasional new boards contrasting sharply with the decayed gray lumber — that is perched on the flat northwest corner of the ranch. Peering across the pens toward the ranch's buckled asphalt road, Odell sees only one trailer truck among the eight automobiles and pickup trucks. The maroon and silver paint tells him that the trailer truck is one that he, not the buyers, ordered to haul the older cows. At a gate, he is surprised to see Skeeter, an old, crimson-complexioned cowboy with both hands buried in a beige windbreaker, walk toward him in high brown shoes instead of boots.

"Hey 'ere, Skeeter, I done quit looking for you four, five years ago for a roundup."

Still grinning, Skeeter quickly glances back at the truck. "Naw, I was ropin' a steer the third of October, nineteen and sixty-nine, and got throwed agin a big gatepost and broke a foot and messed up a shoulder. Couldn't hardly pitch a rope no more. I moved to Fort Stockton and been driving cattle rig ever since eighteen day of May, nineteen and seventy."

"You never did like to work hard no-way, you old rascal."

Skeeter's drawl slows still further. "Naw, I was always kinda a whore cowboy just doin' it for the money. Should've been a railroad man, Santa Fe, and seen the world. But I'm the third cowboy my age I heard of who's gone to hauling cattle. Making more pay."

"Good to see ya," Odell replies. "But 'is keeps up and all the white cowboys'll be driving trucks and it'll just be me and bunch Mexicans gathering cattle." He continues through the alley that divides the pens as he looks for the two brothers buying the cattle. Seeing B.L., the older of the two brothers, Odell wipes his right hand against his pants.

A tall, broad-shouldered, and dark-complexioned man, B.L. is resting the heel of his lizard-skin boots on a board. A pair of glasses and three ballpoint pens, filling the pocket on a western-style maroon shirt, and a thick pad, pressed into the hip pocket of olive-tinted pants, make him appear much heavier than his 215 pounds. His voice is congenial. "Hey 'ere, old buddy!" he jests good-naturedly. "Getting on late as it is, I was beginnin' to think you was cuttin' out all the prime ones on me, huh."

Laughing, Odell shakes B.L.'s hand. "I don't know what it is, but you fellows always end up with best ones ever' time. Anyway, I don't need ask if 'at airplane of your'n got here O.K." Odell glances toward the pickup trucks.

Sonny, who pilots the men's Cessna, frowns. A short man, with a gray Stetson tilted forward enough to hide his thick eyebrows, he continues to rest both thumbs inside the diamond-shaped belt loops, pulling his pants below a slight paunch. He merely twists a thumb to look at his wristwatch. " 'em old boys ought to done been here with the trucks hour ago," he says. "Hope 'ey ain't off drunk somewheres on us."

"They know it'll be their hide if 'ey ain't here pretty soon," B.L. says, smiling at Odell. "So don't let me keep your boys from penning a bunch up."

"We gonna have a load calves cut out first pretty soon," Odell replies. "I reckon Warren's done told you the scales done been proved up by the state 'is fall. But if you want go ahead and test it, go right ahead and we'll get 'at out the way first."

B.L. raises his hand as if taking an oath. "When I'm doing business with you and Warren, I ain't worried one bit."

Odell walks to the pickup trucks. He waits until Warren, sitting on a running board, finishes recalling the time that blackleg killed several hundred cattle during his early years as owner of the ranch. Three elderly cowboys, and nearly a dozen teen-agers who have driven out to watch the end of a roundup, all shake their heads. Moving away from the men, Odell tells Warren that he is holding one group of the handsomest heifer calves to keep on the ranch and another extra group to sell; thus, if B.L. and Sonny press to buy more calves than they contracted, he can pretend to yield to their pressure and sell them the choicest heifers for the same price that they pay for steer calves.

"Still be doing 'em a favor," Warren says, with a wry smile. "These feeder boys, they'll buy ever' good clean calf they can get off a ranch, won't they?"

"I know one favor 'ey ain't gonna get," answers Odell, walking toward the rear pens. "That's us waiting no more 'fore we put 'em on the scales."

Before the men fill a pen with calves, Odell spots two double-deck trailer trucks turning off the county road. He leaves to tell Sonny to position the trucks, their sides covered with manure, near the loading chute beside the scale.

One driver waves at Sonny. A pale, bony man in his early thirties, with a package of cigarettes rolled in the sleeve of a dingy T-shirt and a book of matches tucked in the band of a straw hat, he swaggers forward swinging a long three-cell cattle prod that resembles a Geiger counter used by amateur treasure-seekers.

Sonny hollers cheerfully, "There's old Junior. Five more minutes and we'd had the law out lookin' for you."

Junior, seeming mildly surprised, snaps his head. "Other boys be here pretty quick. They just mile or two back last I seen of 'em."

B.L. turns toward Warren. "I want you and Odell to hear Junior tell about the time he had keeping his drivin' partner sober last year. I guarantee you, if you ever heard anything like 'is before, I'll buy you a new hat."

Odell realizes, from experience, that a shrewd cattle buyer can keep cattle standing longer in the sun with a series of short subtle delays — often going unnoticed at the time — than with one long delay. He continues to walk toward the calves.

"Naw, I'm gonna wait until Odell has time to hear this," B.L. says buoyantly. "But thing I ain't putting off is me and you, Warren, notching 'ese calves. Could you have your boys put about three, four head on first?"

Some of the men chase four calves through an alley and onto a fenced platform atop the scale.

B.L. lays a brass weight on the scale to balance it. "What'd you say, Warren. Huh?"

Warren answers quickly, "Wouldn't be much a cowman if I didn't have a calf 'at'd go four hundred and fifty with this good grass."

Sonny scratches an ear. "Four, forty-eight."

B.L. smiles again. "Good calves from 'is part the country — they'll go four, forty-two."

The men watch the scale balance at 1810 pounds. B.L. scribbles on the back of his pad. "Damn, if they don't go four, fifty-two apiece."

Odell's voice rises above the chorus of bawls. "O.K., down the alley."

Eight men drop down from the sides of a pen ajam with calves nervously stretching their necks to look for their mothers. To drive out the calves, most of the men either fling stones or swing slabs of the decaying planks.

Woody, his torn shirt flopping and eyes fixed elsewhere, casually waves one arm. Yet, characteristically, Willie snaps his yellow popper with all the zest shown on the early days of the roundup. Suddenly, as several calves wheel back into the pen, Chili grabs one around the neck and wrestles him through the gate. As Pancho grabs another calf's ears, J.J. twists his tail; then, kicking him in the rump, he sends the calf scrambling through the gate.

With two other men charging behind them, most of the calves move suspiciously through the alley and then, discovering a lane, rush through an opening that traps them on the scales. Each time a calf stops or turns back, the three elderly cowboys atop an empty pen, seemingly envying the men on the ground, throw stones and holler, "Ho! Ho! Ho!"

Panicking, one calf crashes against a gate and, breaking a plank, runs into another pen. Without the slightest hesitation, a retired cowboy looking at least eighty years old jumps into the pen. Bracing his squat, bowed legs, he jabs a stick into the calf's rib cage, driving it toward the scales.

" 'at's forty-one," J.J. shouts. "Cut the gate!"

"Shit fire!" some one hollers.

Spinning, J.J. sees Pancho grab the gate. Dairy, backing away from it, shakes his left hand. The knuckle bleeds slightly.

Odell walks to the scale, mopping his brow with a sleeve.

Sonny circles the scale's platform, kicking off two small clods.

"Better let the scales settle down first," says B.L., shaking his head. After waiting a minute, he points his pad at several men slouching against the side of the nearest lane. "Don't touch the scales, boys. I ain't buying no cowboys."

Odell picks up a weight. But, before he can balance the scale, B.L. again waves his pad at two other men leaning in a pen about fifteen feet from the scales. "Hey, Odell, could you shoo 'em boys off the scale?"

"Yeah, stand clear," Odell says dryly. Lowering his voice, he turns toward Chili. "Can't nobody be stepping on the scale this far away."

The men, after waiting another two minutes, agree that the calves weigh 18,491 pounds.

Odell hurries back to the pens. "Roll 'em again."

The longer the men drive calves toward the scales, the dirtier their work grows. Anywhere around the stirring cattle, the balmy air is so heavy with dust that, when someone wipes the perspiration from his face, the fingers leave an imprint. As the men dash around inside the pens, there now is little time to avoid the urine and manure that splatters under their boots. By ten o'clock, with every weaned calf sent to the scales, the men drive the remaining cows and their calves into the pens; then, one by one, the men chase the cows into adjacent compartments until they are left with a pen containing only calves. But at nearly all times at least one enraged cow is wheeling, kicking, hooking at the men. Occasionally, as he dodges a cow, a younger cowboy stumbles or is knocked to the ground.

Worse yet, from Odell's viewpoint, B.L. and Sonny continue to slow his pace. Always friendly and soft-spoken, B.L. periodically saunters to the water jug, stops to compliment Odell and Warren on the reputation of both the Double Diamond's cattle and horses, or offers to bet fifty dollars on the next football game played by either the Universities of Oklahoma and Texas. Now, as the cattle's reddish hides gleam under the brightening sun, Odell remembers prior roundups when buyers managed to leave a herd of cattle standing in the sun all day — causing each head to lose as much as ten pounds — before weighing them.

Looking harried, Sonny plants the toe of a boot between two slats. "Hey, B.L.," he says, "you all give me a second here to get figured up."

After huddling with Sonny, B.L. turns to Warren. "Way it is now we done got a hundred seventy-nine head weighed up and Odell said 'ere's a hundred eighty-five head of yearlings to go on after the calves. Overhead's so high, how 'bout letting me have forty-five head extra? So my trucks won't have to half dead-load it back."

Warren shakes his head slowly. "Hell, B.L., them be my prime heifers, you know that. Real good boned ones I got my heart set on."

B.L. slaps his pad against a wrist good-naturedly. "Yeah, I'll forget the two-cent discount for being heifers. Same as steer calves."

"I don't know why I let you talk me into this," Warren replies slowly. As planned with Odell, he gives the cue to sell the group of heifer calves considered less than prime. "Odell, I'm gonna let B.L. and Sonny have forty-five them real prime heifers you liked so well."

Odell nods weakly.

Squinting into the sun, B.L. watches a cowboy scrape the manure from his boots. "Your men's getting awful tired," he says. "Look 'bout as hungry as I am for 'at good Double Diamond chuck. Why don't we go to dinner, huh?"

Turning quickly, Odell twists his lips. "Wouldn't be right to 'ese boys been out a month without getting to town. They want to work straight through. Tell you what. We'll work another load — 'em heifers if you want to — and 'en go to dinner."

Eating hurriedly, the cowboys return to the pens to sort the remaining calves and steers into compartments while

Warren, B.L., and Sonny linger over their cherry cobbler and coffee.

As soon as a cow is separated from her calf, she is driven through a lane leading to the opposite corner of the pens. Here, as Odell studies each cow running toward him, he hollers "Back" if she is to be returned to a pasture or "Cut" if she is to be sent to a stockyard. Except for an occasional cow suffering from pinkeye or cancer, most of the culled cows seem just as healthy as those that will remain on the ranch. But to Odell's trained eye, either the slightly different shade of horns or width of mouth indicate that she is about eleven or twelve years old. Now, after bearing nine or ten calves, she has reached the age that increases the possibility that she might not produce a calf some year and, consequently, will be replaced by a heifer that is almost certain to bear a calf. As a cow is chased through a lane, she often seems dazed from both the trauma of losing her calf and the strange experience, after an entire life on a range, of rushing up a wooden chute and into a trailer truck. Nearly all stop or wheel, but, reacting to the sting of a whip or stick, stumble up the ramp. Others kick or toss their horns. Still others, crazed with grief and fear, try to climb over the sides of the chute. After all but four cows are in the truck, one rears and somersaults toward the three remaining cows. She crashes through the aged boards. But before the cow regains her balance, four men pummel her until she is locked in the trailer.

For Odell, the scene means the culmination of a year. All of the older cattle are on trucks or are being returned to a pasture; all of the calves and yearlings are sold. Before the sun recedes behind the mountains to the west, all of the temporary cowboys will have left the ranch with virtually no plans for another job, probably never to work together again as a roundup crew. After two days, away from cattle, the full-time cowboys at the Double Diamond will resume the unhurried but endless routine, barring blizzards, that prevails during the six months between the fall and spring roundups. In November and December, preparing for winter, they will spend one day either moving a few heifer cows, turning out new bulls, or culling the lame and older horses, and a month to finish breaking the younger colts. Periodically, as they leave blocks of salt in their assigned pastures, the men will search for cattle that are ill and, starting in early February, the young cow having difficulty giving birth to her first calf. Between these chores, the men know, is the sundry labor that has never made anyone feel like a cowboy: During this roundup, Odell filled two and a half pages of a notebook with locations of fences, gates, corrals, and windmills in need of repair.

As two trucks draw away from the pens — one bearing south, the other north — the cows and calves travel in opposite directions to their fates. By tomorrow afternoon, each of the cows will have been auctioned at the El Paso Stockyards under the classification of "canners and cutters" and, within twenty minutes after reaching a slaughterhouse, they will be almost simultaneously stunned by a blow to the head and hoisted by the hind legs onto an overhead conveyor belt. Then, as men work with the specialized efficiency of an assembly line, the cows' throats will be sliced with a suspended electric saw, their hides pulled away, and their carcasses split. As tougher cattle, auctioned for only twenty-five to twenty-nine cents a pound, much of the cows' carcasses will be quickly ground and sold to two chains of hamburger houses and several drive-in restaurants; other parts, mostly their shoulders, will be sent to companies preparing frozen stews and canned beef-vegetable soup; their tongues, hearts, and livers will be flown in dry ice to butcher shops in Rome and Tokyo; and every remaining ounce of tissue and bone will be converted into dog food, soap, or fertilizer.

On the other side of the Double Diamond's pens, the remaining calves are wedged so tightly in a trailer that, while riding northward to Central Oklahoma, they will be unable to kneel or lie down. There does not appear to be enough space in the trailer for even one more calf. But, seeing another three calves being chased up the loading ramp, a driver repeatedly jabs his long cattle prod into the hips of every calf on the edge of the truck. Jolted by the electrical shock, the calves heave forward. The three calves scramble to the top of the ramp and, as the prod again touches their tails, kick and force themselves into the truck. The driver continues to press the prod against any hip or leg protruding through the tailgate. Finally, the other driver is able to lock the gate.

Warren frowns. "I wish they wouldn't use them old hot shots on good calves like that, you know."

Odell stares at the diesel fumes pouring from the exhaust pipe and into the cracks in the trailer. "Sure ain't no wonder why feedlot fellows complain 'bout calves gettin' shipping fever all the time, is it? They done look like 'ey stunned." Turning toward Sonny, he raises his voice: "How long 'ey gonna be on the road?"

"Make it in eighteen hours straight driving," Sonny answers, "if 'em boys don't tree some old girl at a truck stop. Before 'ey get to Oklahoma and unloaded 'morrow, I'll guarantee you we'll be over by Alpine weighin' up another load."

During a year, B.L. and Sonny load as many yearling steers and weaned calves (29,000) as are raised on 650,000 acres of ranchland. Entrepreneurial instead of landed, but always familiar with the inner workings of cattle buying, this relatively new breed of cowmen adds another dimension to the cattle industry. Giving ranchers higher prices than meat packers would bid at stockyards, such men collectively buy 2,500,000 young cattle a year in Texas. If the calves have just been weaned, such as these leaving the Double Diamond, they usually are placed in small "background pastures" to eat both the residue left in wheat fields and eventually sorghum-sweetened grains. After four to six months, the calves will be conditioned for a starkly different environment: they will change from grazing among an average of only one cow and calf per forty-five acres on a grassy ranch to eating a new feed, while either inhaling the swirling dust or plodding through ankle-deep manure and mud, beside 400 to 500 other calves filling just one acre of a feedlot. For example, in the 102 commercial feedlots in the Texas Panhandle, a high plain accessible to interstate highways, railroads, and granaries, anywhere from 2000 to 78,000 young cattle (or a total of 1,600,000) stand at all times.

Here, as a yearling calf stands beside a trough as long as a city block, he is programmed to eat, every day, an average of twenty-five pounds of a steamed mixture of soybeans, corn, sugar-beet pulp, and five or six antibiotics, chemicals, and stimulants. On many large feedlots, electric lights encourage calves to eat throughout the night. At others, pronged plastic pellets, clinging permanently in a sensitive part of a calf's stomach, create the feeling that he already has eaten grass, hay, or fodder (a roughage that he prefers) and thus causes him to actually eat more fattening carbohydrates. And regardless of the type of feed, it usually is laced with either liquid or powdered urea, a tasteless nitrogen refined from animal urine, that creates a profitable chemical reaction as it meets the bacteria in cattles' stomachs: It changes into carbon dioxide and ammonia and, then, an artificial protein that serves as one third of all their protein. Though such large

amounts of feed often cause a steer to bawl from indiges-
tion, his weight still increases from 2.7 to 3.3 pounds each
day.

Under this routine, a calf leaving the Double Diamond
for a feedlot during this roundup will reach the ideal
slaughter weight of 1100 pounds about the time of next
fall's roundup. By contrast, a steer calf remaining on the
ranch, continuing his diet of only grama grass and salt,
will weigh about 800 pounds. He will either stay on the
range until the following spring roundup or be sold and
sent to a feedlot for about two months before he is
slaughtered.

More and more buyers will be seeking the calves that
are kept on ranges. Located primarily in a belt extending
through Oklahoma, Texas, Colorado, Arizona, and California, a growing breed of feedlot operators also has buyers
searching for calves that they can fatten for what is called
"Wall Street cowboys." With the help of investment
houses and mailing lists, these men buy 1,500,000 calves
a year from the estimated $350,000,000 that they solicit
from individuals such as doctors, executives, professional
athletes, or anyone who envisions far more romance and
safety in investing "in cattle ranching out west" than the
turbulent stock market. As a further inducement, the
feedlot operators often depict themselves as an Old West
tax shelter enabling investors to postpone any tax on
profits for up to six years and still claim an immediate
deduction from taxes. In a typical sales letter, Western
Beef, Inc., a conglomerate of cattle feeding and buying
companies based in Amarillo, Texas, mentions little more
than how anyone investing, say, $10,000 in a "limited
partnership" may deduct $15,000 from his current tax:
"The first limited partnership formed for 1973 is struc-
tured with approximately 150% [tax] writeoff."

In other feeding funds, a prospective "limited partner"

receives color brochures depicting cowboys observing Herefords in shaded green pastures or a steer posed on an Oriental rug and captioned: "He may be hard on my carpet, but he's great on my 1040" (as a 200 percent deduction). But if a man wants to play Wall Street cowboy, maintain promoters of some funds, he has to risk the "cowboy arithmetic." A "limited partner" subsequently finds that one such limitation is that he has no voice in the management of his cattle or, when he has attempted to see them, is not even welcome at the feedlot. Meanwhile, using "cowboy arithmetic," the managements of some feeding funds are systematically charging a limited partner's account as many as a dozen fees for "yardage," "subscription," "receiving," "buying," "spraying," "veterinarian," and "shipping." Moreover, as the Securities and Exchange Commission has required some public feeding funds to disclose a "conflict of interest," the feedlots often obtain such services as feed and transportation from their own subsidiaries or associates. Not unexpectedly, many limited partners find that profits are illusive. With all the satisfaction of a cowman finally trading an erratic horse, though, a buyer for one feedlot sees nothing unusual or unethical when a Wall Street cowboy fails to regain even half of his investment when the fattened cattle are sold. "Hell, buddy, when's an old city boy," he asks, "ever had a chance to do any good playing cowboy, huh?"

If a city cowboy could see the men leaving the Double Diamond's pens, he no doubt would find their appearance the antithesis of the cowboy's image. Climbing into the pickup trucks, squeezing between their saddles and bridles, the men seem too happy to even notice the condition of clothing that, with few exceptions, has been worn during the entire roundup. Several shirts are torn, stained, or darkened with perspiration. Two shirts, with most of the buttons missing, are held in place by vests, another by safety pins. Still another wrinkled shirt remains open, exposing a gray T-shirt that doesn't reach a navel. Aside from some places shielded by chaps, denim and beige pants resemble the color of coffee or the earth. Soles are so heavily encrusted with dried manure that dust spreads from them when men kick against a tire. Perspiration that soaks through hats, especially those of the experienced men, has held enough dust to form a band around the base of the crown. Several hats are as hopelessly misshaped as the tan one that Chili drops beside him. Someone accidentally steps on it. But Chili merely punches his fist into the crown, then slaps the top to return it to the usual shape.

Odell doesn't even bother to pull his hat out from under a bridle and rope. Shaking his head, he subconsciously holds his right thumb and crooked finger about two inches apart.

Woody laughs. "You ain't gonna grow no finger back."

"Shoot," says Cecil, " 'at's just how big a swig he's gonna take soon as he gets to his house."

Reaching the graveled area around the corral to the left of Odell's house, the men notice that Rio, Sheep, and Dairy already have returned the horses to the holding pasture. Not bothering to change his clothes, Rio sits against the shady side of the tack room. A can of warm beer rests between his knees.

Routinely, Odell glances to see that Rio has left in the corral four horses that will enable the men to gather all the horses later. Then he speaks appreciatively. "Them boys might've crippled up a few," he says, "but, buddy, you didn't lose a one, did you?"

Rio smiles.

Frosty jumps over the side of another truck. "I'd want to be with old Rio 'ere if I was drilling a well. He'll hit you whiskey or beer one 'nother."

Odell points toward the smoke curling up behind the cook's shed. He faces the men, backing toward his house as he talks. "Might not be no hot pie," he says. "But I got Cookie staying to fix you all bunch a steaks so won't have to spend half day's pay eating on the road."

"Way I look," Frosty snaps, "only places 'at'd let me in be 'em old joints you go to, Chili."

Once they carry their cots and mattresses into the barn, their saddles and bedrolls around their automobiles, many of the men begin to clean themselves. Several of the regular cowboys fill the bathroom in the bunkhouse. After relieving themselves around the barn, the other men groom themselves in much the same manner as Willie. He turns the short hose, hanging from a faucet, under his face and armpits. Drying himself with the old shirt, he puts on a pale green western shirt with artificial pearl buttons. He looks at his undershorts, tosses them away, and pulls on both a tight pair of khaki pants and his dirty boots. After wiping the boots with wet burlap, he continues to stomp so hard on planks, hoping to remove all the manure, that his spurs rattle.

Billy Bob's eyebrows arch. "He never did quiet 'em old spurs down the whole roundup. Another day of 'at and I'd cut 'em off some night."

Warren, Odell, and Specks, the business manager of the ranch, stroll toward the men gathering under the cook's shed. Though he has handled the ranch's receipts, payroll, taxes, and correspondence since 1951, Specks visits the Little Hills Division so infrequently that he doesn't know all the full-time cowboys. He hands Odell the checks made out for the regular monthly wages for the full-time cowboys: $345 for each of the seasonal hands.

Since it is too late to reach a bank today, Specks digs into a zippered pouch to exchange several endorsed checks for new currency.

Odell turns toward Warren. "As many more as we shipped 'is year and way prices are up," he says, "we probably sold 'bout six hundred thousand dollars' worth — 'at is going by what we sold last year."

Warren gazes upward, smiling ambivalently. "You know, Odell, I hope you ain't sold off too many now and put me in higher tax bracket. Way government takes much as it does now, be practically half communist to sell off any more."

When Odell returns to his kitchen, Warren watches Chili pack his wallet with ten-dollar bills. He takes a calfskin wallet from his pocket. "Chili, you ever see one of these, huh?"

Chili backs away, motioning with an arm. "No want to see."

J.J. stops near Warren. "You got one of ever' bill 'at's been made, ain't you? Hundred, five hundred, all?"

"Every single one," Warren replies proudly. "If the government's telling the truth."

Circulating between the cook's shed, bunkhouse, and trucks, few of these men seem to contemplate a quiet evening. True to character, Half Breed tosses a beer can toward the pile of refuse. "Ain't gonna beat 'round the bush about it — before it's good'n dark, I'm gonna get drunk, get laid, and whip hell out anybody who starts something."

He reflects, with some moderating allowances, a wide and enduring sentiment. Neither changing markets, taking fewer and fewer men around stockyards, nor the availability of pickup trucks, providing greater mobility, has inhibited many a cowboy's instinct to compress into one hour or day what geography denied him during a month or more in a line camp or roundup, to revel, much the way it rains in the West and, in Odell's view, "get practically a half year's worth at one time." To a large extent, such men unwind at sites which, like the working cowboy, remain obscured by isolation. For example: In the desert reaches of Nevada, with nothing in the state laws to prohibit Old West whorehouses, a cowboy's background sometimes dictates a choice: He may pick one of the young girls lined up in a house, licensed by a county, carrying a name such as the Mustang Bridge Ranch or Cottontail Ranch. Or, if life in batch camps has conditioned him to less formal surroundings, he favors a tawdry "hog ranch" where usually one plump woman, or occasionally two sisters, provide the only liquor and sex within seventy-five miles. When he hauls a few cattle to the Fort Worth Stockyards, an area separated from the mainstream of the city, a cowboy finds the street leading to the entrance lined with wooden sidewalks and porched boot and beer joints with signs that beckon: "Howdy, Cowboy!" "Come In," "Handmade Boots & Saddles," and "Dancing." Most of the time, red-faced men sit on the wooden benches outside the saloons. But a portly rancher was quick to volunteer, "They probably just used to be cowboys. Real cowboy — he gets in and gets out a place quick."

Some men from the Double Diamond will only drink bourbon from a cup while their families watch. But for many others, their choice is suggestive of the rowdier Old West: "Head for the border." Specifically: Ojinaga, Mexico. Here, sun-backed adobe buildings, many of them the same color as the earth, rise up from the creosote bushes and gleaming sands of Mexico's huge Chihuahuan Desert and spread to the banks of the Rio Grande. In any of a dozen closely bunched saloons, collectively known as the

"zone," the men find the familiar raciness of other cowboys, *vaqueros*, minor *bandidos*, and daydreamers. More
important to the cowboys, four or five women, all in low
blouses and large jewelry, are seldom more than a drink
and six dollars away from their beds in the back rooms.

On the other side of the Rio Grande, standing in the
little town and cattle crossing of Presidio, Texas, a one-
time mission believed to be the oldest settlement in the
United States, travelers leave little doubt that the saloons
of adjacent Ojinaga are prepared for the end of the
roundups. On a recent morning, as Odell led his crew
away from Echo Canyon, an old truck filled with lean
Mexican steers — some of the average of 2000 head of
cattle that pass through Ojinaga each week — eases onto
the concrete siding at the U.S. Bureau of Customs station
in Presidio. The driver gets out of the truck. A relaxed
man, with two shortened right fingers and "BUCK" tooled
into an undyed belt, he studies the tarantula crawling
under the edge of a rock. He walks around as the inspector for the Department of Agriculture's Animal and Plant
Health Inspection Service looks at the steers for indica-
tions of diseases or ticks.

A man nods a greeting at Buck. "Didn't happen to see
'em getting ready for a cowboy or two over in the zone,
did you?"

"Hot damn if 'ey ain't," says Buck, snapping his full
fingers. "Bunch old boys up north 'at's done got their
roundup over with done been 'ere already. Been a heap a
fights, they say, and some shootings. Police, he even got
shot bad. But I'll tell you — with 'at hardback road 'ey
got now, all 'em bars beefed up their girls good and got
some new bunches all the way from Sonora, or someplace. One of 'em girls 'at's been 'ere a while said she's

lookin' for cowboys she knows. Make more money outta the deer hunters who come in after the cowboys get through, but she says she still likes cowboys best."

Across the lane, Elmo Miller, the director of the Bureau of Customs station, and sometimes the only "law" in this part of Texas, knows to expect a predictable pattern from passing cowboys. "They raise enough hell over in Ojinaga," he says, "that about the biggest commotion we've had with cowboys this side of the Rio Grande is a carload coming down to the zone for the first time. They didn't know that in Old Mexico there — they take a three-hour siesta every afternoon. Here the saloons and girls all quiet down and these boys were banging on doors and can't figure out what's happening. They came back mad as all get out."

Pausing, Miller glances at the Rio Grande. "Except for smuggling wetback cows up the river," he continues, "mostly what we get is a little gun-running to Mexico and people coming back to Texas smuggling gold jewelry and liquor under the front seat. But hardworking cowboys — Gringo or Mexican both — never smuggle anything like that at all. Roundup time, they'll get couple of bottles over there. But happy as they are, they don't leave much doubt they've done finished off one bottle and fairly well got rid of the other time they get this far."

Even at the mention of Ojinaga, Woody's eyes light with boyish exuberance. "Damn, if I ain't gonna go in 'at Red Mill bar, too, just for heck of it. See if 'at girl with the long hair and green fingernail polish on is still 'ere."

Three younger men turn toward Woody. "Can you get fixed up pretty good, huh?" one asks.

Woody gestures his head. "Whiskey 'bout half price in Texas. Haircut for forty cents. Real good piece of tail, I'll tell you, for six dollars."

"All of it the same price?" Billy Bob asks.

Woody motions toward Cecil, Chili, and Pancho. "Old bastards like 'at over 'ere get 'at three-, four-dollar stuff. They just walk up to one and say, 'Come on, let's go.' Hell, you can tell already 'at it won't be no good." Pausing, he begins to grin. "I tell you. You talk to 'em little bit. Dance. Brag on 'em. Talk about getting your own little place and settlin' down. Come back for 'em, maybe. You get 'em all worked up and get a six-dollar piece for three dollars."

Half Breed's voice hardens. "You still paid'm six dollars after all 'at talking last year."

Piqued, Woody clears his throat. "Not tonight, I ain't."

As the men talk, stirring memories and fantasies, two of the married cowboys recall alibis that enabled them to also travel to Ojinaga. Frosty struggles to keep from breaking into laughter. "Boy I know with a wife 'at knows ever' thing. He stops in home long enough to leave most his paycheck with her and say he has to take 'is Mexican boy home who saved him from getting killed by old bull. Wife gives him dirty look. But he says, 'Yeah, wasn't for him, kids wouldn't have no daddy. I wouldn't even be standing here.' When he gets back home, he kinda mentions Ojinaga and his old wife says, 'Why 'at's nothing but a cowboy whorehouse 'ere.' He says, 'Boy I sure wouldn't even drove in 'at town if I knowed 'at.' "

Half Breed tucks thirty dollars in a shirt pocket and the remaining wages inside his boots.

Leaning into a pickup truck, Frosty turns up the volume of a radio station playing a recording of "Faded Love." He snaps a thumb rhythmically. "Boy, if you couldn't write a good song about 'at jail in Ojinaga," he says with a smile. "The Oakie pokie. Square hole about big as back 'at pickup and you stick your cup out twice day and get some frijoles. Have to escape or pay off somebody, I reckon, to even get fried baloney on Sunday. You young boys 'at ain't been 'ere — I'd sure 'member 'at if 'ey try to take you alive."

Woody whirls toward Chili. "They done got it saved for Chili, ain't 'at right? Tell 'em why you can't even go 'ere without getting your hind end shot."

Chili shakes his head.

J.J. recalls the incident. "See, old boy used to work here was foolin' with an old girl's tits in old bar 'ere and tore her dress and old son-bitch calls the law on him time he gets outside. Police came up and sees 'is old boy lay 'is three-fifty-seven Magnum pistol on the seat of the truck."

J.J. rises and coils both arms over his hips. "Here 'is old police had his gun out and was on his tiptoes and grinning from ear to ear. Daring 'is old boy to run or reach in for his gun so he could shoot him. 'is old boy just freezes and the police's getting madder 'cause he won't escape. Here old Chili sneaks up behind and knocks gun out the police's hand and throws it 'cross the road. 'ey got in 'at pickup and tore ass out for the river."

Chili, trying to spit and grin at the same time, spills tobacco juice on his collar. "I no afraid to go back if I want to," he says, pounding a fist into a palm.

Dairy turns toward Billy Bob. "How long's it take to get 'ere?"

Cecil chuckles. "Depends on if you ridin' with a Mexican or white boy. Drive like wild Mexican boys won't take no time a-tall."

"Mexicans like to drive fast," Chili says.

Frosty points to a rusted figurine of a bull ornamenting the head of a pickup truck. "You just follow 'at old bull's butt 'ere and pour the gas to her. Time you drunk half pint, you're practically 'ere."

Odell strolls back from his house to shake hands with each of the temporary cowhands.

The gravel around the corral crackles. A pickup carrying two men speeds away. Chili's wife and children, along with her sister, drive up in their gray Ford, causing an embarrassed expression that ends Chili's conversation. In minutes, driving as fast as the men departing, Pauline returns from meeting her and Odell's three children when they got off the school bus. She and the two daughters walk promptly into the house, suggesting that they will greet Odell later. Kenny, his jaw already packed with tobacco, rushes toward Odell. His eyes lock on the remaining men.

"Hey, roundup ain't over with yet," Warren says, turning to Odell. "Not till I get settled up with old Kenny for taking care of the dogies. Wait'll I get old Specks 'way from the chuck and get you paid, too."

" 'at's O.K.," Kenny says softly. Looking impressed, almost envious, he continues to watch three men laugh as they pile into a 1968 Pontiac and speed toward the horizon, leaving a line of brown dust behind them. "They kinda ready, ain't they?"

"Aw, I couldn't say they no different from no other roundup," Warren says, very slowly. "They just 'nother old bunch of cowboys."